Russell Rob ... ırnalist who has worked in ... Kong. He is the co-author of ... *The Story of the Painters and Dockers*, also published by Pan Macmillan. He lives in Melbourne.

Also by Russell Robinson

*Shotgun and Standover: The Story of the Painters and Dockers*
(with James Morton)

# KHAKI CRIMS & DESPERADOES

RUSSELL ROBINSON

MACMILLAN
Pan Macmillan Australia

*For the grandfather I never met, Captain Thomas William Thrupp, 2/4th Field Regiment, accidentally killed in Syria, June 1941*

First published 2014 in Macmillan by Pan Macmillan Australia Pty Ltd
1 Market Street, Sydney, New South Wales, Australia, 2000



Cataloguing-in-Publication entry is available
from the National Library of Australia
http://catalogue.nla.gov.au

Index by Sue Jarvis
Typeset in 13/15.5 pt Granjon by Post Pre-Press Group
Printed by McPherson's Printing Group

Papers used by Pan Macmillan Australia Pty Ltd are natural, recyclable products made from wood grown in sustainable forests. The manufacturing processes conform to the environmental regulations of the country of origin.

# Contents

Introduction 1

Part I: Military Misadventure
1 Brothers in Arms 7
2 The Types You Meet in Camp 22
3 All Aboard! 38
4 Bad to the Bone 54
5 An Unlikely Hero 70

Part II: Services No Longer Required
6 On the Lam in London and Glasgow 89
7 The Train of Shame 109
8 A Day in Court 126
9 Addicted to Love 143

Part III: The Professionals
10 The Bruhns Again 169
11 One Enemy and One Friend 182
12 More of Squizzy's Soldiers 203
13 Racetrack Spivs and Shockers 217

Part IV: Beyond the Reach of Law and Order
14 War's Long Shadow 239
15 The Thirties 256
16 Two Brothers 272
17 Three Lives 284

Acknowledgements 300
Bibliography 301
Notes on Images 308
Index 309

# Introduction

When Australia answered the call to arms in August 1914, its response was overwhelming. Volunteers flocked to enlistment centres in their thousands. From every walk of life they came: lawyers, accountants, clerks, labourers, stockmen, shearers, farmers and teachers – they all signed up for the great adventure. Yet lurking among them were recruits with shadowy credentials; police records that many enlistment officers conveniently overlooked.

Some were career criminals, fresh out of jail or on the run from the law. Others took on new identities to escape family commitments, avoid debts, or both. Some simply wanted a new start. For them, overseas service was an opportunity to put past misdeeds behind them.

Some Australians who went to the war committed heinous crimes, either overseas or after their return. A percentage of them were damaged by the terrible ordeal of trench warfare with its remorseless tension and relentless shelling; men who otherwise might have lived different lives. But there were also men for whom soldiering presented welcome opportunities to handle guns and consort with other criminals – often with the worst of the worst. Their military experiences were simply part of their training for post-war criminal careers.

The impact they had on the Australian Imperial Force was negative and unwelcome. Many of the soldiers in this book would not adapt to the regimented life of military service. Useless for front-line duty, they were shunted off to supply depots or other bases to work out the war there. Some of them stuck it out, others deserted. These were the men who Australia's first official war correspondent, Charles Bean, dubbed the 'hard cases' and 'ne'er-do-wells'. Persistent deserters, he said, 'were always men of this type – in some cases actual criminals who had enlisted without the intention of serving at the front, and ready to go to any length to avoid it'.

Nevertheless, there were plenty of Australians who, despite their criminal records and extensive military rap sheets, showed great courage in war, and served with valour at Gallipoli and in France. Their stories are represented here, as well as the stories of the hard cases.

It was while I was researching a book on the history of the violent Ship Painters and Dockers' Union that the theme of *Khaki Crims & Desperadoes* first came into clear focus. Many of the characters associated with the union, the murderers, standover men, drug traffickers, armed robbers, muscle-for-hire and moonlighters, had spent formative years in the armed forces, notably the army. As a veteran prison officer commented to my co-author James Morton and me, the painters and dockers had 'almost a military aspect. They had blokes over them who would tell them what to do, and when they came to jail it never changed'.

Military historians who have studied criminality in the AIF have evidenced the problems it caused for army discipline and morale. Edward Garstang concludes that the AIF had a deserved reputation as an effective fighting force yet, when compared with the British Army and other Dominion forces, the worst disciplinary record away from the front line.

Former historian at the Australian War Memorial Peter Stanley says, quoting Charles Bean, that the finest tribute we can pay the Australian digger is to tell his story straight, better enabling us to see him as a real person rather than a cardboard cut-out Anzac hero. This book is written in that spirit. It is not intended to besmirch the hard-fought reputations of the honest Australian troops who laid their lives on the line.

The Australian military command's problems with indiscipline were widely known during World War I. Even the reputation of Australia's most celebrated military leader, John Monash, became collateral damage when en route to Egypt 200 men under his command jumped ship at Colombo to frequent the city's bars and hotels. The commandant of the European garrison there wrote an exaggerated report of the incident, which was inflated even further by rumour. Monash felt obliged to write to the Australian defence minister, George Pearce, to reassure him that it had been a one-off incident.

Garstang writes that official figures show that one in 14 Australian soldiers in the first AIF were court-martialled, compared with one in 50 New Zealanders and one in 25 Canadians. More than 340 Australian servicemen faced the death penalty in World War I, although none were actually executed, mainly because of the AIF's hard-line opposition to capital punishment except in cases of mutiny, desertion to the enemy, or traitorous conduct. Nevertheless, they incurred severe sanctions. Between August 1914 and March 1920, more than 140 soldiers were given life sentences, while 46 received 15 years' jail and close to 7000 were slotted for between 3 and 12 years.

More than 38,000 serving Australians were imprisoned with hard labour for terms ranging from six months to two years, and more than 105,000 spent from three to six months in detention. Almost 1000 were discharged in disgrace.

At home, many magistrates and judges did their level best to keep offenders out of the military by imposing stiff jail sentences, in the hope and expectation that on their release their applications to enlist would be rejected.

'A criminal had no right to be associated with honourable men offering their lives for the safety of our homes and the defence of the Empire,' thundered one Sydney judge, Sir Ernest Brougham Docker. 'It was such a degradation, shame and insult that such persons should be permitted to associate with them. I will take care that in my judicial capacity the army is purged of such characters.' The judge had a personal stake in the war effort: his son Ernest was away in France, where he served with great valour and won a Military Cross.

But in the lower courts, some magistrates were known to offer defendants a khaki alternative to prison garb, and the offer was often enthusiastically accepted. This is how it was for Norman Bruhn, the first khaki crim in this book, a despicable figure well known to aficionados of Australian true crime. Bruhn survived the war only to die on the streets of Darlinghurst in 1927, gunned down in a payback killing. His legacy of violence lived on. Some of his grandsons became major players in the painters and dockers group in the 1970s and early '80s, and in the gangland wars that followed.

Norman Bruhn and others like him survived the war because they spent as much time as possible far from the front line.

# PART I

# Military Misadventure

# 1

# Brothers in Arms

NORMAN BRUHN ENLISTED A FEW weeks before Christmas 1914. By the look of police records, he didn't have much choice. In August that year a warrant was issued for his imprisonment for 14 days for failing to pay a court-ordered fine for offensive behaviour. He went to jail and was released in September. On 1 December, he paid the two pound penalty. Three days later, he enlisted. Gallipoli was a long way to go to escape further police attention.

Bruhn was 20 years old, blond-haired, blue-eyed and fresh-faced according to the *Victoria Police Gazette*, but he was a young thug in the making. He and his brothers had grown up in the port city of Geelong, their last address in Corio Street, a stone's throw from the waterfront. Norman's father, Oscar, had been before the court for larrikinism from an early age. When he was 19, he and a mate brought an action against two magistrates alleging that they had erred in sentencing the young pair for armed assault and bad language. The claimants' objection was not that they were innocent – their guilt does not seem to have been at issue. Rather, they claimed 500 pounds compensation from each of the magistrates for exceeding their brief by sentencing them to jail for three months with hard labour. The two young prisoners used the ancient writ of *habeas corpus* to get themselves out of the nick to make their case. History does not record what happened next, but no doubt the newspaper accounts gave locals in the tough inner suburb of South Melbourne a bit of a giggle.

It was probably from this moment that the name Bruhn gained wide notoriety in Victoria, for thereafter it featured often in the country press, usually in stories that were improbable, inaccurate in some key detail, or so vague as to be almost meaningless. Someone called Oscar Bruhn had allegedly assaulted a woman at Connewarre and police expected to lay charges soon. A man named Oscar Bruhn from South Geelong had attempted to throw a goal umpire over the fence when the Barwon Football Club played at Kardinia Park. Oscar Bruhn, 48, had arrived home in a violent mood and thrown his 'little son, William George' through a glass window. Even if there was no truth in them at all, these published rumours left no doubt in the observant reader's mind that the Bruhns were not a soft family.

At 14, Norman went to work in a local woollen mill, where his lower arm was drawn into a loom and fractured, and he got his name in the newspapers for the first but definitely not the last time.

Like any novice hoodlum, he had a magnetic attraction to guns, and was keen to learn how to handle them. His enlistment papers reveal that before he joined the AIF he belonged to a Geelong-based company of the 70th Infantry, which was part of the 18th Infantry Brigade headquartered at Ballarat. This was one of the many civilian militias, Commonwealth-funded and equipped, that were set up to save Australia if it was ever invaded. It was an army of volunteers, often drawn from local rifle clubs.

On his return from war, Norman Bruhn would carve himself a brutal reputation in Melbourne and Sydney, building a rap sheet that ranged from larceny to vagrancy to pimping, from housebreaking to indecent exposure to extortion. He became a firm ally of the high-profile gangster, little Leslie 'Squizzy' Taylor. After moving north, he quickly aligned himself with a reviled Sydney razor gang whose membership included George Wallace, an enforcer who raped and slashed the faces of prostitutes who failed to hand over a large slice of their takings.

After Norman was gunned down in the street, his embattled widow, Irene, was forced to defend her man when newspapers published accounts of his violent criminal history. Their descriptions of the prominent scars on his body mentioned a bullet-shaped wound on one knee, which particularly excited the press. Irene attributed this scar to a war wound suffered in France. Yet, while Bruhn's service record refers to a septic knee, nothing else there suggests it was from a gunshot wound earned in battle. The extensive medical treatment shown on his war service record was mainly for VD.

Attached to the AIF's 6th Battalion, Norman Bruhn embarked for active service on 2 February 1915, shipping out from Port Melbourne in the *Clan MacGillivray*, a converted merchantman. The main body of his unit had arrived in Egypt a couple of days before Bruhn enlisted. As part of the 2nd Australian Infantry Brigade, the 6th would participate in the second wave of the landing at Anzac Cove on 25 April 1915. Norman, however, was in the battalion's 2nd Reinforcements and did not arrive at Gallipoli until mid-May.

He not only missed the Anzacs' landing at Gallipoli, but also the Second Battle of Krithia. In early May, the 2nd Brigade was redeployed to Helles, two hours south by sea. The Australians' task was to reinforce Allied troops there who, after a previous failure, were about to stage a new assault on the strategic peak of

Achi Baba, held by Turks and Germans. This engagement was the first time during the Great War that the AIF fought on an open field of battle. As they rushed up a narrow valley towards Achi Baba, the Australians were exposed, making them easy targets for the well-equipped enemy's artillery and snipers, who picked them off like flies. By the end of the first phase, the 2nd Brigade had more than a thousand men dead or missing.

By the time Bruhn's troopship steamed into the Dardanelles, his battalion had been relieved at Helles and sent back to Anzac Cove. The disadvantages of that location for an army of invaders have become part of the Anzac legend. The terrain was a nightmare of steep escarpments, deep ravines and narrow gullies descending to an exposed beach. And as the Australians dug in they created a crowded, smelly system of trenches and posts, in many ways akin to the filthy back streets of a city, as Charles Bean observed in his book *The Story of Anzac*:

> In these deep narrow alleys the front-line troops and supports lived as completely enclosed as in the lanes of a city, having their habitations along them in niches undercut in the wall, some times curtained by hanging blankets or waterproof sheets. Meanwhile the company and battalion headquarters, the medical aid-post, the quartermaster's store, and other offices became gradually as fixed and recognised as the public offices of a metropolis. The bivouacs on slopes behind the lines resembled the clustered booths at a great fair. In some respects most men came to regard the routine as one of city life.

Bruhn landed at Gallipoli during a period of high tension. The Anzacs were constantly harassed by the enemy at close quarters – an enemy commanding higher territory and much better armed with big guns. Unloading supplies from ship to beach was dangerous. At night men slept crowded in the trenches, wearing their greatcoats and armed with their guns, ready to respond to attack. Under cover of dark, some brave Anzacs headed into no-man's-land to reconnoitre. Had the enemy changed position, and were they preparing for a fresh attack?

Norman Bruhn lasted just a couple of months before he was hospitalised with influenza at Mudros, a small port on the Greek island of Lemnos. Illness was rife among the Anzac troops that July, with hundreds of men hospitalised with dysentery and fever. The bodies of the dead, the accumulation of refuse, the manure of pack animals, the flies – all contributed to the unsanitary conditions at Gallipoli.

The crowded tent hospitals of Mudros were no picnic, especially once the dysentery cases began arriving. Bruhn stayed in for 11 days, and was discharged to duty in time for the Battle of Lone Pine in August. The 2nd Brigade distinguished itself in this engagement, winning nine Victoria Crosses. What role Bruhn played, if any, is unknown. In September, the 6th Battalion was relieved, and sent to Lemnos. There, on the 17th, Norman Bruhn was readmitted to hospital, again suffering flu. The patient finally rejoined his battalion on 6 November.

Back in Egypt after the Anzac forces evacuated Gallipoli in December, Bruhn went AWL early in the new year and as a result received 28 days of field punishment no. 2. This meant that he was handcuffed, and possibly fettered as well, and forced to carry out heavy labour. Unpleasant as that undoubtedly was, it was still an improvement on field punishment no. 1, in which the offender was not only shackled but also tied to a fixed object such as a gun wheel for up to two hours at a time. If the army manual was followed to the letter, the offender's arms would be outstretched and his legs bound together, giving the appearance of crucifixion. At its extreme, FP no. 1 was a cruel punishment that even some officers abhorred.

In late February, Bruhn was assigned to the 46th Battalion, formed from Gallipoli veterans and reinforcements newly arrived from Australia. In late March, the new battalion marched out to Serapeum, in desert near the Suez Canal. The Turks had been active in this area, and the 46th's job was to help defend it. None of the members of the unit, Norman included, could have enjoyed the three-day march across such unwelcoming territory, each man wearing new boots and carrying 25 kilograms of kit. 'Weather – hot, Water – scarce, Surface of ground – very deep sand,' the battalion diary recorded. By the third day, many men had exhausted their ration of water and food, and had to complete the journey on an empty tank.

It was all too much for Norman: a week after the unit's arrival at Serapeum, he went AWL for four days. Where he went remains a mystery, but for that offence he received seven days close confinement and forfeited five days pay. This was the straw that broke the camel's back. Two days later, Norman exited camp again and was AWL for a month, probably reacquainting himself with the booze and other temptations on offer in Cairo's sleazier quarters.

Returned to camp, he copped 28 days of field punishment no. 2 and forfeited 30 days pay. The day this sentence was over, the army shipped him out from Alexandria, bound for Marseilles. The rest of the 46th had already left for France a few days before, and he was to join them. They would soon play their part on the battlefields of northern France. The question was whether Norman would be there with them.

*

Lieutenant General Sir William Birdwood had a message for the Anzac forces heading to France: 'You will undoubtedly be faced with temptations in France, for we shall have to pass through and be billeted in densely populated villages. Drink will, I am afraid, be obtainable, while villages will mostly be full of women and children, whose fathers, husbands and brothers are fighting for their country in the trenches against our common enemy.'

This account of France's temptations must have been music to Norman Bruhn's ears. It appears he missed the rest of the general's appeal for good behaviour, particularly the part about booze: 'That you will respect the women I have not the slightest doubt, because I know how absolutely repugnant the idea of any offence against a defenceless woman is to every Australian and New Zealander. It is against drink, however, that I particularly wish now to warn you, and to implore you to take hold of yourselves, and in the case of every man to absolutely make up his mind and determine for himself that he will not give way to it, and that he will remember that the honour of either Australia or New Zealand is in his personal keeping . . . Remember that a few black sheep can give a bad name to a whole flock.'

The 46th ended up near Bailleul, between Hazebrouck and Ypres, before moving on to Fleurbaix where they went into the trenches, sustaining a couple of casualties before the battalion was relieved. The war in France was very different from the war at Gallipoli, where the Australians were pinned down to a small area. In France they were deployed and redeployed, often by train, and often at short notice. In this fluid situation, Bruhn found his way west to Étaples, near Calais, and went AWL there for 11 days.

Étaples was a working port and a major railhead, with all the hustle and bustle and illicit opportunity which went along with that. Perhaps it reminded him of Geelong. It was also the site of a big military camp, at the height of the war bursting at the seams with 100,000 men. The camp had a detention centre run by a provost marshal and was thick with military police. When Norman was picked up, his penalty was FP no. 1 for drunkenness and being AWL. While still under this punishment, he copped another seven days of FP no. 2 for making a false statement to an officer in the field.

His unit meanwhile had had their first really serious taste of action. On 4 August, they were called in to supply the front-line troops of the 2nd Division at Pozières. Over late July and early August, three Australian divisions fought to take this French village that would become a byword for blood sacrifice. More than 12,000 Australians perished at Pozières, many blown to bits by almost constant German bombardment. The 46th battalion, to which Bruhn still belonged at least on paper, was mainly used as supply and reserve troops in the first stage of the action. But they had two stints in the trenches, and managed to defeat a German counterattack.

The story of Sydney's gangland crime in the 1920s might have played out differently if Norman Bruhn had been at the Battle of Pozières, but by then the authorities had apparently assessed his character as a soldier, and temporarily parked him at the Australian depot at Étaples, where he could do least harm.

In early September 1916 Bruhn was admitted to hospital with myalgia (muscle pain), then on 15 September discharged. Three days later he was off again, and not sighted until 14 November. He was found lying down drunk seven kilometres from base in a wood at Camiers. One of the arresting officers told the subsequent court martial that Bruhn 'smelt strongly of drink' and became 'very abusive' as he was being 'assisted' to a lorry for the drive back to detention at Étaples. But the accused man protested that he was innocent. 'I never went to sleep after it and I remember quite plainly seeing the police arrive. I was not drunk,' Bruhn told the hearing.

He had spent the day of his arrest with friends, he said. They went to a hospital to see 'a chum'. Afterwards, 'we had three or four bottles of wine between four of us, not more'. The charges against Bruhn were drunkenness and desertion. If he had been in the British Army, he would have been dead: deserters were shot. But the leadership of the AIF refused to impose the death penalty on their volunteer army.

He was sentenced to two years imprisonment with hard labour. Only a couple of weeks later the sentence was suspended, probably because Bruhn's battalion was moving on. The 46th were briefly at Dernancourt, then St Vaast, where their time was filled with general training and musketry while they waited for their next engagement.

A week after rejoining his unit, just before New Year's Eve, Norman Bruhn broke camp and went missing until the second week of February. He was now classed as a deserter.

A dose of the clap landed Bruhn in hospital in Étaples in early March 1917. There he stayed for almost seven weeks before rejoining his unit, only to last a day before being readmitted under arrest to hospital for 'VDG' (venereal disease, gonorrhoea). This became the pattern of Bruhn's war, shuffling constantly between the field punishment compound, the hospital, then back to his unit, where he would break out again.

He had been AWL for more than two months when the Armistice was declared on 11 November 1918. On 23 November he was arrested, and a few days later admitted to hospital at Le Havre for VD. He escaped again and was eventually arrested at Amiens in February 1919. He was held there by the provost marshal, 'pending disposal', but then escaped from the escort taking him back to his unit.

It was not just that Bruhn had developed a taste for life on the lam in France: he knew that now the war was over the military authorities would have the time and attention to discipline him properly.

At last, on 23 October 1919, he was sent to England. Eight days later he was court-martialled in London, charged with being AWL in France between 29 March and 17 October. He was sentenced to nine months detention and admitted to Lewes Detention Barracks. A bit over a month later, he was shipped home and the unexpired portion of his sentence was remitted. The authorities had washed their hands of him.

Norman Bruhn's war finally ended on 4 February 1920 when the disgraced digger disembarked in Melbourne and was handed his discharge papers, stamped 'Services no longer required'. Befitting his misconduct, Bruhn forfeited his entitlement to the standard military decorations and medals. The only reminders of his war service were his scars and tattoos. On his left forearm '1915' and 'Egypt' were inscribed above and below a Union Jack and a French flag.

*

Norman was not the only Bruhn who went to war. His younger brother, Stanley, had joined the 6th Battalion a month before him, and his older brothers William and Oscar also served in France.

Stanley Bruhn was probably the military lion of the family. Just 19 when he landed at Gallipoli, he became well known there for his souveniring. On 28 August, he and another private, Harry Lane, were in a party detailed to help unload a barge moored just off the beach and were copped for pilfering a case of whisky. Both men received 90 days imprisonment, without hard labour. The penalties were later suspended, as sentences often were at the front. When Lane's record of conduct was read to the hearing, it was without blemish. Bruhn's file was not quite as glowing. It stated: 'Has been with the Battalion about three months. During that period his character and general conduct may be classed as fair.'

Next, Stanley earned himself 40 days field punishment for taking a boat while he was stationed at Lemnos. The vessel belonged to a local Greek resident. A month or so later he was off to Marseilles where he joined the British Expeditionary Forces and soon found himself in more strife. He got drunk and threatened an NCO, for which he received 14 days field punishment. But unlike his brother Norman, the 6th did not dispense with Stanley's services, and even promoted him. As the war chewed up Australian lives, and officers and NCOs died in their hundreds, replacements had to be found. In 1916, Stanley Bruhn became lance corporal.

As part of the 1st Division, Bruhn's battalion played a key role in France. It served in the Battle of the Somme, then was sent to Flanders. Later it returned to France and played its part in the Battle of Bullecourt. It participated in the Third Battle of Ypres, and was involved in staving off the massive German assault of early 1918. Bruhn played his part but, as at Gallipoli, it was booze that brought him down.

In May 1918, at Hazebrouck, he was pinched for stealing champagne. This village had been under sustained German attack before it was saved by the Australian forces. The locals were naturally grateful – up to a point. Madame Gabrielle Smeets Leroy told a court martial how a group of Australian soldiers, which included Stanley, had arrived at her house one day and sat themselves down in her kitchen. It was an hour or so before midday so she fed them some soup. They repaid her by raiding her cellar.

'I saw the accused [Bruhn] go into my cellar and pick up some bottles of champagne,' she told the hearing through a military translator. 'I closed the door of the cellar at once. Then someone took me by the throat. Then the accused and another man ran away with the champagne.'

Mme Leroy said she often sold champagne to soldiers, but Bruhn and his pals had not parted with any cash. 'No one paid me. They went to the cellar without asking.' Some time later, Bruhn returned to her house with other soldiers. 'The accused stayed in the kitchen while another soldier with a revolver in his hand went into the cellar. The accused had a stick in his hand. They all went away with bottles of champagne.'

The following morning Bruhn and yet another contingent arrived at the house and headed straight for the kitchen, where this time Bruhn descended into the cellar, emerging with more of the sparkling stuff. The tribunal found him guilty of stealing. He was sentenced to five years, which was later reduced to two years imprisonment with hard labour. The army council reviewed the case and promptly quashed the conviction.

The incident is sketchily referred to in *As Rough as Bags*, a history of the 6th Battalion. Without naming Bruhn, it tells of how a group of soldiers had vanished from the lines, 'and to the astonishment of their sergeant, reappeared two hours later, somewhat the worse for wear, and carrying a pack full of Gold Top champagne bottles':

> It appears that a well-stocked, but deserted cellar had been found some nights earlier . . . and they had been sneaking out each night for unauthorised refreshment.

Stanley (Stan to his mates) appears to have been a popular member of the battalion, particularly when it came to sporting contests. He starred as bowler in a cricket match played during a stop at Racquinghem camp near Hazebrouck, with figures of 8 for 20 in one match and 9 for 22 in another.

Six days after the Armistice, Lance Corporal Stanley Bruhn was promoted to corporal and appointed acting sergeant, a sign of how depleted the NCO ranks were by the end of the war. It would be another seven months before he made it home and was discharged. Unlike Norman, he earned his war medals.

Older brother William George Bruhn was 28 when he pulled on a khaki uniform in December 1916. His enlistment papers showed he had a large scar on the right forearm and another on the left cheek. A locomotive fireman by trade, Bill Bruhn had already been in trouble with the law.

By late 1916, Bruhn, Service Number 452, was in France with the Railway Unit, 2nd Section. Things went well until early 1918, when he was severely reprimanded for giving out locomotive coal. It is not stated whether the Australian corporal sold or traded the coal, only that his actions were prejudicial to good order and military discipline.

William Bruhn saw out the rest of the war without a further blemish on his record. But on a cold afternoon in Flanders, in late January 1919, he accidentally shot a citizen: a small boy, in fact. He was charged with conduct to the prejudice of good order and military discipline, and true to the Bruhn family tradition, pleaded not guilty at his court martial.

The evidence against him was overwhelming, however, beginning with fellow soldier, Sapper David Harper, who said that on the afternoon in question he was sitting in the back of a truck with Bruhn, who was checking a malfunction on his automatic revolver. It was an American service model owned by Bruhn. He'd only had it for a few weeks and had never fired it. Harper gave evidence that the weapon had jammed and Bruhn had asked for a knife to prise the bullet free.

'I heard the report of the discharge of the revolver,' Harper said. 'Bruhn then said, "My God, I've shot a boy." On looking out the door I saw a boy lying on his back and blood coming from a wound in the front of his forehead.'

Bruhn immediately reported the incident to his superior officer. Questioned by Charles D'Haenens, Chef de Gendarmerie at Roulers, Harper said he did not see Bruhn point the revolver deliberately at the boy. Crowds of children often approached the military convoys for food and small change. The panel heard that Bruhn had previously dispersed a small gathering.

In his evidence, Bruhn said he had obtained the address of the dead boy's parents and paid for the funeral out of his own pocket. 'I feel the death of the boy very acutely,' he told the hearing. He was found guilty and was ordered to forfeit his seniority.

Despite this incident, the stocky fireman and the AIF parted company on amicable terms and he collected his war medals and tucked his honourable discharge under his arm, then re-enlisted in the family's criminal empire. Like many returning veterans who could not keep out of trouble with the law, his war service record came in handy whenever he was asking for a lighter sentence.

*

Last but not least, there was Oscar Charles Bruhn, another son of the original Oscar, who signed up with the 3rd Machine Gun Battalion. After his wife died, the 26-year-old engine cleaner left his daughter in the care of relatives and enlisted in October 1916. His was an undistinguished war, disrupted by VD. Two weeks after disembarking in England, he was admitted to hospital in Bulford suffering from the complaint. In December 1917, he was back in hospital with another dose, this time for 140 days. In between treatments, he went AWL.

As the war ended, authorities remained alarmed at the number of infected servicemen, particularly diggers, who were still in England, spreading VD through the local community. By late March 1919, Bruhn returned to Bulford with VD, where he remained for 62 days.

Eventually he shipped back to Australia with a clean-ish record. He had spent most of his war in and out of hospital with a series of unsavoury conditions. In addition to recurrent treatments for VD, there was a spell at Belton Hospital in the Midlands for a tumour on the penis, and treatment at Eastbourne Military Hospital for a painful anal fistula.

Whether they were contracting the clap, going AWL, pinching booze or mishandling firearms, the Bruhn brothers had undistinguished careers in arms. No doubt the military authorities thought that Norman in particular was more trouble than he was worth.

They were not the only crime family to answer the call to arms. Clans like the Cutmores, Devines and Taylors all contributed more than one member, though some didn't actually make it out of Australia.

# 2

# The Types You Meet in Camp

CLAUDE TAYLOR, BROTHER OF THE more famous Squizzy, was one of the first men to enlist in the AIF, signing up with the 5th Battalion within weeks of Britain declaring war on Germany. On his enlistment papers, he described himself as a 25-year-old labourer. In fact his age changed from one court appearance to the next, and his real occupation was gangster. He may have been pint-sized, but there was an edginess in his intense stare. Claude was an enforcer in Squizzy Taylor's fledgling army of street rats, pickpockets, touts and thugs.

He had run with his brother's gang as far back as 1907, when the group mounted a vicious attack on a rival in the gritty inner-Melbourne suburb of Fitzroy. The thugs laid into their victim, one Thomas Prentice, with pieces of timber and an iron bar, boots and fists. A pistol was held to the head of Prentice's young female companion, who was forced to witness the assault. When the injured man finally made it to nearby St Vincent's Hospital, 17 stitches were inserted into his lip. In a separate assault on the same night, the Taylor brothers were charged with attacking a man named Christopher Williams. While one of the Taylors took to him with an iron bar, the other covered him with a handgun. Both were given a week's jail and ordered to serve it in solitary confinement.

The following year Claude Taylor landed in the watch house after he and two cronies robbed well-known photographer Charles Gray of his meagre takings. The trio entered Gray's Bourke Street shop and one man, pointing to Taylor, said: 'Say, mate. This bloke wants 'is picture took.'

Taylor was placed in a chair, his hair hurriedly combed and the wrinkles in his jacket smoothed out. Gray took one or two pictures and then, as he was about to change the pose, Taylor's mates ran out carrying the cash register. Gray rushed after them but soon gave up the chase. By the time he returned to the studio, Taylor had also vanished.

In a plot twist worthy of an Agatha Christie mystery, Gray's photographs provided the breakthrough police needed to solve the crime. When the pictures were developed, the rozzers immediately recognised Taylor. When he was arrested, the suspect agreed the photograph represented a faithful likeness of him, but denied any knowledge of the heist or the participants.

As the years went on, Taylor's offending became more violent. In 1912, at the Maryborough Court of General Sessions, Taylor was sentenced to two years hard labour for assault and robbery. He had taken seven pounds – more than a fortnight's wages – from a man named David Quinton Clark. The judge stiffened the sentence by ordering that, two months into his term, Taylor was to be flogged with fifteen strokes of the cat-o-nine-tails.

Rather like Norman Bruhn, Taylor's experience on the inside was enough to persuade him that he needed a fresh start and the AIF was just the place to find it. But Private Claude Harold John Taylor lasted only two months under canvas. Just prior to embarkation for Egypt, he quit the army, his brief career summarised in a handwritten note across the top of his file: 'Absent without leave from 17th October 1914.' By then, newspapers had begun to tell the story of the slaughter that was twentieth-century trench warfare, and the *Emden* and other German warships were threatening Australian shipping routes to Europe. War was looking less like a big adventure and more like a serious commitment.

Taylor was a deserter, but it appears his absence was not noticed. His mother, Rose, certainly didn't notify the authorities. She continued to receive three shillings a week from his soldier's pay, and it wasn't until early February 1918, four years after he deserted, that the army realised the error. On 30 April 1919, in a memo to the 3rd Military Division from the Officer-in-Charge of Base Records, information was sought about the missing private.

'Will you kindly advise this office as to whether there is any information available which could assist in tracing the whereabouts of the abovementioned soldier who enlisted at Prahran, Vic. on 19–8–14.' Three weeks later came the reply confirming: 'Soldier D.N.E. [did not embark].'

Unfortunately for Taylor, the police and prison authorities did a better job of keeping a trace on him after he returned to civvy street. Images of his rapidly receding hairline and increasingly hangdog stare featured frequently in various state police gazettes. The entries were always blunt and to the point, with labels such as 'rogue' and 'vagabond'. His body art was a sight to behold, and no doubt assisted police in his identification. Added to the five-pointed star on the back of his right hand was a cross and wreath on the inside lower right arm. An anchor with an entwined snake was tattooed on his right arm, a bird on the right shoulder, a heart on the back of the right hand, and on his left wrist, clasped hands and a rising sun.

*

Australian soldiers were paid more generously than their comrades in other Allied armies: six shillings a day on active service, a decent plug that made service attractive enough to some men. However, the training camps were completely inadequate at first. Word quickly spread and as a result there were many nonstarters. By mid-1915, the federal government had called a royal commission into conditions in the camps: it heard evidence that 33 per cent of men who enlisted did not proceed to camp. The head of the inquiry, Justice Sir George Rich, recommended that men should be sworn in as soon as they passed fit, so that those who later changed their minds could be charged with desertion.

Conditions were so unsanitary that men risked permanent incapacitation without ever seeing the front line. Latrines were open to the weather, and facilities for bathing, laundry and dishwashing were grossly inadequate. Pots, pans and eating utensils were cleaned with water mixed with soil and sand, a mixture that Sir George noted would surely have contained spit and urine. He found that conditions in some camps were not merely cruel but calculated to endanger the lives of recruits.

In Victoria, most recruits went into camp at Broadmeadows on Melbourne's north-western outskirts, where a tent city had been flung up on a farmer's fields. There was a shortage of uniforms and underwear. As winter approached, the wet conditions and poor drainage resulted in colds and flu.

In Western Australia, the main camp for infantry was at Blackboy Hill, east of Midland Junction. The first recruits who signed up found themselves detailed to carve their new home out of bush. For a long time, the camp was a rough and ready collection of corrugated iron huts and canvas bell tents, and a parade ground where, as A.B. Facey recalled in his famous memoir *A Fortunate Life*, raw recruits unused to drilling occasionally punched the sergeant on the nose.

The main camp in New South Wales, at Liverpool, outside Sydney, was particularly subject to complaints. Joe Maxwell, who would go on to win a VC and a Military Cross and to write a knockabout memoir of his wartime experiences, recounted entering the camp in February 1915:

> I tramped into Liverpool Camp as a recruit, filled with as many illusions about war and soldiers as perhaps ever fluttered in the minds of adventurers in fiction. Nineteen of us were allotted to one tent. It was a group that seemed to include all the dead-beats, out-of-works, and hard citizens of Sydney.
>
> Then came that ritual of camp which to the novice was terrifying. To be plucked from the comforts of home, to be given a regimental number and dumped into a packed tent to sleep with feet to the centre pole was, to say the least, a little shattering.

In the early days of war, and in the immediate aftermath of the Gallipoli landing, men volunteered in droves. Not everyone signed up for patriotic reasons. As one regimental history retails, some blokes who found themselves 'jobless, homeless and broke' at that particular moment in history solved their immediate problems by enlisting. If the People's Palace was booked out, then the AIF could put a roof over their heads, albeit a rudimentary one.

Major training locations like Liverpool, Broadmeadows and Enoggera in Brisbane were relatively close to town, which led to problems with booze and women as many men made the most of their newly found freedom. The royal commissioner recommended that military police should crack down on the 'women of loose morals' who operated close to the camps. He also noted that the new recruits had easy access to local pubs. They were getting drunk and sleeping outdoors in the cold and wet, which led to illness. His final report recommended a comprehensive ban on the sale of liquor to soldiers. Alternatively, pubs within a radius of five miles of the Liverpool camp should be closed to soldiers from 6 pm. 'Pickets should be placed in or near hotels and instructed to see that no drink is carried away from the hotels by the soldiers in bottles or other receptacles for liquor.'

For some of the young recruits, the sudden promotion to manhood was more than they could handle, particularly once they had a drink in them. William Edward Gruner was looking forward to heading overseas to fight for his country. It was an opportunity to follow in the footsteps of his older brother, Hubert, who had signed up in Bendigo in late July 1915. Hubert was a driver who had seen action in France; he won a Military Medal in recognition of his conspicuous service in the field of battle.

The younger Gruner had a lot to live up to.

He was short but extremely powerfully built, and a scrapper. In his many police profiles he is described thus: 'Farm labourer, 5ft 3¼in, fair hair, blue eyes, nose has been broken, scar on back of right hand and scar on left wrist.' He had been raised in Richmond, one of the toughest working-class areas in Melbourne, an Irish 'struggle town' that was home to some of the most notorious gangsters of the era, including Squizzy Taylor. His own father, Albert, was a petty thief and minor local crim. In Richmond, the boot and the blade ruled, and military service was an escape from poverty and lawlessness.

William Gruner had been in the training camps for more than six months by the time his embarkation date came around in late April 1917. With a leave pass in his back pocket, he arranged to meet his father at the Prince of Wales Hotel in Richmond. The Gruners arrived at the popular pub at about 8 pm, where they drank and played cards and drank some more. By 11 pm the booze was taking its toll and a dispute arose with the barmaid over the bill.

The licensee, Robert Walker, stepped in and admonished the pair, telling them, 'You are a pair of @#$! mongrels, scaling a woman for sixpence.' Walker was a local identity, a former policeman who had worked the district for 20 years and also acted as assistant watch-house keeper.

The Gruners were escorted out and the door locked behind them. Witnesses said the young soldier started to kick the door. Walker, followed by his own son, went out to investigate. In court later, witnesses could not agree what had happened next, but the thrust of it was that the licensee had had enough of young Gruner's objections and told him, 'I don't want to talk to you, go away.'

He felled the young soldier with a slap to the face. Private Gruner leapt up and struck him. Walker retaliated with another slap. Walker's son, Robert, warned his father that Gruner had pulled a knife from his pocket. Like many young roughs around Richmond, Gruner carried a folding clasp knife. Albert Gruner was not impressed. He warned his son: 'No knife play while I am here; you are not going to use that.'

Too late. The inebriated young soldier sidestepped his father and ran at the publican, thrusting the knife into his side. A witness, Private Richard Thomas Harrison of the Army Medical Corps, told police that William Gruner had been 'very drunk'. He overheard him tell his father, 'Do you think I am going to stand a big @#$! doing that to me? I will kill the @#$!'

When police arrested him later at the family home in Richmond, they found the bloodstained knife in his pocket. In his court evidence, Gruner could not recall using the knife, nor could he remember how many drinks he'd had that night. In court, his father suggested that his son had been provoked: just before the knifing, Walker called his son a disgrace to the uniform.

Gruner was sentenced to five years jail with hard labour for manslaughter, with the judge describing it as a 'wicked and villainous crime'. With that, his military career came to a resounding end, unlike his criminal career. After his release, Gruner was back and forth before the courts on theft, vagrancy, obstructing, unlawful possession and obscene language charges.

*

By late 1915, as the war continued to use up men like cannon fodder, Britain's demand for troops grew. In January 1916, the UK government introduced conscription to raise the numbers needed. In Australia the federal government led by Billy Hughes ambitiously raised its targets for voluntary enlistment by a further 50,000. Even men with extensive criminal records made it into the army, thanks to the rush to enlist able-bodied volunteers.

Among the worst of the worst was Arthur Geoffrey Oldring, who volunteered two days after Christmas 1916. He signed up in Adelaide, describing himself on his papers as an engine driver. Oldring's real name was George Farrow Blunderfield, and he was an escaped prisoner who had been on the run from Western Australian police since April 1914.

An English immigrant who had come out via South Africa, Blunderfield had begun his criminal career in Kalgoorlie, where in the late 1890s he led a gang of bicycle thieves and earned himself the nickname 'Bicycle George'. On one occasion he was arrested for stealing a bike, and while he was out on bail he attacked the police's principal witness against him, one of his own friends. Blunderfield lured his victim to a campfire, where he struck him a heavy blow to the back of the head with a piece of iron. He watched callously as his injured mate staggered off into the distance.

Tried at the Perth Criminal Sessions for wounding with intent to murder, Blunderfield was acquitted but fined five pounds for stealing. Four months later he was convicted of raping a six-year-old girl, for which he was sentenced to twelve years jail. Evidence indicated that Blunderfield had been seen loitering around the house where the little girl lived and had entered through the back door and kept her subdued with lollies. Her mother was alerted to the assault by the blood on the youngster's bedclothes.

Blunderfield served seven years of this sentence and was then issued with a ticket of leave for good behaviour. His freedom was short-lived. Two years later, he broke into the Hopetoun Post Office, on the south coast of Western Australia. The postmaster, Charles Efford, was an agent for the State Savings Bank and known to hold hundreds of pounds on the premises.

Late one night in October 1909, Blunderfield paid a visit to the Efford household to spread news that an insulator was broken on the telegraph line near the building. Mrs Efford told him she would inform her husband the following morning. Some hours later Efford, unable to sleep because of the stifling heat, opened the bedroom window to let in some cool air. Within a short time, the postmaster was startled by the rustling sounds of an intruder.

Blunderfield had broken in, armed with a revolver and an iron bar. As Efford climbed out of bed to investigate the noise, a shot rang out. A bullet grazed his face and put a hole in the pillow, before lodging in the wall. Aroused from sleep, Mrs Efford screamed at the dark form of the intruder in their bedroom. Blunderfield immediately struck her on the head with an iron bar wrapped in a cloth and tied with fishing line. Only the thick hair pad she was wearing saved her from serious injury. Dazed and frightened, she scrambled through the open window, Blunderfield following in hot pursuit. Once in the street, she ran screaming to her neighbours.

Blunderfield kept running and disappeared into the bush. Charles Efford, with blood streaming down his face, recovered his wits and rushed to the police station. While the Effords were unable to identify their attacker because of the darkness, their young children, Samuel and Ivy, gave police the lead they needed. The children named George Blunderfield as the man they'd seen in the passage before the attack on their parents. He had been carrying a candle, and they recognised Blunderfield as a regular visitor to the Efford family home. He'd even played games with them.

At the crime scene, police located a bag on the back verandah containing 2000 detonators and a bottle of kerosene. Blunderfield had planned to blow the safe if the postmaster refused to hand over the keys. Accompanied by a black tracker, police headed for Blunderfield's camp nearby. There they found cloth similar to the material wrapped around the iron bar. The suspect was located and charged with attempting to kill Charles Efford. Midway through his trial in December 1909, Blunderfield changed his plea to guilty, and the court was told of the previous attempted murder charge involving Campbell.

Blunderfield's defence in the Efford case was that he remembered nothing, thanks to a skull fracture he had suffered 12 years earlier. This didn't wash with the court-appointed doctors, and the judge was equally unimpressed. In sentencing, he said of Blunderfield: 'If he is sane, the best place for him is prison, because he is a dangerous man.' Blunderfield was given nine years, which included the three unserved years from the previous rape sentence.

After three years in the Fremantle Gaol, he was sent to Wadjemup, on what is now called Rottnest Island. It had been a notoriously brutal prison, used mainly for Aboriginal offenders. The bodies of hundreds of Aboriginal prisoners were buried within the prison grounds, a grisly testament to the inhumane treatment inflicted on those in custody. By the time Blunderfield arrived on the island, however, the conditions were more relaxed. Blunderfield had freedom in his sights. He became cook to a group of prisoners who were given the freedom to walk about the island. One Sunday in 1914, he and his group went fishing. At Porpoise Bay he peeled off, telling the other men he was going to return to the jail. That was the last they saw of him.

Blunderfield never made it back. When he was discovered missing, a search party was sent out and reported seeing tracks along the beach leading to a pile of clothes and a towel. It was thought that he'd gone for a swim and drowned or been taken by sharks.

Later, a relative claimed that Blunderfield had retrieved a set of civvies he'd earlier stowed in the sand dunes and had boarded the *Zephyr*, a ferry which regularly serviced Wadjemup. By the time his absence was officially recorded, he was back on the mainland. A month after his escape, the Perth *Daily News* reported: 'Blunderfield, the long-sentence prisoner who was thought to have drowned at Rottnest, really escaped to the mainland. Blunderfield is a distinct menace to the community, as he is evidently of homicidal tendencies, being the author of many crimes, including attempted murder, brutal assault and rape.' Sunday newspapers published his photograph and described him as 'a most desperate criminal' whose recapture 'is earnestly to be desired, for while he is at large he is a distinct menace to the community'.

When he signed up almost 18 months later, Blunderfield, now using the alias of Oldring, was passed fit, though living rough had left his teeth in bad repair and he required substantial dental treatment. He enlisted in the 8th Machine Gun Company in Adelaide and was posted to the training camp at Seymour, prior to embarkation.

Recruit Number 767 was, by his personnel records, a sound soldier, though he was older than most recruits. He trained well and was generally well regarded. He was careful not to stand out from his group, for fear of inviting questions or checks on his background. Even so, Oldring was on for a good time before packing his kit for a new life overseas. The day he met a 50-year-old widow called Margaret Taylor, the complex web of lies Oldring had spun to cover his tracks began to unravel. The pair's paths crossed in North Melbourne in August 1917, when Oldring was on leave.

Mrs Taylor's older children, Violet and Elizabeth, had little regard for their mother's new beau, though she herself seemed oblivious to his violent criminal past. She followed Oldring to Seymour and the two were often seen strolling together around the town, accompanied by Mrs Taylor's youngest daughter, 12-year-old Rosie. The widow wanted marriage and suggested that Oldring could avoid being sent overseas by deserting. Little did she know he was already on the run from authorities.

In early November 1917, Oldring's unit was about to embark for France. He arranged to meet Mrs Taylor and her daughter on 11 November, at a bridge crossing the Goulburn River about five miles from the Seymour township. As police said later, it was a lonely place. What Margaret and Rosie thought they were doing there is anyone's guess. They took a horse-drawn cab to the rendezvous point, telling the inquisitive driver that they were meeting Margaret's sister, who would take them on.

When the driver left, Oldring emerged from the bushes where he'd been hiding and carried their luggage to a nearby campsite he'd prepared. Whether Oldring had lured the pair there to murder them is not clear. He said later that he'd been with Margaret Taylor the day before she and Rosie met him at the bridge. They'd had words over his desire to go to war instead of marrying her.

'She was continually asking me to desert the Forces and get married. I always told her no that I would remain in the army,' he claimed in a police statement.

Oldring returned to base late on Friday night. 'My head felt very bad and I was despondent,' he said.

It was in that frame of mind he met Mrs Taylor and her daughter the next day. After an argument, he stove in Margaret's head with her own tomahawk, then turned on the terrified young girl.

It took police almost a week to find the bodies. Rosie's semi-naked corpse was discovered first. A post-mortem examination revealed she'd been savagely struck about the head with the back of a tomahawk. Three deep wounds were located: the depressions matched the shape of the tomahawk, which had been fished from the river near the murder scene. Her skull was extensively fractured and the brain beneath lacerated. The police surgeon determined that young Rosie had been bashed to death before being flung into the swirling waters. One of the garters she had worn at the time was missing, and surgeons also discovered her hymen had been lacerated.

Four days later, detectives found the decaying remains of Mrs Taylor. Her body had floated to the surface quite close to the bridge and had snagged on a large tree branch. She too had been savagely battered about the head.

The Goulburn River had been in full flood and the killer had undoubtedly banked on the bodies being swiftly swept downstream. He must have assumed that by the time the bodies were located and identified, he would have embarked with his unit for Europe. However, on the eve of departure, Oldring was told by a friend that Rosie's body had been discovered. He immediately swapped his khaki uniform for civilian clothes and fled, heading straight into the bush.

A few days later, he secured a job on the Small family's fruit farm in Lancaster, but the orchardist had his doubts about the secretive and nervous labourer. After a few days, he got his wife to ride into Tatura to get the police. Oldring told the officers who came to arrest him that he was Arthur Brakespeare. He denied that he had ever been a soldier, just as he would later deny at trial that he had ever been in jail. Sergeant Coote later told the court: 'The prisoner was very nervous; was trembling violently and made very contradictory statements to me during the interview.' They found him in possession of two striped rugs belonging to Mrs Taylor – and Rosie's missing garter.

At his trial, Oldring's defence was 'mental derangement'. He said that he could remember nothing of the weekend of the killing, until he woke in his bunk at the camp on Monday morning. 'It would be about 6 o'clock. I had my uniform on. I felt very ill – my head was dazed and I could not remember where I had been since Friday but I felt as though something dreadful had happened.

'I was shivering all over, but I could not recall anything what I had done. All the following week I was in a dazed condition and tried to remember where I had been on the Saturday and Sunday – that would be the 10th and 11th of November.'

The jury was unmoved. He was found guilty and sentenced to hang.

On the morning of 15 April 1918, Oldring was escorted from his cell at the Melbourne Gaol to the gallows, where the noose was placed around his neck. Asked if he had anything to say, Private Oldring mumbled a few incomprehensible words.

The trapdoor was released.

*

Oldring was not the only member of the Blunderfield clan to enlist. One of his brothers, Charles Farrow Blunderfield, signed up in December 1915 in Brisbane, after serving time for his involvement in a botched payroll robbery. But if his brother was an amateur thief, Oldring was a case apart, an evil man who repeatedly attempted to kill people who knew and trusted him.

He claimed in his defence that he suffered memory loss caused by an old bike accident. He also said that mental illness ran in his family. It was true that his father had committed suicide in 1904, and that other members of his family suffered mental distress. A third brother also enlisted in World War I and was sent abroad, but was diagnosed in July 1915 as being of 'unsound mind'. After stints in British hospitals, he was sent home in 1918, just after Oldring's execution.

Then there was Oldring's sister, Jessie Ward Farrow Brown, who took her own life because of the shame he had caused her family. Jessie had married a hairdresser and settled in Port Melbourne. She had had no contact with her brother for many years when he suddenly turned up on her doorstep, wearing his AIF uniform. After that, he began to visit occasionally, usually on a Sunday. After the murder of Margaret Taylor, police interviewed Jessie, who told them she was sorry he had made contact, as he was a disgrace to the family. She didn't want her children exposed to him.

Her innocent involvement in Oldring's deception was just too much for Jessie. Within a day of her brother's arrest, she told her husband that she needed a rest, and went up to their bedroom. After locking the door, she opened a bottle of Lysol, a popular cleaning agent, poured it into a glass and drank it.

When the family discovered her some time later, her husband took her in his arms and heard her whisper: 'You have been a good husband to me.' She died in hospital soon after.

In her suicide note to her husband, she wrote: 'I blame myself for allowing that monster to come here and now you have to suffer for it. I made a great mistake in letting him come down on Sundays and I do hope they won't blame you for harbouring him.'

# 3

# All Aboard!

AT 6 AM ON 1 November 1914, a convoy carrying almost 20,000 Australian troops to the war sailed from Albany in Western Australia. In three lines, almost forty navy vessels and converted merchantmen steamed out of King George Sound, headed for Fremantle to embark troops from Blackboy Hill camp.

National security required secrecy: no coverage of this momentous departure appeared in the papers. The *Albany Advertiser*'s shipping column even went so far as to report that only three steamships bound for Fremantle and the east had sailed that day. But for anyone who witnessed its departure early on that Sunday morning, it must have been a stirring sight: the biggest military convoy ever assembled in Australian waters up to that time.

The British armoured cruiser HMS *Minotaur* led the group, which included troopships from New Zealand and their Japanese escort, the cruiser *Ibuki*. Once the ships reached open water, the Australian cruiser HMAS *Sydney* rode shotgun on one flank, and her sister ship HMAS *Melbourne* brought up the rear.

Over the following four years, such transports wore out the carpet between the ports of Western Australia and Colombo or Cape Town. They carried reinforcements to the Middle East and Europe, and fetched home the wounded and sick. They also brought back the 'incorrigibles' who were considered too much trouble to keep overseas, and – until October 1915, when the authorities decided there were just too many of them – Australian servicemen infected with VD.

The first convoy was ready to sail by mid-September 1914. The plan was that troops would embark on requisitioned liners and cargo ships at Brisbane, Sydney and Melbourne for the journey to the west, where they would be concentrated into a large group heavily defended by naval escort. But its departure from Australia was delayed by the *Emden*, a notorious German man-of-war playing cat and mouse with Allied shipping in the Indian Ocean. It had captured British steamers, stealing their coal and cargo, and had sunk Russian and French naval vessels, and as a result the British and Australian authorities were on high alert.

So thousands of Australian troops were stuck in camp, performing endless route marches and scoring leave when they could. Others who had already embarked from their home ports found themselves cooling their heels in Melbourne or Adelaide or Perth. Many men availed themselves of this unforeseen opportunity for an extra party, and restrictions on newspaper reporting of the convoy's delayed departure meant that coverage of the troops' carousing was muted. When the 10th Battalion, a South Australian unit, arrived at Fremantle on 25 October, two companies allowed shore leave 'immediately began to take Perth apart', as journalist Robert Macklin put it. For the rest of the ranks, leave was quickly stopped. When the *Ascanius* sailed on 2 December, two men were still AWL.

Despite military command's efforts to prevent it, many soldiers enjoyed a month of mayhem. The law-abiding citizens of Perth became tired of troops bent on a good time at all costs, overstaying their welcome in the city's watering holes or getting themselves into trouble with the opposite sex. As last stop for departing troops, the Western Australian capital proved an irresistible magnet for camp followers, prostitutes, and 'amateurs' who couldn't resist a man in khaki.

This was the start of a pattern of departing troops making trouble in Perth and Fremantle. Some men drank until they picked fights they could not remember later. In a typical case in 1915, a police constable passing the Imperial Hotel in Perth heard a row inside. Going in to investigate, he found a soldier, Patrick Ryan, aggressively wrestling with a returned serviceman who had been wounded in action. He separated the pair, then left the hotel after extracting a promise from Ryan to behave himself. But after he left, Ryan knocked the returned soldier down again, even though the man's leg had been badly injured in war and he could only hobble about on a stick. The magistrate sent Ryan to jail for 21 days.

Drunkenness and jail time caused soldiers to miss their ship. The judge threw the book at Harold Edwards, a young reinforcement in the 3rd Battalion, from Kurrajong in New South Wales, who had embarked on a burglary spree after becoming stranded AWL in Fremantle. When his troopship had docked there in January 1916, Edwards and three of his mates had disembarked and got drunk and had been left behind. The enterprising Edwards, a plumber by trade, had turned his hand to breaking and entering.

On his first appearance before the courts, just days after his ship had sailed, the 22-year-old soldier copped three months. Weeks later, he was back before the bench, pleading guilty to ransacking a house and taking a camera, a leather case and jewellery. Justice Burnside judged that he was 'not an amateur' and sent him down for three years. Passing sentence, he observed that the soldier might have reported his absence to the military authorities instead of embarking on a crime spree, but in any event 'his Honour did not think he would have been a credit to his country if he had been sent to the front as a soldier'.

Some of the men who got stranded in Perth were tragic cases. Private William Robert Ure missed his boat and went on a pub crawl that ended with his death. Ure, a 44-year-old labourer with a wife and family in Sydney, had signed up with the 15th Battalion in Brisbane. Reaching Perth aboard the HMAT *Warilda*, Ure and a mate went ashore; when the *Warilda* sailed a few days later, they were not in it. They handed themselves in and were sent to Blackboy Hill camp to be assigned another ship.

On 31 October 1915, Ure collapsed in Wittenoom Street, Perth. Witnesses said that he looked up, clutched his head and fell forward. Passers-by rushed to help the soldier, who was barely conscious, his face twitching. He died in hospital an hour later.

The inquest that followed heard evidence that a small amount of strychnine had been found in his stomach. It was suspected that Ure had killed himself because of remorse over missing his ship. His mate, who had been AWL with him, told the hearing that Ure had been worried about whether his wife would be docked his pay for the extra time spent in Perth. A finding of suicide would have prevented Mrs Ure receiving a war widow's pension. Fortunately for her, the jury decided that the soldier had died of acute heart failure.

Police told the inquest that Ure had spent the days before his death with a bar fly named Nellie Elliott, visiting one pub after another. On the last night of his life, the couple had booked into a coffee palace together – which did not mean they shared an evening of sobriety. Coffee palaces in Perth were more akin to hostels for the homeless, frequented by prostitutes and notorious for their squalid conditions. Elliott was signed in as Mrs Ure.

Ever since the gold rushes of the 1890s, Perth and its port of Fremantle had had a flourishing sex industry, which included an exotic collection of French and Japanese prostitutes who had come out to the goldfields as part of international syndicates. With the outbreak of war, the vice scene became frenetic.

In Perth, the industry was situated on the wrong side of the tracks, quite literally. Most of the brothels were in Roe Street, which faced the train line that separated the business district from industrial suburbs. Some train travellers objected to the fact that what they first saw as they pulled into Perth was a row of brothels.

A year after the war started, there were 15 brothels operating in Roe Street. In the first two years of the war, convictions for soliciting doubled, and the press called for stronger controls of the women who worked in them.

The upshot was that police insisted on regular medical examinations of prostitutes; any found to be infected with VD were hauled up before the courts on vagrancy charges. Their clients were not charged, but military records tell us that many soldiers had been infected after assignations with the 'ladies' of Perth just before the troopships departed for overseas.

Some women operated solo in the streets, pubs and coffee palaces. Increasingly, though, police pushed prostitution back into Roe Street, where it could be unofficially regulated. The most successful of the brothel keepers there was Frenchwoman Josie de Bray (real name Marie Louis Monnier), who at the height of the war owned the biggest brothel in Roe Street, and two others to boot. She was a sly-grogger as well as a brothel keeper, selling beer at five shillings a pop to the soldiers who frequented her houses.

Italian-born Marie Guidotti was another prominent brothel keeper, often described as a 'low woman', whose fortune was built on providing sexual services for soldiers and sailors. She had an extensive criminal record, principally for brothel-keeping, and had also served time in jail for her involvement in sex slavery. Twelve years before the war, Guidotti and her partner, Charles Cozzi, had recruited a 16-year-old girl in Rome to work for them as a servant in Australia. Cozzi presented himself as a mining executive. The couple paid her fare and promised her a decent wage. In Kalgoorlie, the couple had set up a household in Brookman Street, one of the streets notorious for prostitution. Their young servant guessed her fate when she observed that every day the other verandahs in the street were full of women sitting or standing in their doorways, 'dressed in coloured, gay, loose wrappers'. Even though Cozzi beat her, the girl would not cooperate. She screamed at would-be clients until they retreated. At last, a young tradesman working at the house helped her escape. She went to Perth and told her story to the authorities.

After Guidotti's release from jail, she rebuilt her business empire. By 1913, at the age of 34, she was running a busy brothel in Fremantle. Her name was often invoked in the Western Australian parliament, which heard she was 'a notorious law breaker'. Her establishments, it was often alleged in court by military authorities, were responsible for spreading disease among soldiers stationed around Perth.

From early in the war, venereal disease showed signs of becoming a major problem. Even before they left the country, many men were infected. In August 1915, the *Sunday Times* told its readers: 'We all know what happened at the start of the war – how some filthy disease-laden young prostitutes of Roe Street were engaged in the wholesale contamination and ruination of a number of our soldiers until the police stepped in and placed these women where they could do no further damage.'

At Blackboy Hill, medical officers set up a 'prophylactic tent' which was open day and night 'for the convenience of men returning to Camp': remedies aimed at preventing VD were available. 'Men are advised to use this tent immediately they return if they have had sexual intercourse, and they will not be penalised for so doing,' the camp adjutant reported.

The epidemic was not confined to the West. Authorities at Liverpool in New South Wales periodically diverted new recruits there to Brisbane and other training centres, to avoid an outbreak of infection. Further south, Melbourne at that time had a worryingly high rate of VD among its general population. John Daniel 'Snowy' Cutmore, who would tangle fatally with Squizzy Taylor a decade later, was one recruit to become infected there. Cutmore enlisted in April 1916 but went AWL from Broadmeadows within a few months. When he was picked up in July, he was suffering from gonorrhoea.

Australian troops travelling overseas were lectured about the dangers of VD and issued with a prophylactic box that contained tubes of calomel and carbolic cream and a packet of potassium permanganate tablets – good old Condy's Crystals, more commonly used for treating nits. According to the instruction manual, the calomel cream was to be applied before and after intercourse. Condoms were also recommended, but these had to be purchased separately.

The soldier was encouraged to keep his instruction card on him at all times and at the first sign of infection to attend an early treatment centre or 'Blue Light Depot'. Troops were told that treatment within the first 12 hours of the first indication of infection was effective in 86 per cent of cases. As an inducement, soldiers who attended the early treatment centres would not have their identities recorded or lose pay.

As part of the lecture, troops were given a sort of Life Education rundown on sexual behaviour. 'Many of you have probably heard that it is somehow or other harmful to the physical wellbeing to refrain from indulging in sexual intercourse,' the audience was told. 'From the medical point of view, that statement is absolutely false. Physically there is no necessity for it, and good health is not injured by avoiding sexual intercourse . . . The finest and healthiest man is he who is master of his passions, not their slave. Such a man, at any rate, will not suffer the penalties associated with venereal disease.'

To add to the sombre mood of the briefing, soldiers were warned that those who drank 'more than is good for him' would lose control and yield to the temptation of a disease-carrying prostitute.

Emphasising the need to take proper precautions, the authorities warned that no woman who 'allows you to have irregular sexual intercourse' could be regarded as safe. 'She has probably granted the same favour to others. The amateur, no matter how clean looking, is just as dangerous as the regular prostitute.'

*

The news that the first Australian convoy was destined for Egypt rather than England caused consternation among the military authorities, partly because of concerns about VD. The Australian war correspondent Charles Bean described Egypt as a 'hotbed of disease', and he wasn't far off the mark. In 1915, he penned a guidebook for the touring soldier, in which he sternly warned the men of the sexual pitfalls in the Land of the Pharaohs.

> Cairo has made itself a name in the world as a hotbed of both gonorrhoea and syphilis . . . Egypt has been an ancient home of syphilis – it was

> certainly here in Roman times; and there is found in the skull bones of mummies a disease which is almost certainly syphilis. Almost every village contains syphilis. And if a man will not steer altogether clear of the risk by exercising a little restraint, his only sane course is to provide himself with certain prophylactics beforehand to lessen the chance of a disastrous result.

Many men paid little heed. The troops from that first convoy landed in Egypt in December 1914, and by 1915 the Australian government issued orders that 'no pay will be issued while abroad for a period of absence from duty on account of venereal disease'. This rule often had more impact on the offending men's families, who were in receipt of a portion of their pay, than on the men themselves. The number of soldiers under treatment for VD grew by the week. By February 1916, almost 6000 men had been infected and more than 1000 of them shipped home.

One of the problems was that Australians had gone to war to fight, but before 1916 there was little fighting to be had in Egypt. The Aussies spent most of their time training in camps outside Cairo, and when off duty in the city's bazaars and brothels. Soon, the Australian VD camp at Mena was packed with patients.

Even Joe Maxwell, who would go on to become one of the most highly decorated Australian diggers, with a Victoria Cross, a Military Cross and a Distinguished Conduct Medal, was not immune. Egypt disappointed the impressionable Private Maxwell, who was only 18 when he landed there. He had expected romance and glamour, but all he found was 'a stifling heat that stewed the brain, a penetrating desert dust that scraped the flesh, sweat, boots, thirst, utter weariness, swish of sand, and the flame that poured from the sun and made men mad'. The young soldier succumbed to the charms of the ladies of the night 'who flaunted sex before the weary warrior'.

'I was destined to live and learn and see much,' Maxwell would recall in his memoir in characteristic understatement.

Buried deep in his official papers is a reference to the 37 days he spent in the Australian Dermatological Hospital, Abassia, being treated for venereal disease. His dose could be traced back to a brief visit to the notorious rue des Soeurs, or Sisters Street, a red-light district in Alexandria.

As historian Joan Beaumont says in *Broken Nation*, in Egypt Australians were 'happy to play "lords of the desert", exploiting the cheap labour and sexual services'. Phillip James Humphries was one notable example. He was almost 40 when he signed up with the 6th Light Horse Regiment in October 1915, and had no time to waste. Within a month of disembarking in Egypt, the trooper from Oberon in New South Wales was being treated for VD. He remained a patient for 17 days before rejoining his unit at the training camp at Tel-el-Kabir. A fortnight later he was back before the medicos with a 'sore penis'. After 15 days he was sent back to his unit, only to return less than a month later with the same affliction.

A year later Humphries came before a full court martial, charged with an unlawful killing. The hearing was told that a bedouin, Mahomed Ali Kagi, had been slain by the soldier who was on active duty. According to newspaper reports, Humphries had criminally assaulted a bedouin girl in Palestine and 'shot a native who went to her assistance'. He pleaded not guilty, but was found otherwise, and sentenced to penal servitude for life. Near the war's end, he was shipped back to Australia to serve out his term in Goulburn Gaol. His service medals were forfeited.

Sex and booze made a volatile combination for many troops, especially in an exotic location where the locals and the visitors did not particularly understand or trust each other. On occasion, this ill will boiled over into violence. The legendary Battle of the Wazzir was not just one but two stoushes involving misbehaving Australian and New Zealand troops in Cairo's red-light district, an area officially known as Haret al-Wasa'a. A collection of seedy bars, brothels and street prostitutes, the Wazzir's exotic offerings attracted diggers in their thousands, many of them keen to cast off their virgin status before heading to the front line. But Cairo's prostitutes exacted a heavy toll on Australia's fighting forces in more ways than one: high prices and venereal disease.

On Good Friday 1915, in the same month men of the Australian 1st Division landed at Gallipoli, a group of angry Australians converged on the Wazzir. In the confrontation that followed, the soldiers threw clothes and furniture out into the street. The fracas quickly drew a large crowd, and the violence and vandalism escalated. In the end up to 400 men joined in the attack, storming the brothels, setting fire to rooms, and robbing and bashing the inhabitants before driving them onto the streets. Firemen called to put out the blazes had some of their hoses punctured by knives. After the smoke had cleared, eight diggers, six British tommies and one New Zealand soldier were injured, including four with gunshot wounds.

The next day, a military inquiry met to try to establish the facts of the case and who to charge. It heard that two or three disgruntled Australians had demanded that some prostitutes reimburse them for the pay they had lost while they had VD. Graham Wilson, a former Australian Army officer who has investigated the incident in his book *Bully Beef and Balderdash*, calls the episode 'far more sordid' than the legend that has grown up around it suggests.

He describes how the women stood firm in their refusals to give the men any money. 'At this, the Australians became more aggressive and at least one of the defenceless women was struck down by an Australian soldier. The women then ran into their building for shelter, only to be followed by the Australians who broke down the front door of the building, broke into the women's rooms and began to throw furniture and clothing out into the street. Two fires were also lit in the prostitutes' rooms.'

The court of inquiry ordered that the Australian and New Zealand government should pay damages for the property that had been destroyed.

Three months later, on the last day of July, the Wazzir again erupted. Yet again the row involved a handful of Australians standing over prostitutes. The diggers claimed they'd been robbed by the prostitutes, who in turn accused them of not paying for their services. The women were physically assaulted and, fearing for their safety, fled to their apartments, only to be followed by the rampaging soldiers, who broke down the doors and destroyed their clothing and furniture. Two buildings were set alight and the blazes spread to four adjoining houses. When the firefighters turned out, their hoses and appliances were again damaged by some of the crowd. The affray was eventually broken up by the Military Mounted Police, with the assistance of picquets (lines of soldiers).

The area was placed in lockdown, and entry into Cairo by road and tram was blocked to diggers by military police. There was a violent aftermath the next day at Heliopolis, a swanky suburb 10 kilometres from the centre of Cairo, a resort area between the capital and the coast. When a large contingent of Australians en route to Cairo on leave were informed of the lockdown, they did not take the news well. They cooled their heels in the bars and hostelries of Heliopolis until the booze began to run out. Fearing another riot, military police cleared the venues of everyone in khaki – except those of warrant officer ranking and above. It was a stupid decision, and the resentful troops reacted.

As the angry soldiers spilled onto the streets, mayhem erupted. Rocks and other missiles rained on carriages carrying officers, bars were broken into and looted and some civilians seriously assaulted. Calm was finally restored just before midnight. In the wash-up, 19 diggers were rounded up and put before a court martial sitting at Zeitoun.

Seven of the men were named as ringleaders, including Private George Bickerstaff from the 27th Battalion. Bickerstaff was arrested while trying to break into a locked bar, allegedly 'demanding drink'. He was also charged with throwing rocks at senior officers. In his defence, he claimed to be a 'total abstainer'. He said he was knocking on the door simply enquiring about the latrines, and his arrest for rock-throwing was a case of mistaken identity. He said he was unable to call character witnesses because they were all at the front.

Bickerstaff was indeed found to be sober at the time of his arrest. But Captain Sydney Herbert Worthington, who described himself as commander of the Light Horse picquet responsible for 'quelling the riots', was sure of his guilt: 'I recognise the accused as having taken a very prominent part in the disturbance. There is no doubt as to his identity.'

Worthington said his memory was clear because he'd been one of Bickerstaff's targets. 'I recognise him as one of the men who tried to burst open the door of the Grand Brasserie Bar. I tried to arrest him and he resisted me and with the assistance of the crowd he got away.'

Evidence was also given that when Bickerstaff was taken into custody, stones were found in his pocket. He was sentenced to 112 days detention and three months loss of pay. His mate, Joseph McQueen, was also arrested, but seems to have escaped charge.

Bickerstaff was one of the 'Kibble boys': teenagers from a charity school in Paisley, Scotland, who went out to Australia under a farm apprentice scheme run by the South Australian government just before the war. Sixteen of the boys later enlisted, some of them perhaps hoping to see Scotland again. Bickerstaff and Joseph McQueen signed up within a month of each other, and shipped out together at the end of May 1915. Their friendship would be further strengthened in Egypt, as shown in a studio photograph depicting them in an upright stance, dressed in their uniforms, and looking into each other's eyes and gripping hands firmly.

There were Kibble boys who served with distinction, such as George McPhail of the 50th Battalion, who survived some of the worst battles on the Western Front and finished the war as sergeant. But Bickerstaff and McQueen were cut from somewhat different cloth.

When his battalion finally made it to England for training, Bickerstaff went AWL from the base at Perham Downs on the edge of Salisbury Plain, eventually turning up in his home town. There he remained until he was apprehended two months later. That cost him 60 days detention and more than 34 pounds in pay.

When Bickerstaff was demobilised he resumed residency in South Australia, where he married and settled down. But his life took a dramatic turn in July 1920 when he fronted the Adelaide Criminal Court charged with sexually molesting a six-year-old boy. At his sentencing, Bickerstaff's lawyer pleaded for clemency, invoking his military contribution, his Scottish background, his strong family roots and his one-time membership of the church choir in Paisley. His wife took the stand and gave a glowing character reference. So did his friend McQueen, by then a labourer. It is unlikely that McQueen gave a full account of his association with the defendant, because if he had, questions would undoubtedly have been raised about the interruptions to Bickerstaff's time in khaki.

In the end, George Bickerstaff was found guilty and slotted for 12 months. Somewhere along the line, he contracted TB.

He died in Melbourne, in the Heidelberg hospital for chronic diseases, in 1932.

After his adventures with Bickerstaff in Heliopolis, McQueen had a tough war. He saw action in France and suffered shell shock, trench fever and injuries to his right knee and leg that required hospitalisation. By mid-July 1918 it appeared it was all too much for the young private. After securing four days leave, McQueen went to Scotland 'to see my people', as he later told a court martial hearing.

He claimed that his visit coincided with the Stanrigg Colliery disaster, near Airdrie, Lanarkshire, in which 19 people perished. Layers of saturated moss had collapsed on the mine with such force that witnesses described it as 'making noise like thunder'.

One of those entombed in the coal seam was his uncle, 59-year-old John Queen. Seven of the dead miners were children, some as young as 14. Four of the teenagers were found clinging to each other in a manhole which was choked with wet moss. Rising floodwaters impeded rescue efforts and by the third day all hope had been lost of finding alive those trapped.

Joseph McQueen told his superior officers he had answered the colliery workers' call for volunteers to help in the rescue mission. 'Before volunteering I sent a wire to my CO, but got no reply,' he said in his statement. 'We were unsuccessful in getting the bodies and I continued working there till the 7th of November when the bodies were recovered.

'I was weak after working so long and I also had an attack of the flu. When I was better I reported myself. I considered it my duty to remain at home.'

McQueen emphasised his Anzac credentials, noting, 'I believe I was recommended for the Military Medal at Pozières.' He eventually handed himself in at London on 18 November – a week after the signing of the Armistice – and was immediately taken into custody.

A five-line notation, signed by pit manager George Johnstone and detailing John Queen's death and the fact that his body had not been recovered until 7 November, was presented at his court martial. Johnstone closed by writing: 'Trusting this will find your sympathy . . .' No such luck.

Not surprisingly, given McQueen's four-month absence in the critical closing stages of the war, the young soldier was sentenced to nine months jail and taken to the Lewes Detention Barracks. The following July he made it back to Australia in the troopship *Mahia*, and four months later was discharged as being medically unfit on account of an old injury to his right knee.

# 4

# Bad to the Bone

MANY DIGGERS WHO CAUGHT VD ended up in Langwarrin, an isolated military camp more than 40 kilometres from Melbourne. It had been a training camp for Boer War soldiers at the turn of the century, and at the start of the Great War was recommissioned as an internment centre for German and Turk civilians. But with the dramatic emergence of VD among enlisted men, the facility became a 'pox camp'.

Set well away from the township of Langwarrin in an obscure bush setting, the former prison camp was hated by the VD patients who were despatched there: out of sight of polite society and out of mind. The men were herded behind barbed-wire enclosures, and slept in tents with rubber sheets and blankets for bedding. The tents were leaky and the dirt floors quickly turned to mud when it rained, but as medical historian Audrey Mulder writes, in the first years of the VD camp lack of water was the most common problem.

> The small medical staff found it impossible to treat the men adequately. There was no proper water supply and a severe drought existed. All the water

> was carried by train from Mordialloc and thence by water cart to the Camp. The lack of bathing facilities implied habitual personal uncleanliness. The attitude of the general public and the authorities to the men was that they were 'untouchables'. Naturally they were disgruntled, spiteful and insubordinate.

Two hundred militiamen were set to guard the patients, and many of these guards were also resentful about the conditions. They too were ill-equipped, to the point where some uniforms were provided by public donation, such as the 12 oilskin coats given in May 1915 by a Melbourne clothier to keep the sentries warm and dry on winter nights. Some guards pilfered the Red Cross parcels intended for the patients.

Until the primitive conditions improved, recovery was difficult. Little wonder that soon after his diagnosis, Snowy Cutmore went AWL from Langwarrin and never returned, or that group escapes were relatively common. In October 1915 there was a mass break-out involving 50 patients who had been refused leave to visit the township. They fought the guards, broke camp and headed for the local railway station, where they caught the train to Melbourne.

Newspaper reports of the escape coyly described the wanted men as being 'encamped at Langwarrin, where men suffering from certain diseases are held'.

'An armed guard left Melbourne and intercepted the men at Caulfield, where the Frankston train arrived at 11.23 pm. The carriages were surrounded and the men ordered to retrain,' the *Argus* reported. 'Slight trouble was experienced with the more rowdy members of the party, who were handcuffed.'

The men were then taken on to Melbourne, where they were met by more police 'to guard against any possible demonstration on the part of the camp breakers'.

Not all the runaways had taken the train. Some of them went across country, headed for home or interstate. After a week, military authorities enlisted the public's help to smoke them out. A large notice was placed in newspapers across Australia.

> Members of the Australian Imperial Force who broke out of the Langwarrin Island camp are hereby notified that they must report at the Guardroom, Victoria Barracks no later than 10am on Tuesday, 26th instant, without fail.
>
> In the event of any person failing to obey the above order his full name, address and description will be published in the daily press, and he will be arrested for desertion. The public are cautioned against harbouring any deserter. Any person concealing or assisting in concealing him is liable to imprisonment with hard labour for 12 months.

By and large, the threat of public shaming worked and many of the escapees made their way back. But the incident shone a spotlight on the unsavoury nature of Langwarrin and its appalling conditions.

Residents of the Langwarrin township also raised concerns about the infected men sharing amenities with the rest of the community. In November 1915, the Mornington Progress Association was up in arms about the soldiers using the same drinking vessels and other amenities as locals at the railway station. The association urged the Victorian Board of Health to use its influence to have the Railway Department refuse to serve VD patients in the refreshment rooms. The health board passed on the association's concerns to the defence authorities. The campaign got into the papers, and the *Argus* urged the Railway Department to set aside special carriages for the sick men, and to disinfect them after they had completed their journey.

Public fear of a VD epidemic was understandable, because even before the war the disease was a serious public health problem. At the Australasian Medical Congress in Melbourne, a Dr Bennie told delegates that 10 per cent of Melbourne's children were infected with syphilis. A federal committee looking into the causes of death and invalidity in 1917 heard that three years earlier more than 3000 children across Australia had died from inherited syphilis and gonorrhoea. VD crossed all social barriers.

It was the same within Australia's armed forces. Even highly decorated war heroes were not immune. About 10 Victoria Cross winners were, at one stage or another, in designated hospitals being treated for the condition, as their war service records reveal.

Private Edward John Francis Ryan was one VC winner who contracted the 'scarlet scourge' or 'red plague', as the disease was often referred to in polite circles. A labourer born in Tumut, New South Wales, Ryan was with the 2nd Reinforcements of the 55th Battalion and spent two months in Egypt before heading on to Fleurbaix in France. From mid-October 1917 he was laid up with VD for 39 days. The following September, during the Allied advance against the Hindenburg Line, he led a party in an attack against a German unit which had cut him and his comrades off from their own lines at Le Catelet, in Picardy. According to his Victoria Cross citation, Ryan and his comrades killed three Germans. Acting alone, he rushed at the rest with bombs, forcing them back to no-man's-land. He was wounded but survived.

Eight months later he was presented with his VC by King George V at Buckingham Palace. The following month he was back in hospital with another dose of the clap. On his release, he fronted a court martial hearing on charges including failing to appear at a place of parade, disobeying a lawful command and using insubordinate language. The VC winner was found guilty on all charges – and ordered to forfeit one day's pay.

Insubordinate, occasionally disobedient, not immune to a good time, Ryan might have displayed a larrikin streak, but he was no crook. Like many veterans, he struggled to hold down a job after the war, and in the Depression years he marched hundreds of miles looking for honest work.

Another Australian who won the VC during the same campaign was a courageous sergeant living with a secret. His real identity was Trooper Maurice Buckley, and he had joined the 13th Light Horse Regiment the week before Christmas 1914 and was sent to Egypt. Like many of his comrades, however, the young soldier contracted gonorrhoea and syphilis, and in late 1915 was shipped home, banished to Langwarrin. After five months, Buckley could take no more. In March 1916, he slipped through the gates, never to return. His papers were stamped 'deserter' and he was struck off the army roll.

Buckley's reputation was shattered. The Christian Brothers–educated soldier had been sent home without firing a shot, and he had to explain to his proud family why his military expedition had been cut short.

The Buckleys gathered for a family conference at mother Agnes's house in Malvern, a leafy Melbourne suburb. With the military police combing Melbourne for the deserter, Mrs Buckley suggested her son re-enlist, but under another name. The last place the MPs would look, she calculated, would be under their noses.

So the fugitive travelled to the army recruitment centre in Sydney, where he signed up as Private Gerald Sexton. Sexton was his mother's maiden name, and Gerald was the name of his brother who had died in an army camp almost a year earlier of meningitis.

The 'new recruit' was assigned to the 13th Battalion of the 4th Division, embarking shortly after for Plymouth and then France. In the battle of 8 August 1918, he earned a Distinguished Conduct Medal for his bravery in the Morcourt Valley conflict. Three weeks later at Le Verguier, armed with a Lewis machine-gun, Sexton turned his attention to a group of Germans and a field gun, rushing towards them while still under heavy fire. After killing the gunners, he headed in the direction of the machine-gun fire and, shooting his Lewis gun from the hip, cleared a dugout and took 30 prisoners. Sexton then continued to advance on the enemy.

On 9 December 1918 he was awarded the Victoria Cross. But three weeks later the commanding officer at Langwarrin notified military command of Sexton's false identity. At the end of the war, Buckley was returned to Australia and medically discharged suffering shell shock. He didn't lose his fighting spirit. Buckley, a strong Catholic, was openly aligned to the controversial Archbishop Daniel Mannix and marched ahead of him in the St Patrick's Day parades. The war hero also established a strong kinship with the equally controversial John Wren, whose suspect business empire had its roots in SP bookmaking, sly grog and prostitution. Wren bankrolled the VC winner into a road-contracting business in country Victoria.

When Buckley died in January 1921 after a horseriding incident, he was buried in the Brighton Cemetery. Fittingly, he was laid to rest alongside the brother whose name he'd borrowed to restore his reputation.

*

No doubt about it, VD caused mayhem. Archibald Murchison enlisted at Beaufort in country Victoria in late March 1915. Within months the 19-year-old labourer was in Langwarrin with a nasty dose of gonorrhoea.

The young private wasn't for hanging around, though, and through the gates he walked, straight for Melbourne, where he might have blended into the background had he not partaken of drink and addressed passers-by from the top of a lamppost. His antics caught the eye of the passing constabulary, and the soldier was taken to Melbourne's City Court, where he was fined three pounds then promptly returned to the VD hospital. His conviction whetted the interest of the court reporter from the racy tabloid, *Truth*, who filed an account, accompanied by the lurid headline: LOOSE FROM LANGWARRIN. BAD BOY'S BOISTEROUS BEHAVIOUR. NINETEEN-YEAR-OLD SOLDIER FINED.

The following February, on a very warm evening, the ruddy-complexioned Murchison would again be in the headlines, but on a much more serious matter. This time he was fighting a manslaughter charge, after killing a soldier named John Heath.

The 43-year-old cook from the Ascot Vale military camp had confronted young Murchison, who had been drinking in a King Street hotel in the city. According to witnesses he made a 'very offensive expression'. Given that Murchison had just returned to the Broadmeadows camp from Langwarrin, Heath's insult more than likely centred on the private's manhood.

Murchison admitted striking Heath, who fell to the footpath. After getting to his feet, Heath ran towards Murchison brandishing a piece of wood. A woman standing nearby screamed, and Heath immediately threw it away. With that, Murchison punched him again, causing him to fall again and fracture his skull. He was dead inside 10 minutes.

Murchison was cleared of any blame by the coroner, who declared it death by misadventure, adding that Heath had 'really invited the trouble', and the response was simply 'what any man would do'.

Homicide detectives saw it differently, and Murchison was immediately arrested for murder. The soldier beat the charge several weeks later when a criminal court jury returned a not-guilty verdict.

As for young Archie, he was unceremoniously dumped from the army a month or so later for being 'medically unfit' – venereal disease again. The unambiguous notation on his military record states: 'Discharged at Broadmeadows being worthless and incorrigible and services no longer required – 17 May, 1916.'

In an attempt to improve the running of Langwarrin, the authorities came up with a plan. From August 1915, the guards there would be men who had been treated and recovered from the disease. They thought it would free the militiamen for other duties and offer recovered patients useful employment. But it didn't keep a guard named Michael Cook from offending.

Cook was a tall, strapping 22-year-old labourer when he enlisted in January 1915. He came from Victoria's Western District and must have owned his own horse, for he was attached to the 13th Light Horse Regiment and served at Gallipoli. He had got himself into a spot of bother while in Egypt and had copped 28 days detention for begging, but otherwise his military record was unremarkable.

He was invalided home from the Middle East in January 1916 and immediately diagnosed with enteric fever. When he recovered, he returned to duty at the Broadmeadows military camp, but a few months later was diagnosed with gonorrhoea. In May, he entered Langwarrin, and there he eventually became a guard. Pencilled on his hospital admission form is the notation, '160 days' – the total time he'd spent in both facilities.

On 31 October 1916, Cook was absent from duty, and the reason soon became apparent. An 18-year-old girl accused Cook of violently raping her during a chance encounter at Melbourne's botanical gardens that afternoon.

In court, the victim calmly told her story. She had had lunch in town with her father and was walking home to South Yarra when she stopped and sat down on a bench near the Queen's statue. For half an hour she sat and read, until she was approached by a soldier who asked if he could share the bench. He sat and smoked while she continued to read. He asked her where she was going later, and when she said she planned to walk home along the river, he suggested he accompany her part of the way. He lied and told her that he was quartered at the barracks in St Kilda Road.

They set out, but a thunderstorm struck and the pair sought shelter under a tree in the gardens. According to the girl's evidence, Cook then seized her by the wrist, dragged her to the ground and proceeded to rape her. They were just 25 yards from a public pathway. As the *Truth* newspaper delicately explained:

> When she remonstrated with him, he announced that he intended to be intimate with her, and would not let her go until he affected his purpose. A struggle ensued and the prisoner eventually threw her down. She screamed and he clutched her throat, threatening to choke her. Her answer to that was that she would sooner be choked than ruined, whereupon he tightened his hold, and she was nearly breathless before he loosened his grip.
>
> When she besought him to desist, he replied: 'No girl who has ever been in my clutches has got away from me.' The victim gave evidence that he had thrust his thumb into her mouth and his fingers under her chin, and pushed her back onto the ground.

> Then he violently disarranged her clothing, tearing portions of it in his endeavours to effect his purpose, and at length discovering that she was in a certain condition of health.
>
> To which he remarked: 'You needn't be afraid. I run more risks than you.' He then forcibly removed the last obstacle to his gratification.

Presumably he meant that he knew he was clean of VD at the time of the rape.

The heavy rain and thunder continued and when Cook readjusted his own clothing, it was covered in mud and grass – and blood. His victim was soaked to the skin, her skirt and blouse torn and badly soiled. As he was preparing to leave, she asked him why he'd done such a thing to her and he answered: 'While I was away the @#$! Australians ruined two of my sisters, so I vowed vengeance on other fellows' sisters.' Bizarrely, he then scrawled what purported to be his name on a piece of paper and left it with her, saying he could be found at that address 'if anything went wrong'. The name was a 'Private Souter, military police, Frankston'. His trial would be told Private Souter was one of his army 'cobbers'.

Cook was not averse to misrepresenting himself. On his enlistment form he had declared himself as John Edwards, which was later amended to Michael Cook after his long-suffering wife, Minnie, blew the whistle.

Unsurprisingly, he denied the rape allegation, claiming his victim was a willing participant and that they had 'kissed and spooned'. But this was fiercely rejected by the young woman, who was also challenged as to why she had not informed Cook about her menstrual cycle – or 'condition of health' – before he'd made clear his intentions. 'I was not going to speak to a strange man about a matter like that.' She told the court that until that day she'd been a virgin.

The woman, dishevelled, bruised, bloodied and in great distress, eventually reached home where she broke the news to her mother. She could not bring herself to tell her father. 'I've been outraged by a soldier,' she sobbed. Her mother immediately insisted she go to the police. Cook, who was still in the vicinity, was soon tracked down.

The victim was taken to hospital.

Her family already had its own problems. Her father was a returned serviceman whose stint was dramatically cut short by his addiction to booze. He was a chronic alcoholic who had been unceremoniously shipped home from Egypt. One official memo from his training battalion commander to the medical officer over a mislaid conduct sheet pulls no punches: 'He has a bad record, however, having been awarded punishments on several occasions, for drunkenness and absent without leave.'

The disgrace would not have been lost on his relations, who had influential political and financial links in Queensland. His late father had been a prominent member of that State's parliament.

At trial Cook was found guilty of criminal assault. In his summing-up, Justice Henry Edward Agincourt Hodges took direct aim at the disgraced soldier. He indignantly questioned Cook's sense of military respect, adding that his behaviour was 'a disgrace not only to the uniform, but also to his Majesty's forces'.

Justice Hodges told the guilty man: 'It is not part of my duty to deliver a moral lecture to you, which I do not think you are in a position to receive. I have only one duty to perform.' With that, he sentenced him to death.

A month later, the capital sentence was commuted to seven years by order of the State Executive Council. Cook's time in the army ended ignominiously with an official discharge and the forfeiture of his service medals and ribbons.

*

For many Australian soldiers based in England, the Australian VD hospital at Bulford had a revolving door. Set on the Salisbury Plain in Wiltshire, the hospital was taken over in August 1916 by the Australian Dermatology Hospital, with instruments and appliances largely provided by the Australian Red Cross Society. Within a short time it was also taking in infected Australians from France, where VD was rampant. Edward Garstang, in his thesis on crime and punishment on the Western Front, notes that by 1918 Australians were 'becoming reckless' when it came to exposing themselves to VD: 'considering the increasing numbers contracting the disease, despite the thorough education program and safeguards in place regarding the disease, the high rates do suggest that some men were contracting the disease to avoid frontline duty'. It was a 'self-inflicted' wound that gave them a break of several weeks from the fighting without incurring a military charge.

Bulford became widely known as 'the College' – because so many Australians had 'graduated' from there. The worst of the AIF's recalcitrants flooded into this hospital which, unlike military prison hospitals, had no system of quarantining the bad characters from the rest. Consequently it was hard to maintain discipline, and adequate exercise could not be given for this very reason. Some men had to be restrained or placed under heavily armed guard.

Near the end of the war, it became a near-permanent address for William Ness Hutton, a young private attached to the 54th Infantry Battalion. Hutton had joined the army in early October 1916, no doubt at the insistence of his family, straight after walking out of the gates of Goulburn Gaol.

The 17-year-old miner had been given a year with hard labour after being charged with carnal knowledge of a girl under 10 at his home town of Neath, between Cessnock and the Hunter Valley in New South Wales. At the expiration of his sentence, the judge told him, he would 'be required to find sureties for his behaviour for three years'. The army would be the answer, although according to his enlistment papers Hutton had tried before and failed – because of bad teeth. Nonetheless, the newly released prisoner was accepted for the military and embarked on 11 November 1916.

Aside from a relatively minor matter of going AWL for five days for which he forfeited ten days pay, Hutton's war was uneventful – until late June 1918 when he received a battlefield gunshot wound in France and was invalided to a medical centre in Cambridge, England. Hutton had been shot in the thigh, but this wasn't going to dampen his sexual drive. From late September 1918 through to the following August, Hutton was in and out of Bulford and Parkhouse and spent more than 200 days being treated for VD.

A notorious Bulford detainee was one Private George Vaughan, a walking disaster where the opposite sex was concerned. Young Vaughan was hospitalised five times with the pox between September and early December 1918. Even on the voyage home, Vaughan was admitted to the ship's hospital suffering 'VD and gonorrhoea'.

In a letter from the AIF command, his doting wife, Florence, was given a detailed list of her wandering husband's VD visits. The 21-year-old labourer had been AWL seven times, and clearly his free time was taken up by various sexual activities. At his final court martial appearance, Vaughan explained his absence from camp was out of concern for the young local woman he'd been squiring.

'I was a patient in the 1st AGH Bulford and while undergoing treatment I received a letter from my young lady stating that she was in trouble, which I admit was caused by me,' he said in his statement.

'She stated that she informed her parents to the fact that she was in trouble and unfortunately her father was unexpected to live and she was very worried about things. And he wanted to see me urgently to discuss the matter and to find out my intentions for her future welfare.

'Now Sirs, you can just think what state of mind I was in. I at once proceeded to the orderly room – showed the letter to the Colonel Commanding and applied for leave, which he refused to grant me.

'Knowing that her father was near his last, I thought it my duty as an honourable man to satisfy her Father before he died, that I would take the proper course and marry his daughter.

'I left the camp and came to London and visited the hospital with my young lady and we both sat at his bedside while he passed away. That is my reason for absenting myself from Camp.'

It appears the only misty eyes in the rooms belonged to Vaughan, because the court martial panel immediately slotted him for two years. After a brief time he was shipped home, first to a jail cell and then into the frosty embrace of the long-suffering Florence.

A year or so after his return, Vaughan added bigamy to his rap sheet. He tied the knot with an Annandale woman, and together they set up home. When Florence appeared in the Sydney divorce court in late February 1922, newspapers described the betrayed wife as being 'a small woman, dressed in black'. She told of how she'd married Vaughan in Pyrmont on 13 November 1916, just before he went off to war. Vaughan wasn't in court to hear Florence; he was already behind bars doing nine months for bigamy. Seven years later, he was back in jail for neglecting a maintenance order for the upkeep of his child. His service medals were forfeited.

Another out-of-control private soldier did manage to keep his medals, and also made it onto the Australian War Memorial's Roll of Honour. Edward Woods was a serial escaper and a notorious 'sandbagger' who preyed on citizens and soldiers alike, coshing them and robbing them of their cash and valuables.

He had no doubt been engaged in his own street wars before enlisting in Melbourne in early February 1915. His physical description notes the scar above the right elbow, another scar on the lumbar region and evidence that his left arm was once broken. But if the army thought he was up for the fight, they were mistaken.

Within a year of signing on, Woods was in the Middle East and laid up for 19 days with VD. Six weeks after his release, he was reinfected, this time with a strain of gonorrhoea, and immediately despatched to the 17th General Hospital in Alexandria. The following March he was again being treated for the pox in Alexandria, where he remained for close to three months.

Within days of his release, Woods was sent to France but a few weeks later found himself before a field general court martial sitting at Étaples, charged with escaping while in confinement. He was sentenced to 56 days of field punishment no. 1. The following March he was again struck down by VD, but this, all things considering, was the least of his problems. Just days earlier he'd been before another field general court martial, this time charged with desertion and striking his superior officer in the execution of his duty. Woods pleaded not guilty to both charges, but took the rap on the striking charge. On the desertion count he appears to have dodged a bullet – it was downgraded to AWL. Nonetheless, the 20-year-old private was given a four-year custodial sentence, which was shortly after commuted to two years.

While on the run in France, Woods' life took a predictable turn. In his book *Bad Characters,* Peter Stanley tells of how he linked up with a band of like-minded deserters who ran amok behind the lines in France, raking in the cash through gambling and armed robberies.

> Its head was 'Bluey' McKinnon, an 11th Battalion man who had been absent for nearly a year. Good looking and smartly dressed, he commuted between Paris and his gambling schools at Etaples. McKinnon's sidekick was Edward Woods, a Liverpool-born cook who cheekily wore an officer's tunic. He had been arrested by the 5th Division's APM (when he was found with double-headed pennies and an APM stamp on him), but escaped, only to be recaptured and imprisoned for two years.

On 20 July 1918, Woods was released, the remainder of his sentenced being suspended, and he was returned to the 58th Battalion.

Less than two months later, on 2 September, the infantryman was killed in fierce action which helped drive the Germans from the town of Péronne, during the Battle of Mont St Quentin. According to his file, Woods was hit by a piece of shell and killed instantaneously.

# 5

# An Unlikely Hero

In Parramatta Gaol, George Harris was a prisoner to be feared whatever side of the bars a man stood on, a desperate and dangerous criminal beyond redemption. The crowning moment of his career in jail came when he tried to stab the prison's deputy governor to death.

By the time he enlisted in 1916, he was 34 and had spent almost half his life in jail for crimes of violence. Harris was born in Dubbo but never knew his parents: he was educated on the dangerous streets of Surry Hills and Darlinghurst. By the age of 18, he was well known to police as a bag-snatcher, petty thief and member of a larrikin gang which used the Liverpool Arms Hotel in Surry Hills as its base.

Then Harris and a fellow gang member got their names in the papers over a shooting incident in Oxford Street. A police constable had tried to apprehend Harris for a street robbery a few days before in which he'd snatched a handbag with eight shillings in small change from a young married woman. Harris struggled violently with the officer, Constable George Edward Ward. As Ward dragged him to the nearest police station, Harris's associate, Robert Shaw, intervened and fired his revolver at the officer's head.

Shaw's bullet struck the policeman's helmet and glanced off his skull. With blood streaming down his face, the constable clung to Harris until back-up arrived. At Shaw's trial for unlawful wounding, the wife of the publican of the Liverpool Arms was called as an unwilling witness. Sarah Carley told the police court she saw Harris and Shaw in the bar before the shooting: they were checking their revolvers and openly discussing shooting police.

According to Mrs Carley, Harris said to Shaw: 'If I get caught you blow him out, and if you get caught I'll do the same.'

After the incident, Shaw returned to the hotel, where he told her: 'Harris has gone off, missus, a copper took him, and I shot him.'

The following day she overheard Shaw talking to a gang member, who said to him: 'You ought to have finished him off altogether.'

The Central Criminal Court jury found Shaw guilty of maliciously wounding with intent to inflict grievous bodily harm. Harris went down for six months with hard labour for purse stealing. When he was released, Harris quickly reverted to his old ways, spending another three years in prison.

In early 1905, he was convicted of assaulting and robbing a widow named Ada Linklater. The woman wasn't going to give up her bag easily and tried to fight off Harris. He seized her by the waist and dragged her into a lane, where he threw her down, punched her in the chest and kicked her thigh, while wrenching the bag out of her hand. It contained one pound, two shillings and tuppence, about half a weekly wage. Mrs Linklater went to the police station to report the theft. When she left, she noticed Harris lurking across the road and immediately raised the alert.

Harris vigorously denied any involvement and in court produced his own alibi witnesses claiming he was miles away at the time. He complained that because of his record, every time a bag was snatched in Sydney he was blamed. He claimed that he'd tried to get a job after leaving jail but was restricted by the lack of a reference. And because he was an orphan and had been brought up on the streets, the only education he'd received was in jail.

His pleas of innocence failed to sway the Darlinghurst Sessions jury, and the judge sentenced him to the maximum possible stretch – 10 years in jail.

He was about a year into his sentence at Parramatta Gaol when he lined up for the muster one day in November 1906. The daily rollcall was conducted by the deputy governor, James Quaine, a respected career prison officer. He and Harris had clashed earlier when they were both at the Darlinghurst lock-up. As chief warder there, Quaine had stopped one of Harris's jail visits as a penalty for bad conduct. The powerfully built Harris did not forget it.

Late in the afternoon of 17 November, Quaine, in the company of two warders, conducted a rollcall of prisoners, lined up outside the prison workshop. Just as he called Harris's assigned number, 19, Harris sprang forward and struck Quaine on the left side of the face with his fist. The force of the blow momentarily turned the senior warden around.

Just as Quaine began to recover his balance, Harris stepped in with a bootmaker's knife. He had smuggled it out of the workshop, sharpened it and hidden it in his sleeve. From a distance of about two paces, he lunged at Quaine, piercing his left breast with the tip of the knife, shouting something like: 'Take that you dog . . . I'll teach you to lock up a man for nothing.'

The two warders rushed in and grabbed Harris from behind. As they scuffled, the knife fell from Harris's hand to the ground.

The blade had penetrated the warder's skin just below the fourth rib and punctured his left lung. The wound was close to two inches in length. The force of the attack was such that the tip of the knife had snapped off and remained embedded in a rib. Quaine was haemorrhaging internally. In a state of shock, he appeared unaware that he'd been stabbed, and continued the rollcall. Remarkably, not one prisoner stepped out of line during the attack.

When Quaine returned to his section, he collapsed. By then he was bleeding freely from the chest wound. He was rushed to the prison's hospital, where doctors found him 'almost pulseless'. One of them later gave evidence that 'he was in a state of complete collapse and in a dying condition'. For a fortnight, Quaine remained in a critical state.

Harris was isolated in a special supervision cell with grated doors. As officials later acknowledged, he unsuccessfully attempted suicide. A 24-hour watch was kept on him, and he was deprived of sharp objects, even down to his eating utensils, which comprised just a wooden dish and spoon. A local newspaper, the *Cumberland Argus and Fruitgrowers Advocate* took particular interest in his case. It painted a horrific, if not unsympathetic, picture of the young prisoner, calling him 'a character that needs watching':

> He is a blonde lad with a square-cut head, forehead projecting, deep-sunken eyes, thin, close lips, denoting a passionate temper. The chin, though rather square, inclines inwards, and gives one the impression of a temperament that would brood a good deal over any matter that did not please him . . . a creature of fits and starts, and likely to burst out like a latent volcano at any moment.

At his trial, Harris pleaded not guilty to feloniously wounding Quaine with intent to murder him, and used his appearance as a forum to also proclaim his innocence of the crime that had landed him in Parramatta for 10 years. That had been a case of mistaken identity, he said. Since entering jail, he'd suffered sleep deprivation which had affected his wellbeing. His explanation for having the knife was that he used it to shave because 'the clip he got every two weeks' was not enough to satisfy a man with pride in his presentation.

Harris claimed he had no grudge against Quaine. Addressing the jury, he solemnly declared: 'I thank God, gentlemen, I have not got that gentleman's blood on my mind.' He said he could not recall the moment he allegedly plunged the knife into his jailer's chest. Since he had been wrongfully imprisoned for robbing the widow, he had suffered from sleeplessness and worry. At the time of the muster he was ill and hadn't slept the previous night.

The jury returned after just two hours with the inevitable verdict: guilty. With that, the judge sentenced him to death. Quaine survived, and the sentence was later commuted to penal servitude for life. But no jail was going to hold George Harris.

He managed to get a transfer to the Parramatta Hospital for the Insane, a somewhat less arduous institution. In late October 1909, he fled the asylum on the eve of his return to Parramatta Gaol. With the assistance of a friend, Harris slipped away from other inmates in an exercise area and made for an outhouse where he collected a set of clothes. He left his asylum clothes under the toilet seat, beside the slop bucket.

Dressed in his civilian attire, the man described by police as a 'dangerous criminal lunatic' walked out of the asylum undetected. From there he travelled to a house in Redfern, but his freedom was short-lived. The newspaper headlines trumpeted: DANGEROUS CRIMINAL AT LARGE. Someone dobbed him in. After several days, police sprang an early morning raid on the house in Redfern and arrested Harris in a bedroom. He was taken away without incident.

Harris was returned to Parramatta, where he became prisoner number 57. His file was none too complimentary, describing him as 'nursing imaginary wrongs; very cunning, irritable and easily upset'.

It goes on: 'He has made violent, treacherous and unprovoked assaults on prison officials and his fellow prisoners.' The journalist from the *Cumberland Argus* who had watched him defend himself at his 1906 trial was more sympathetic:

> When he appeared in public in connection with the trial for the attack upon Mr Quaine, Harris struck us as very much the ordinary type of citizen, a fair, blue-eyed man of about average build, with a hard but far from unpleasant face . . . No wonder it was hard. Ten years, with the immediate prospect of being hung, was enough to make a man's face look hard. Yet we could not help thinking that the human material might under different conditions have turned out 'not so bad after all'.

*

The state attorney-general at that time was David Hall, a barrister and Labor radical. He wanted to improve the lot of working men and women and was also a prison reformer. That did not mean he was soft. During the war, he was a founding member of the Universal Service League, a group set up across political lines to lobby for the introduction of conscription. (Hall had tried to join up himself, but was rejected on medical grounds.) When the ALP split over the issue of conscription, Hall joined the pro-conscription side, for which he was evicted from the Labor Party.

Harris asked to see the attorney-general, to plead for an early release. Hall took a keen interest in the notorious prisoner's case, even after a prison official told him that he would be dealing with 'the worst man in the jail'.

'I never remembered my parents,' Harris told the attorney-general when they met in prison in 1912. 'My earliest recollection was when, at the age of three, I was handed over to some people in Sydney to be cared for. By the time I was twelve I was on the *Sobraon* (a sailing ship used to teach wayward and deserted children). Leaving that at about 16, I at once got into trouble, and was in and out of gaol until I became 21.

'On my 21st birthday I determined to reform, and to earn an honest living. I didn't know one respectable person in the whole world. I went to live in the house of a prostitute in Surry Hills; bought a basket and went hawking. The work was hard, but I made a living out of it for some time.

'Every time a crime was committed the police naturally suspected me. Twice I was arrested and held in prison, and then let go because no evidence could be obtained against me.

'Then a woman was hit and robbed of her handbag. I was arrested, and she wrongly identified me as the offender. At the time of the offence I was playing cards with two women and a man in the house where I lived. I called these people at my trial. They bore out my story, but in cross-examination the man admitted he was a thief and the women, that they kept a brothel. The jury did not believe these people could speak the truth. I was found guilty of a crime that I never committed and was sentenced to 10 years imprisonment.

'In serving my previous sentence in gaol I was always regarded as a good prisoner. When there I just made the best of it, but this time to be wrongfully convicted after I had worked so hard to live an honest life, made me so depressed that I went nearly mad. I was continuously in trouble in the gaol, and after two years, having a knife in my possession, as the governor of the gaol went through the workshops, I rushed at him, stabbed him, and left him for dead.

'I was charged with attempted murder, found guilty and sentenced to death. On the governor recovering, my sentence was turned into one of penal servitude for life. Then I went quite mad. I was taken from the gaol and put into the hospital for the criminal insane. After nearly a year there my senses returned, but I pretended insanity until I got a chance to escape. My chance came, and I escaped. I was free for a few days, when I was reported by a man who knew me, and again arrested. I did not resist, but went with the arresting constable in a car to Darlinghurst. As we drove along I said to him, "You know, I have had bad luck. I was not guilty of that robbery for which I got ten years."

'He replied that he had heard of a number of people who said the same regarding me.'

Harris implored the attorney-general to vigorously review his case: 'If you come to the conclusion that I was not guilty of the crime of which I was first convicted, and for which I got ten years, I do not ask you to let me out at once. All I ask is that you put a limit on my sentence, and do not leave me here for life.'

Hall thoroughly reviewed the case and came to the conclusion that there were significant flaws in the Crown brief. He also interviewed the police officer who recaptured Harris after his escape from the asylum. 'He was unable to give proof of his innocence, but what he had to say served to very greatly strengthen the doubts that had risen in my mind as to the man's guilt,' Hall noted in a minute to his department.

Harris was behind bars for an unprovoked attack on a prison official, for which he deserved to be penalised. But Hall accepted that Harris's mind was 'unhinged' at the time of the attack, and that he was suicidal. He noted that Harris had attempted suicide, and expressed concern that the prisoner had not given up on trying to end his own life.

In an official memo, Hall urged that in six years time, if the prisoner's mental health had improved and his conduct and industry were up to measure, he could be released. When Hall visited Parramatta the following year, he saw the prisoner, and the 'bright, smiling man' thanked him for his help. The jail's overseer told Hall: 'Prisoner No 57 is the best prisoner in the gaol. I think he has quite reformed.'

A few years later, the state Labor government was in disarray over the conscription debate. After Hall's departure from the Labor Party, he lost the justice portfolio. He decided that his last act would be to cut Harris's sentence by two years and release him straight away. The two men met just days before Harris's release. The grateful prisoner told the attorney-general: 'I am 34 years of age, and I have spent 16 years in gaol. I have not a relative in the world. There is only one thing that a decent man in my position ought to do, and that is fight for his country. If you will let me, I will enlist.'

Hall wrote in a newspaper article at the end of the war that it wasn't he who suggested Harris enlist.

> I did not ask him to do so, nor had I hinted at it in any way. He had been the victim of such misfortune, and from childhood had received, at his country's hands, such shocking treatment, that it did not seem fair to me to ask that man to fight for the land that had treated him so badly. But of his own free will he chose to do it.

Harris walked through the Parramatta gates for the last time in late 1916. Instead of heading for his old criminal haunts, he went straight to Brisbane where, true to his word, he enlisted and was detailed to the 13th Machine Gun Company of the 13th Training Battalion. Within six months he had embarked for France.

As his enlistment papers later revealed, he had another benefactor. Esther Bennett did not occupy any positions of power or influence, but her personal kindness helped turn the once vilified prisoner around. She was the unmarried sister of a young man who had served time with Harris, a gambler named Fred Bennett who did a few stretches for illegal gaming and for failure to pay maintenance for the upkeep of his child. One year, just before Christmas, when he was working as a wharf labourer, he suggested to his workmates that they band together and buy Harris a dinner. He asked his sister to take the food to the prisoner. From then on, she took him special dinners for Christmas, Easter Sunday and the King's birthday.

George Harris would always remember the Bennett family's kindness. In his enlistment papers, Esther is named as his next of kin, but marked as 'Friend'. While he was in Brisbane, he also made a will that named her as the sole beneficiary in the event of his death.

At the start of December 1916, Harris sought and was granted five days leave to visit Esther and her brother at 11 Pelican Street, Surry Hills. 'I wish to see all my friends, as I wish to go to England for training as soon as possible,' he wrote. Then he added: 'It will be my last farewell.' He was going back just one more time to his old stamping ground. At the end of Pelican Street was Oxford Street, where Harris had been arrested in such dramatic circumstances in 1905. Most of the events and people that had shaped his life story were located in this neighbourhood. But unlike many other men who returned home on leave, Harris did not go AWL. He returned to his unit on time and slipped easily into the routines of army life.

His group embarked in Melbourne on 11 May 1917 and arrived in England in July. They were destined for Grantham, in Lincolnshire, where the British Machine Gun Corps had its training facilities. He was part of the team manning a Vickers gun, the medium-sized machine-gun which was standard Australian equipment. This gun had a barrel a bit over a metre long, and could fire up to 500 rounds a minute. Its range was 2000 to 4000 metres. It was water-cooled, and in two pieces, weighing about 25 kilograms. It was not as light and portable as the newer Lewis machine-gun and required a specialist machine-gun team.

The Vickers gun was manned by at least three soldiers: one to fire, one to load and one to carry ammo and perform other support tasks. Harris carried the ammo – perhaps not surprising, given his history of violence and mental illness.

In England, despite a barrage of plentiful temptations to go AWL, George Harris kept his service record in impeccable shape. In months of training in England, all he suffered was a sprained ankle. Not one instance of missing parade or being insubordinate in the field – let alone of contracting VD. Harris had joined the so-called suicide club and was focused on reaching the battlefields of northern France.

*

It was still a war of inches when Harris signed up, although some historians say the tide was slowly turning the Allies' way. All through 1916, Britain and the former British colonies struggled to replenish their stock of fighters and build and develop superiority in arms. In 1916, Australia lost about 40,000 men on the Western Front. But in 1917, the losses for Australia were even higher: more than 76,000 troops were lost. This was the theatre of war that Harris entered on New Year's Day 1918, when his unit shipped out to Étaples. He was posted to the 24th Machine Gun Company, which was sent into the mud of northern France.

In March, the German army launched its final major offensive, aimed at winning the war. In three great assaults over the following months, it inflicted huge losses on the Allies, who fought desperately and managed to stave off defeat.

George Harris's unit was in the thick of it. In April, the Australian Army rationalised the organisation of its machine-gun units, and the 24th became part of a larger 4th Machine Gun Battalion attached to the 4th Division. That division, in turn, was part of the Australia Corps led by the Australian general, John Monash.

Harris's neatly penned letters to David Hall were positive and told of the 'grand work' by the machine-gunners 'in stemming the German offensive' and that in time they would 'give the Huns the surprise of their lives'.

In July, Harris was sent to the 4th Army rest camp for a week. Monash liked his front-line soldiers to be fit. As he wrote in *Australian Victories in France in 1918*: 'Troops destined for battle must be kept in the highest physical condition. This means good feeding, comfortable housing, and adequate rest. A couple of weary days and sleepless nights spent in crowded railway trains, with cold food and little exercise, are sufficient to play havoc with the fighting trim of even a crack battalion.'

George Harris was prepared for whatever came next. Sometime in late July he wrote to Esther Bennett informing her precisely of the contents of his paybook and wallet, which were to be sent to her in the event of his death.

The war was about to enter its final stage. The Allies planned an all-out offensive against the Germans for early August. It would combine many thousands of men from different armies and deploy masses of tanks, light machine-guns and other weapons in an elaborate, coordinated surprise attack that some experts have dubbed one of the first examples of modern warfare.

It was a combined effort, quietly planned by the British, Australians and Canadians at a pretty little village on the

Somme one sunny summer afternoon in mid-July. From the outset these generals went to much trouble to preserve the element of surprise. To prevent the Germans realising the massing of troops and tanks near the front line, much of the preparation was completed at night, under cover of rain and darkness. Monash gradually withdrew his men on the right flank, to prevent the enemy realising that the Canadians were moving into position near the Australians. The Allies also went to a great deal of trouble to disguise the sudden proliferation of tanks (168 of them in all, in the lines Monash oversaw) by hiding them in bombed-out farm compounds or deep woods until the day for action arrived.

By this stage of the war, the British finally had the know-how to pinpoint precisely the position of the enemy's guns. But that needed to remain a secret. For days, Allied gunners pounded German gun emplacements that had recently been vacated, so that the Germans would not suspect anything.

Monash planned to send the Australians a very long way through the German lines. This was something Australian troops were good at, fighting their way to objectives not reached before. The problem in the past had been that they often had to abandon them for want of back-up from the British guns and reinforcements. This time, Monash had five divisions of Australians at his disposal, and the Canadian corps protecting his right flank.

The Australian attack would be staged in three phases. The first phase was fairly conventional. The troops advanced under the cover of a barrage, their objective to take the enemy's front-line trenches. In the second phase, two more divisions of men would enter the fray, running past their comrades and into open country. Their objectives were the German guns and other key installations. It was this phase, the most dangerous, in which George Harris was involved. The 4th Machine Gun Battalion was ordered to cover the weaker left flank, and Vickers machine-guns were tasked with protecting the men of the 4th Division as they fought their way forwards.

The Battle of 8 August, as the Australians called it, began in darkness, at 4.20 am. The day dawned with a heavy ground mist, which only added to the element of surprise. By 7 am the first phase had succeeded completely. At 8.20 am the second phase began. It met remarkably little resistance, except on the left flank, where, as Monash's biographer later recorded, 'German artillery shooting across the river knocked many tanks out, and some astounding artillery duels followed'.

From the five Australian divisions mobilised that day, only about two thousand men died: extraordinarily few, especially as the Allies had achieved the most sweeping advance they ever made in a single day in France.

Private George Harris had played his part in a pivotal battle, but on this day of victory he was one of those killed in action. He'd been carrying ammunition to the gun posts when he died. His body was retrieved and buried a few days later at a nearby military cemetery that had been designated before the battle began. His company captain, Harold Alexander Sheridan, a Gallipoli veteran and himself once wounded in battle, later wrote to Harris's mentor, David Hall:

> Private George Harris, 634, joined the 24th M.G. Company early in 1918. I was then second in command of the company and had every opportunity of judging the various qualities of every man in the unit. Harris was greatly liked by all the men of his company and greatly esteemed by his officers on account of his great bravery. He took a prominent part in the company's work in the line during the days in March and April

> when things looked very black indeed, and up to August 8, when he was killed. He was in the front line with his section officers on every occasion that the company was in the line.
>
> He was killed while carrying ammunition to the guns and is buried in a little cemetery at Cerisy-Gailly on the banks of the Somme. I was present when he was buried, and a decent cross marks the spot where he lies.
>
> Harris was one of the most straightforward men I ever met, and one of the best soldiers I have seen in the A.I.F during four years of service. I think it is fitting that those who befriended this man in his hour of need should know how much good there was in him, and that he died like the hero he undoubtedly was.

George Harris was mourned by his friends at Pelican Street, who were the closest he had ever come to a real family. They inserted notices in memoriam in both the *Catholic Press* and the *Sydney Morning Herald*.

> We loved him too dearly in life
> to ever forget him in death.
> Inserted by his loving friends, Winifred, Fred and Esther G. Bennett, 11 Pelican-street, city.

As promised, after George's death Esther received a parcel of his personal effects, including his paybook and the photos that were with him when he died. Esther never married, but continued to live with other members of her family until her death in 1941.

In a strange postscript to this case, on the eve of Harris's departure from Australia, James Quaine found himself entangled in a controversy which saw him sacked as governor of Parramatta Gaol by order of the State Executive Council. The order was proclaimed in the *Government Gazette*, effective on 30 April 1917. Several days later he went missing, prompting a police search. According to a local newspaper report, the jail governor had gone home on the Sunday after completing his duties.

'He had tea; and then went out as if for a walk or to revisit the gaol, opposite to which his residence is. He did not return,' the article stated.

Searching for reasons why the respected 60-year-old prison governor would disappear, the article recounted the stabbing incident at the hand of George Harris, and also the deaths of his two daughters, one of them just a few months earlier, and the other after a long illness, and 'just when she was on the threshold of womanhood'.

But the sting in the article was as follows: 'It is unfortunate that Mr Quaine is away at the present time (wherever he may have got to) because there are a number of matters connected with the accounts on which perhaps he alone can give certain information the department wishes to obtain.'

# PART II

# Services No Longer Required

# 6

# On the Lam in London and Glasgow

AUSTRALIA'S CALL TO ARMS WAS answered promptly by thousands of men across the country, but a year or two into the war, enlistments began to drop. Battlefield casualties and bad publicity about the war's progress – or lack of it – were beginning to bite. Reinforcements were required, and quickly. Some believed Australia's jails could hold the answer.

The war effort could be bolstered by conscripting the underclasses, a New South Wales rural councillor urged, quite early in the war. 'While a large number of our smartest and most industrious youth have volunteered, the more or less useless young men, those in a chronic state of unemployment, are not responding to the call,' the President of the Demondrille Shire Council wrote in March 1915.

He went further, exhorting other shires to support a push for police to be authorised to compile lists of suitable candidates, 'and have them sent to the front, and to give judges in criminal courts the power to send guilty prisoners on active service instead of to gaol'.

It was a radical suggestion, but less than a year later at the notorious Bathurst Gaol, military drilling was introduced to the prisoners' regime of physical exercise. George Steele, a noted reformer who became Comptroller-General of Prisons for New South Wales, was encouraged by seeing some of his released prisoners go straight into khaki, and acquit themselves with great credit in the Empire's defence.

The local newspaper, the *Bathurst Times*, applauded the move:

> It will give those prisoners who will regain their liberty at an early date an opportunity of enlisting in the military forces, joining the recruits with a great deal of useful training already 'up their sleeves'. It may be argued that convicted criminals will not be encouraged by the military authorities, but naturally the prospective recruit recently from jail is not going to make known his shame, and it is safe to say that a great number of ex-convicts are already at the front and in training camps, giving excellent service. And after all, when a man has served his time, he is presumed to be morally purged . . .

By the end of 1915, the push was on to find another 50,000 troops to send into battle. In Melbourne, the State Parliament Recruiting Committee was on the front foot. In a none-too-subtle attempt to relax the background checks made on applicants, the committee expressed objections to some of the questions raised during vetting as being 'too inquisitorial'.

But not everyone agreed, in particular Ernest Brougham Docker, a fire-and-brimstone judge on the New South Wales District Court bench, who preached against sending criminals into the armed forces. One bad man in a regiment, he thundered, would corrupt a hundred.

His establishment credentials were impeccable, as were his church connections. As well as being a member of the Church of England synod, Judge Docker had published a book of sacred verse, aptly entitled 'Hymns of the Kingdom'. His religious zeal was often reflected in his judicial outlook.

With his bushy white beard and Old Testament zeal, Judge Docker left no one in his court in any doubt that he opposed the use of the armed forces as a vehicle for the rehabilitation of thieves, thugs, murderers and other miscreants. In a series of well-reported outbursts in 1916, he said that criminals should not be sent to training camps to fraternise with men of good character: 'It was this evil which made many mothers dread sending their sons into camp life.'

He thought that fighting for the Empire was a privilege, telling one soldier he sentenced to jail for stealing:

> There are too many like you who got into the expeditionary forces, but had no right to be there. A criminal had no right to be associated with honourable men offering their lives for the safety of our homes and the defence of the Empire. It was a degradation, shame and insult that such persons should be permitted to associate with them.
>
> In addition to being an insult, it would be a risk to them having their property stolen . . . there have been a number of complaints already about that. The force seems to be used by criminals as a refuge from the consequences of their crime. I certainly will not assist in allowing a criminal to go to the front with honest decent people.

Perhaps he was thinking protectively of his own boys when he spoke out. One of his sons, Alfred Brougham Docker, had held a commission in the New South Wales military forces. The other, Captain Ernest Noel Brougham Docker, was attached to the 13th Australian Field Ambulance, and returned home with a Military Cross for his bravery in battle at Villers Bretonneux in April 1918.

His sons' military service was the yardstick by which His Honour measured the straggling parade of servicemen who came before him in court. But as fast as his judicial net filtered them out, another crim slipped through and ended up in the army.

One of the most notable Australian crooks to go to war was James Edward Devine, who would go on after the war to build a crime empire in Sydney with his wife, the notorious prostitute Tilly Devine. He was a regular fixture in the pages of police gazettes across the country under his own name or his alias, James Davis, described as a 'bludger, receiver and gunman . . . who associates with the worst type of criminals'. The Australian War Memorial paints Devine as 'quite possibly the AIF's worst soldier . . . with dozens of unauthorised absences, periods in detention and numerous stints in hospital with VD'.

Devine, born in the Melbourne suburb of Brunswick, was a shearer and a small-time racecourse racketeer and thief when he joined up in mid-February 1916 with his brother Frank. Both were destined for the famed 1st Australian Tunnelling Company, which was primarily responsible for placing destructive charges below enemy trench positions. The so-called earwiggers worked in great secrecy, burrowing into dank and dark places, keeping silent and keeping vigil for any sounds, while trying to avoid detection.

On the Western Front, military command was frustrated with the toll that trench warfare was inflicting on manpower and resources. The Germans were well entrenched by the end of 1914, and better armed. Every Allied advance came at major cost, even though the distance between opposing sides' trench lines was often less than 100 metres. So the tunnellers' brief was to attack the enemy underground with explosives. The Germans, however, had the same idea and they would be tunnelling from the opposite end. In this silent war, the claustrophobic and stressful conditions metres below the surface would have terrified the most hardened infantryman operating above ground. Sometimes, one side's tunnel broke into the enemy's and desperate skirmishes ensued.

The tunnellers were made up from a wide cross-section of recruits, ranging from stockmen, engineers, bank managers, tree fellers, dentists, kangaroo shooters, labourers, university academics and, of course, shearers. But some of them were more serious about their job than others.

Big Jim Devine, a strapping 23-year-old with blue eyes, brown hair and a fresh complexion, looked like a picture-perfect specimen of the Australian digger. The reality was that he was a shirker, a deserter and a man not to be trusted. After disembarking in England on 18 July 1916, Devine was sent to Perham Downs, a bleak training camp on Salisbury Plain, which clearly did not suit the young Australian. Knocked up to acting corporal, he was quickly knocked down to sapper again. He went AWL for three weeks and when he returned was sentenced to 168 hours detention and forfeiture of nine days pay.

On 29 August he was shipped to France, to the Australian Divisional Base Depot at Étaples, before being transferred as a reinforcement to the 1st Tunnelling Company. After two months there, he reported sick with pyrexia (fever of unknown origin). By mid-December he'd been marched into the depot at Étaples again, before being shipped back to England for permanent base duties at Weymouth, on the south coast. At least he was above ground and sleeping in a hut, albeit it on a straw mattress.

Around this time Devine was treated for VD after being transferred to the Verne Isolation Hospital at Portland. Several months later he was again on the lam, in and around London. When he was apprehended, he was confined to barracks for seven days and docked 14 days pay. On 9 July 1917, he was marched into the No. 1 Command Depot at Perham Downs. This was a retraining base for soldiers considered too fit for convalescent camp but not yet ready to return to their unit. Some like Devine would never be ready!

The set-up would have suited Devine down to a tee, if the following description of a typical command depot applied to Perham Downs:

> Training was very varied. There were football matches twice a week as well as cricket, tennis, boxing and fencing with inter-squadron tournaments. The gymnasium was under the supervision of a Medical Officer and was well supplied with machines to allow weight training and rowing as well as the conventional vaulting horses and climbing ropes . . . The camp motto was 'Hors de Combat' (outside the fight), which was spelt out in the traditional white washed stones.

A bit over a month after his arrival there, Devine married the nubile but worldly Matilda (Tilly) Twiss, at the Sacred Heart Church in the poor part of Camberwell, south London. On the marriage certificate Devine listed Perham Downs as his address, and soldier as his occupation. Twiss gave no occupation, but was in fact a 16-year-old street prostitute. Her beat was Soho and the Strand, where she encountered many Australians eager to experience her sexual talents. An independent operator, the teenage Cockney worked hard and reaped the rewards.

In Devine, she had not only a husband but a ready-made pimp. Once the newlyweds had exchanged their vows, it was back to business. Matilda returned to prostitution and Devine continued in the army. Six days after his nuptials he went AWL, during which time he contracted another dose of the pox, landing him at Bulford – but not for long. Devine was off again.

London was the place to be for a soldier on leave in 1917. In Australia, it was the worst year of the war. The poisonous public debate over whether to introduce conscription had split the nation, while families fretted about the mounting casualty rate and feared the arrival of the parish priest carrying bad news to their own front door. In that year alone more than 76,000 Australians were killed or wounded or listed as missing on the Western Front – twice the number of casualties in France the previous year and three times that of the Gallipoli campaign. The 40,000 fatalities amounted to two-thirds of all Australian deaths during the war.

Under the shadow of these battlefield losses, many Australian soldiers in London carried on like there was no tomorrow. In 1915, crowds of cheering Britons had turned out to greet the warriors from the dominions, men who had left their families and friends on the other side of the world to help England in its time of need. Two years after their triumphal arrival, the Australians were widely scorned, labelled as drunken, disorderly, rowdy, lustful and even dangerous. The number of diggers before the magistrates courts increased by the day. English criminals consorted with, and in some cases hid, Australian deserters such as Devine.

Much of the crime occurred inside and around the camps occupied by the Australians. A lot of it was kept under wraps until after the war, when returned soldiers tried to open the eyes of their compatriots to the misconduct of diggers abroad.

One returned man writing to the *Daily News* in Perth described how the Aussie 'heroes' sandbagged an 11-year-old paperboy at Fovant camp in Wiltshire, and stole 'his pennies'. He concluded:

> I fear we must make up our minds to it, that there are quite a number of precious blackguards among the members of the AIF; and unless every respectable returned soldier will have the backbone strenuously to resist the 'young ruffians, who get a few drinks in', they must not be surprised if the impression gets abroad that these 'young ruffians' are more typical of the AIF, even than they are. I am not saying that a blackguard may not be a good fighting soldier.

Two-up schools operated in almost every camp in England, and were generally run by outsiders. 'At Codford camp and its vicinity there were dozens of loose-end soldiers who had deserted camp and who were either sheltered by villagers or who had laid perdus [hide-outs] in the woods, thickets, and other places,' another former digger recalled. In a letter to his local paper at Barcaldine, he described these operators as 'wasters who had deserted camp after arrival in England and lived by preying on their fellows': 'It was taking a forward area risk, leaving camp alone after dark. It was quite a common occurrence for diggers to stagger into camp and report that they'd been sandbagged and robbed.'

Women were both victims and accomplices, he wrote. A nurse from New Zealand was knocked down and robbed. But gangs also used female decoys. One gang which operated on the road outside Wilton had a female member who picked up diggers and enticed them into dark lanes or corners; there they were robbed by men in the gang.

Devine was making the most of his time in London gathering together valuable criminal associates through his teenage bride. In 1918, he was on the run and loose for almost three months before being apprehended on 8 August and sent to the notorious Lewes Detention Barracks. Built in 1853 and overlooking the sea on the south-east coast of England, this forbidding prison's inmates included Sinn Fein members arrested during the bloody Easter uprising of 1916.

By the war's end more than 2000 military prisoners would have passed through Lewes, and many more through jails and detention centres across England and northern France. A third of those inmates were suffering from the pox. Aussie prisoners far outnumbered those of other Commonwealth forces, much to the dismay of Australian military chiefs. By the end of 1916 diggers were being imprisoned at double the rate of the comrades from other dominions. A year later, the rate was about three and a half times more.

At Lewes, prisoners slept in single cells and spent most of their waking hours in workshops or in bleak, high-walled exercise yards where the guards vigorously discouraged conversation.

Devine did three months there and was released on Armistice Day 1918. He was assigned to the Overseas Training Brigade at Longbridge Deverill, in Wiltshire. But he still had the roaming spirit, and two days after reporting for duty, he walked out through the gates and remained at large for the next nine months. During this time he no doubt went back to living off his wife.

Big Jim Devine was bad-tempered and often, in a drunken fit of temper, beat Tilly. But he was not a jealous man. If he was possessive, it was only for the money his wife earned on the street. She stuck with her Australian soldier, and in these years bore him two children, a daughter, Alice Teresa, who died at birth, and a son, Frederick James Devine.

By this time Jim's brother, Frank, had been shipped home with an injured left hand. Frank was almost a year younger than Jim, but streets ahead in maturity. His war had been frequently interrupted by illness, not VD, as in the case of his brother, but pyrexia. Nonetheless, he served his country well. The minor blemish on his service record was when he went AWL for four days in October 1917.

With the war's ending, Jim Devine was assessing his family's future. Business was dropping off, as Commonwealth troops shipped out. It was time to head home, Devine decided. Late on the night of 11 July 1919 the deserter surrendered to military authorities. A court martial at Sutton Veny sentenced him to nine months detention. Devine pleaded guilty, but it would be the last time the hard man of Australian crime made such an admission.

Like many others of his kind, Devine received a considerable remission and was shipped home in disgrace, leaving Tilly behind until she could get a berth. Even on the voyage home, Devine couldn't resist thumbing his nose at the army brass. When the troopship docked at Durban, he went AWL for three days, incurring a fortnight's forfeiture of pay.

*

Ernest Edward Sharp and Thomas Vincent Maguire were two more Aussie deserters on the lam in 1917. They deserted their posts and turned to crime for survival. Their support network consisted of home-grown London crims such as the dangerous Joseph Jones, who became a dock worker after being invalided from the military.

Maguire had already spent three years in the Citizens Forces when he signed up in Brisbane in late September 1916. He was a 22-year-old scrapper who gave his occupation as 'pugilist'. Six months later, he embarked from Sydney for overseas, where he was taken on strength into the 26th Battalion.

Sharp, a nuggety Sydney labourer four years older than Maguire, enlisted in 1915 and was assigned to the 4th Battalion. Except for brief periods of ill health and AWL, Maguire's and Sharp's records were unremarkable.

But in 1917 both were being pursued as deserters. The two Australians befriended Jones soon after they'd fled their bases. In a police statement, Sharp described how he'd met the Englishman in a private house in London. Jones was in civilian clothes, but wearing a 'wound stripe', an official recognition of having been wounded in action, and a silver badge on his coat.

'We went for a drink and met another soldier, named Tom Maguire, whom I have known for some time. We again met Jones later, and became friendly with him and his wife,' Sharp told police.

One night in October, Sharp caught up with Jones in the Peacock public house near Westminster Bridge. After a number of drinks they left, walking up Waterloo Road, stopping at a coffee stall on the Strand side of the bridge, scouting for potential targets.

'While we were standing there, someone said, "Tom has just gone over the bridge with two Canadian goats [mugs],"' Sharp testified. The Canadians were Private Oliver Imlay and Private John McKinley, who were both on sick leave that evening.

Sharp and Jones stalked the trio from the other side of the road, only joining them after they had a chance encounter with two women and engaged them in conversation. Jones then asked one of the Canadians if he wanted a bottle of whisky. He invited the pair to follow him up the road, accompanied by Sharp and, later, Maguire. They stopped at a quiet location in the vicinity of Blackfriars Road, Waterloo. In his statement, Sharp said:

> We turned into a passage and stopped. One of the Canadians said, 'Where is the whisky?' Jones

> said: 'Don't make a row; I've got to go into this boozer to get it. Walk up here'.
>
> We walked on to the passage and stopped in a back gateway, and Jones said, 'It will cost 4/6 p each.' I gave him tuppence; Maguire gave him something, I don't know how much. The smaller Canadian gave him some money. The big Canadian said, 'I have not got much.'
>
> I was standing in front of the smaller Canadian, who was standing in the corner of the gateway. Something was said about money, I don't remember what.
>
> Then suddenly Jones pushed me aside with his left hand. I heard something whizz past me from the direction of Jones, and I saw something like a policeman's truncheon in his right hand, and he seemed to hit the smaller Canadian on the left side of his neck. I heard the blow and the man fell backwards into the gate corner.
>
> I saw Maguire hit the big Canadian with his fist in the face, and the Canadian fell on his hands and knees. In the meantime, Jones and I searched the little fellow. The big fellow tried to rise. Jones left me, and hit him somewhere on the back of the head with the truncheon. He tried to get up and Jones hit him twice more with the truncheon.
>
> He tried to get up again, and Maguire kicked him in the face.

The carnage might have been even greater if a man in a nearby building hadn't opened a window and shouted: 'What are you doing there?' The attackers fled, stopping down the street to inspect what they'd stolen. It was meagre takings. 'I put what

I had into my hat,' said Sharp. There were some papers and a paybook, a 10 shilling note, some silver and coppers. The money amounted to 14 shillings. Jones said, 'Here is the four bob I got for the whisky. That makes 18 bob.'

Sharp said: 'I threw the papers and paybook which I had found on the little fellow over the church fence. We cut up the 18 shillings and had 6 shillings each – and went to a coffee stall and had tea.'

The two diggers did not meet until the following week when news of Private Imlay's death was reported in most of the newspapers. Jones told them he'd already got rid of the murder weapon, the policeman's truncheon. Sharp, torn between feelings of panic and remorse, destroyed the false leave pass he'd been carrying.

An intensive investigation was immediately launched by Scotland Yard, assisted by a respected Victorian detective, Richard Brennan, who had been seconded to the AIF. Sharp and Maguire, who were initially charged with murder, received seven years and ten years respectively for assaulting the young grenadier and robbing him with violence. Jones, who was charged with having inflicted the fatal blows on Imlay, was later executed in Wandsworth Prison.

Immediately after the Australians were sentenced, details of their convictions, along with their photographs and fingerprints, were forwarded to police in Queensland and New South Wales. As the war ended, tens of thousands of Australians were being repatriated home, including those prisoners being held in military detention centres in France and across England. The Australian military was keen to repatriate such men, but not those serving civil sentences for murder, manslaughter and rape.

*

Not all gang members were cowards and shirkers. Some were courageous soldiers who displayed extreme gallantry on the battlefield. Martin Linnane was one such soldier who received a Military Medal. But the labourer's valour was overshadowed by his extreme criminality and violence, often fuelled by alcohol, which continued for many years after he was out of khaki.

Linnane was almost 21 when he travelled from Broken Hill to Oaklands, South Australia, in November 1914 to sign up. It appeared a promising start for the Gallipoli campaigner. But within a year he was shipped home in the HMAT *Ceramic* and despatched straight to Langwarrin with the pox. There he remained until he was given the all-clear to resume his duties and sent back to the fray, taken on strength in the 7th Battalion.

Linnane's war was action-packed both on and off the battlefield. In France, he was wounded twice, taking shrapnel to the face and right arm; and then five days after rejoining his unit he received a gunshot wound to the right leg. By this time his senior officers were in no doubt about his courage under fire. After a fierce encounter with the enemy on 8 and 9 August 1918, during the advance on Proyart, a French village in the Somme Valley, it was officially recognised. Linnane's 'conspicuous gallantry and devotion to duty' earned him a Military Medal. His citation read:

> Private Linnane did splendid work in bombing out an enemy post that was holding up our advance in the centre. He crawled up to the post (consisting of 10 men), threw in a bomb, dashed forward and bayoneted one of the enemy. The garrison still showed fight and Private Linnane kept on attacking them, thus, at great personal risk, drawing the enemy's attention from our advance. Finally some more of our men arrived

> and the garrison of the enemy post surrendered. Private Linnane by his gallant action, undoubtedly saved heavy casualties, and greatly assisted in finally capturing the post.

But Martin Linnane's standing was severely undermined by his own reckless and criminal behaviour in and out of camp. A couple of months after the war ended, still stuck in France, he did a runner at a small café when the bill was presented, and copped 14 days of field punishment no. 2. In all, he was illegally absent from duty on half-a-dozen occasions, totalling six months. For which he was sentenced to more than 370 days detention – less remissions – and the forfeiture of 645 days pay.

Many soldiers left in France after the Armistice got themselves into trouble waiting for a ship back to England, and thence to home. Some would rather have stayed on. Linnane, when he returned to England, took to ambushing and robbing unwary diggers and civilians to help make ends meet. He was finally apprehended, and in July 1919 found guilty of assault and slotted for 12 months.

Out of khaki, Linnane's life followed a predictable pattern in and out of jail. He became a petty criminal, drunk and thug, who did not draw the line at assaulting women. The extent of his criminality was on public display when the Military Medal winner appeared in a brief item in the *Adelaide News* during World War II. Linnane faced the local police court on a charge of stealing a pair of cheap white canvas shoes and received two months jail after admitting to 82 previous convictions.

*

Some Australian soldiers were executed for crimes they committed in the UK. Albert James Fraser, a 23-year-old labourer from Geelong in Victoria, was sentenced to hang for his part in luring a discharged British soldier into a Glasgow park in early February 1920, and then robbing and beating him to death.

Fraser, a driver, began the war as a petty criminal with seven convictions to his name. His appearance was unprepossessing: a coarse-featured face and a heavily tattooed chest that featured the words 'I love Becky'. His last conviction at the Melbourne Petty Sessions was for loitering with intent, penalty three months jail with hard labour. In September 1916, he joined the army.

Private Albert Fraser, Service Number 60118, left Sydney on 30 July 1918 as a reinforcement who had already been shunted around between battalions. By the time his ship reached Cape Town he'd already been hit with 96 hours detention and forfeiture of four days pay for disobedience. About a month later he was charged with neglecting to obey an order. He landed in London only a month before the war ended and a week after the Armistice, he took off. Fraser was missing until his apprehension the following June. Marched into Sutton Veny, he cooled his heels for a month before setting off again.

This 23-year-old soldier who'd never seen action quickly found a home in the dangerous back streets of Glasgow, where he teamed up with other criminals and prostitutes specialising in assault and robbery. Late one bitterly cold night in February 1920, Fraser and his associate, an Irish crook by the name of James Rollins, used two prostitutes to entice a returned soldier to the Queens Park Recreation Ground, where they planned to rob him.

Everything went to plan, but the two men went too far. Fraser savagely pistol-whipped their target's face, fracturing his upper and lower jaw, and cutting and bruising his face. The violence caused a lesion of the brain, and his liver was ruptured.

They carried the injured man some distance before dumping him over a fence. They removed his boots, his overcoat and other clothing, cut his pockets away to empty them, and left him to die.

Their victim was a veteran named Henry Senior, who had served with distinction with the 11th Hussars, and fought at Mons. The 35-year-old stonemason lived with his mother.

The killers, 'with bloodstained hands and bulging pockets', were sighted on a tram, but Senior's body wasn't found until the following day. Fraser, Rollins and their molls headed for Ireland, where Fraser and Rollins hid in a cave, in a desolate spot about eight kilometres from Belfast. They were arrested days later after they emerged to join the women, who would later give King's evidence at their trial.

Police located the victim's boots and overcoat in a pawnshop. When Fraser and Rollins were returned to Glasgow, they were booed and hissed at by a hostile crowd waiting for them at the railway station.

The Australian offered no defence during his trial in Glasgow. The army sent a representative to monitor the proceedings and watched as the evidence of 35 Crown witnesses pinned the pair to a series of robberies with violence, which culminated with the murder of Senior. The jury of 15 took just 20 minutes to return guilty verdicts. Immediately donning his black cap, presiding judge Lord Sands imposed the only sentence the law would permit: 'That you both be taken thence and confined in the Dukes Street Prison until May 26th 1920 and that between the hours of eight and nine in the forenoon of that day you be hanged by the neck until you are dead.'

Fraser and Rollins shook hands and smiled and waved to their supporters in the court.

The only argument given in favour of Fraser by his counsel was to have the verdict reduced from murder to justifiable homicide, taking into account his war service. Given its brevity and Fraser's long periods of AWL, there was little surprise when it failed. In his official report, the army observer praised the conduct of the prosecution and defence throughout the trial, and noted that Fraser's nationality had not been revealed to the jury. Fraser's execution not only disqualified him from his service medals but also his war gratuity.

*

Tilly Devine followed her husband Jim out to Australia a year after he returned. The not-so-blushing war bride boarded the *Waimana*, a brideship carrying women to their men in Australia. Many women took children with them, but Tilly left her young son, Frederick, behind.

As the war ended, Australians soldiers in England were marrying at the rate of about 150 a week. In 1919, more than 15,000 women and infants shipped out to Australian to join their husbands and fathers.

Many of these alliances did not turn out happily.

Samuel Pearse was a young Salvation Army bandsman who joined the AIF in July 1915. He was not yet 18, and his parents were not keen for him to go. Pearse served in Gallipoli before shipping off to Belgium. In September 1917 he won the Military Medal for single-handedly raiding a German machine-gun post on the Western Front.

But away from the front line, the young soldier wasn't as disciplined. A glance at his military records reveals a series of offences, including disobedience, neglect of duty, being absent from the guard, and AWL. And in the year that he won the Military Medal, Pearse was also fighting another enemy – VD. Between June and August 1917, the young gunner was out of action for 38 days receiving treatment, and then another four days at the 39th General Hospital in Le Havre.

In January 1918, while on leave in England, the young Australian fell for the charms of Kitty Knox, an English ambulance driver, and the pair became engaged several months later.

Pearse returned to the front in France, was wounded and repatriated to England, where the romance intensified. So much so that the newly promoted corporal went AWL, lost a month's pay and dropped in seniority. He was also despatched back to France, but he still pined for the comely Kitty.

Michael Challinger, in his book *Anzacs in Arkhangel*, writes that by the time the Armistice had been declared, Pearse persuaded a mate to smash his foot with a hammer, so that he could get back to his girl. The injuries resulted in one of his toes being amputated, but he was sent to England for treatment. He was reunited with Kitty and plans were made to sail back to Australia, where the couple would tie the knot.

However, tight shipping schedules and the call of another battlefront intervened. Against Kitty's wishes, Pearse signed up for action as a private soldier with the North Russian Relief Force fighting the Bolsheviks.

The pair married in 1919, just weeks before he embarked for this new front with hundreds of other Australian veterans. Before he left, while he was still in England training with the British forces for the campaign, Kitty wrote to her husband with the news that she was pregnant.

In late August, at Emsta in northern Russia, Sergeant Pearse cut through enemy barbed wire under heavy machine-gun and rifle fire, to clear a way for his troops to enter the enemy's battery position. He then charged the blockhouse single-handedly, killing the occupants with bombs. Moments later he was cut down by a Russian machine-gun and died.

He was awarded the Victoria Cross posthumously. Kitty accepted it for him at Buckingham Palace, their one-month-old daughter, Victoria Catherine (VC) Sarah, held to her bosom.

The story had a sad postscript. Kitty had promised her husband that their daughter would grow up in Mildura, surrounded by his family. The next year, she sailed for Australia on the MV *Baramban*. But a shipboard meeting would have devastating consequences for the young widow and her daughter.

Among the soldiers travelling home was the disgraced soldier Albert Arthur Howard Rose, a mean and violent man who worked as a shearer in New South Wales before the war. His military record, if Kitty could have seen it, would have shown that he had spent more time in hospital being treated for VD and syphilis, and under arrest for escaping from custody and going AWL, than he had in active service. The reason for his late return to Australia was that he was finishing a 15-month sentence at Pentonville Prison for the crime robbery with violence, which he'd committed while AWL.

Whether or not she was aware of his chronic VD and his thuggery, Kitty took a shine to Rose and the pair married that October. Pearse's family naturally disapproved and the ties were cut, leaving Kitty and her child isolated and in Rose's control. He continued on a criminal path and, according to Challinger, Kitty not only took his name but also told Vicky that the abusive Rose was her natural father.

Added to Vicky's misery was her mother's preposterous story that the coveted Victoria Cross was Rose's, for his courage under fire. To maintain the fraud, the little girl was never shown the medal, which would have revealed to her the inscription of the true hero – Samuel George Pearse.

# 7

# The Train of Shame

ANZAC DAY 1919, A SOLEMN day across Australia. It was an opportunity to remember fallen comrades and reflect on lives lost in the ill-fated Gallipoli campaign. In Melbourne, the occasion was marked by the launch of the Anzac Remembrance Day appeal, set up to fund a memorial to honour the war dead. In the city, there was no procession as such, just a gathering of about 700 soldiers who passed through the streets and were given a cordial welcome.

But while the city remembered its war dead, a dissolute group of nine military prisoners was en route from Melbourne to Sydney on a regular train service. The significance of the date was not lost on the six guards and five military policemen charged with getting the disgraced soldiers to Albury, where they would be handed over to another official escort. Many of the prisoners were already drunk when they boarded the train, and all that lay ahead was trouble for both the guards and their charges.

The end of the war had presented the Australian Army with a major logistical challenge: what to do with its khaki crims. Only prisoners who had committed the most serious offences against

British civilians were left behind in British jails. The rest were sent to the Australian prison at Lewes, which became a clearing house. From there prisoners were shipped back to Australia. Most had their sentences fully remitted the day they sailed. The worst, habitual offenders like the men on the Melbourne–Sydney express, were sent to Australian jails to serve out their time.

By far the greatest scoundrel in this group was John Beaumont West, a Sydney butcher who had enlisted not once but twice, and proved to be double the trouble for army command. His first taste of military life was in May 1915, when he was appointed to the Newcastle Depot Battalion. A little over two months later, West was arrested with three other soldiers and charged with assaulting and robbing John George Young. The quartet had laid into their victim and made off with his watch and chain and about one pound in change. Several weeks later West was out of the army. The handwritten note on his military record read simply: 'Discharged – misconduct.'

But on New Year's Eve, as Australians braced themselves for another year of bloodshed, West signed up for another crack at soldiering. He was allocated service number 6662 and after two months of basic training was on his way to Europe as a member of the 20th Battalion. Even the voyage was eventful. At Cape Town he broke ship and went AWL. Later he was found to have pilfered another soldier's clothes, a crime which earned him 72 hours detention.

In his three years of military service, West's list of infringements and crimes was something to behold. He was prosecuted 11 times for being AWL and three times for drunkenness. Twice he was penalised for neglecting to obey orders, once for breaking camp, once for damaging government property, and once for stealing, being improperly in possession of government property. He also made himself known to the civil authorities in Britain during the considerable time he spent there. While he was in training camp in Wiltshire, he appeared before the local bench on shop-breaking charges. The heist included two pairs of riding breeches, two pairs of socks, one cake of shaving soap, two bottles of hair cream, one bottle of castor oil and a tin of tooth powder. He was jailed for one day and lost 20 days pay.

During such escapades on the run, West had difficulty merging into the civilian community, simply by virtue of his extensive and elaborate body art. Tattooed on his left forearm was a pair of clasped hands with the inscription: 'Goodbye Australia'. On the other arm was 'Memory of my dear Mother', with the notation, 'died 1st Novr. 1910'.

Then, down the forearm, was the following in memoriam notice:

*I cannot clasp your loving hand,*
*Your face I cannot see,*
*But lest this token tell,*
*I still remember thee.*
*Elsie, I love thee.*

In June 1917, West got hitched to Christina Towes, the daughter of a British naval shipwright. On 20 September, he was taken on strength to the 18th Battalion. This was the battalion Joe Maxwell served in and it had already seen torrid action that year, at Warlencourt and Bullecourt. West was assigned to the battalion as a reinforcement just as it entered the Battle of Menin Road on 20 September. Twelve days later, he was wounded in action, hit in the thigh. He was shipped back to England where, venturing forth after his convalescence, he caught a dose of the clap and ended up in Bulford.

Several weeks later he was back before the medicos with 'abrasions of the penis'. His subsequent court martial was told of how West had been picked up during a violent encounter with Sergeant Richard George Pennicott, of the Australian Provost Corps, in Piccadilly on 20 December 1918. After his arrest, West shouted: 'I am not going with you bastards.' He ran off, but was quickly brought to the ground, no doubt handicapped by his injured leg. It would have been a fair chase: Pennicott, a strapping labourer from Tasmania, had a knee injury sustained in an accidental wounding six months earlier.

West wasn't going to be taken easily. He continued to kick out at the MP and the melee attracted a crowd of onlookers, many of them barracking for West. The struggling prisoner then called on the crowd for assistance, and some obliged by aiming kicks at Sergeant Pennicott. In the confusion, West slipped away, but 30 minutes later he was sighted, and carried kicking and screaming the police station. He'd been on the run for more than 50 days.

The Australian Army had resisted the British approach of shooting deserters. Instead it gave them stiff sentences, sometimes amounting to years. At his court martial West pleaded guilty and asked for leniency, giving a vivid account of his marital troubles, and accusing his wife of entertaining fellow deserters. He blamed his assault on Pennicott on his frustration at not being able to get the proper leave, owing to his poor record.

'My wife has given me trouble by misconducting herself. I applied but was unable to get the allotment stopped [a portion of his pay], but was told by headquarters I must get further evidence of her misconduct and I went absent without leave to obtain this information.

'Yesterday, I heard that [an] Australian deserter had been taken away from the house. My wife was here yesterday and told me that divorce proceedings were being put into operations.'

West copped a six-month term at Lewes and his papers were stamped, 'To be returned to Australia as an incorrigible at an early date.' His 'bad character' was noted, as was the number of his arrests in London.

Shipped back to Australia in the *Derbyshire* with other crims, they were in a compound in Melbourne awaiting transport to Sydney when one of those lucky chances presented itself. 'About two hours before entering the train, I went to the wash-house, and whilst there someone called out, "Hey Digger."' West said later, in a police statement.

'I looked to where the voice came from, and saw a pair of soldier's boots and puttees. I said, "What's up?" A soldier who was standing at the rear of the wash-house, said, "Could you do with a booze before going away?" I said, "How much?"

'He said, "10/6 a bottle for whisky." I said, "Wait till I see my mates."'

West went back to the room where the rest of the prisoners were under guard, He told two of them, Privates Harold John Neville and William Page, that 'there is a fellow there, who can get some booze'. He collected 14 shillings from each of them, and tossed in some money himself. Then he went back to the washroom and handed the soldier two pounds and ten shillings, telling him 'to bring back four bottles and have a drink with the change'.

West said he was assured by the soldier it would take just 20 minutes to complete the order, and was advised to 'keep your eye open for me coming back under here'.

He maintained he did not know the identity of his supplier: 'From the position I was in whilst in the wash-house I could not see him. The only portion visible was his feet and legs. I handed him the money through the opening at the bottom of the wall of the wash-house.'

About 20 minutes later the soldier returned. West informed Neville, and told him 'ask the corporal to let you go for a piss, and I'll go wash my hands'.

The supplier was true to his word, passing two parcels containing four pints of Bulloch Lade Whisky through the hole in the washroom wall.

'I took one and Neville took the other. We put them down our breeches and went back to the yard, and went into one of the cells. And all hands drank three of the bottles.'

He put the fourth bottle in his kit bag, to drink on the train.

Neville, during his service overseas, had been a serial offender and a serious irritation to the military police. In December 1918, after he was nicked yet again by the Provost Corps, the following communiqué was despatched to AIF headquarters in London: 'This man has been arrested here on more occasions than any member of the AIF. It is requested that approval be given for his trial and subsequent return to Australia as an incorrigible, please.' Neville was placed on a six-month detention order, and then promptly shipped back to Australia in the *Derbyshire* to complete the rest of his sentence.

His real name was Frank Thomas Hyland, but he enlisted twice as Harold John Neville, the first time in early November 1915. Barely nine months into his service with the 19th Battalion, he was repatriated back to Australia, and then discharged after he had complained of defective vision while in Egypt.

Three months later he lined up again, this time at the Dubbo recruiting office in New South Wales. He was answering his country's call to arms, but for the army it would be a decision command would later sorely regret. Neville made it overseas, but the voyage would not be smooth sailing for the young private. Aside from minor shipboard infractions, such as going AWL for six hours and refusing to obey an order, Neville went down with the dreaded pox, spending 21 days in isolation. Once on land, Neville's skirmishes with VD would continue. He would have two major visits to the Bulford Hospital, and while still infected escape from the isolation ward and remain on the run for a fortnight lurking in and around London.

But even the pox could not curtail Neville's romantic pursuits. He claimed an affair of the heart was the reason he went AWL on numerous occasions. Once when he'd been picked up after 77 days on the lam, he told his court martial that he had been called to the bedside of his 'intended wife', a Miss Dolly Wilson, who was suffering a serve attack of bronchitis. His requests for compassionate leave were turned down, so Neville skipped camp.

'I made up my mind to see the girl I loved. I then came to London and went straight to my girl's bedside,' he stated. 'I was not there ten minutes before she took another bad turn. I went straight for the doctor.' Rushed to the hospital, Dolly later died of pneumonia, according to Neville.

He gave the court martial a rundown of his own ailments, his brief time at Gallipoli, his evacuation to Australia on health grounds, and his re-enlistment some months later. Neville stated that he was no shirker and had tried to get across to France to fight with his comrades but was refused 'as I was not fit'. He claimed he'd also tried to return to Australia, but that too had been rejected.

'So I got sick of being in the one camp and I heard several chaps saying that if you went AWL they would send you to France but when I wanted them to send me they refused, then when I was first getting contented to stop in camp, this trouble fell on me when my girl died,' his statement read.

'I did not care what became of me and now I am told that I am being sent home to Australia as an incorrigible.' His request for a review was flatly rejected and on New Year's Day 1919 he was ordered to serve six months, which was how he came to find himself drunk and on the same train as West.

Among the other prisoners travelling north were Privates Harrie Nathan Jemmett and William Page. These men had tried to escape as they were being disembarked from the *Derbyshire* and transferred to the Portsea quarantine station. When the two were recaptured a day or so later, Jemmett struggled so violently that he had to be handcuffed. After being subdued he sneered to one of the police officers: 'If I ever have to go to Sydney and a military guard is put over me, there will be a murder. One of us will go down as I have no time for military police.'

Page was a labourer from Queensland who had served with the 26th Battalion. He was a deserter, a drunk, and had spent considerable periods in hospital being treated for venereal disease. He had a 12-month prison sentence hanging over him, and his military papers had him stamped as incorrigible. Yet for Page, being transported home in disgrace was probably his preferred option. If he'd stayed around London, where he was wanted for larceny in company with another digger, British police would inevitably have charged him, resulting in an even heavier sentence in a punitive English jail.

Jemmett, a 23-year-old miner, had enlisted at the Sydney Showgrounds camp in June 1915 and been posted to the 59th Battalion as a reinforcement. In a burst of patriotism he had had an Australian coat of arms tattooed on his right arm. But his military records reveal a man far from committed to his country's cause.

Within three months of disembarking in France he was fronting a field general court martial charged with conduct prejudicial to good order and military discipline; to wit, negligent self-inflicted wounding. The 59th Battalion had been involved in the Allied advance that followed the enemy's retreat to the Hindenburg Line. Nine days after Jemmett joined his unit in the field, he shot himself in the foot with his rifle. He was promptly dealt with by his commanding officer, who found him guilty and docked 14 days pay. He also spent 67 days in hospital.

When he eventually returned to active duty, it wasn't long before he broke camp and went AWL for seven days. The following month he left No. 12 Camp, Le Havre, and roamed free for just over five months until he was picked up by military police at Cayeux. A field general court martial slotted him for two years but this was suspended the following month, a decision no doubt influenced by the troop replenishment demands.

Three weeks later, Jemmett was being treated for VD in the No. 39 General Hospital at Le Havre, where he spent almost a month before rejoining his unit in late April. A week later he was off again until his apprehension on 25 July. A fortnight later he escaped from the guard room and remained free for two months until he was arrested in early October and returned to barracks under escort.

Jemmett again slipped the guard later that month and somehow made it across the Channel. In London, he roamed free until the day after Christmas, when he handed himself in to MPs. With the hostilities well over by now, the young private undoubtedly wanted to get home. But awaiting him back at his barracks was a two-year sentence to be served at Lewes. This sentence was made concurrent with the previous two-year term military chiefs had unwisely suspended.

In early March he was transported back to Australia to serve the rest of his time.

*

Jemmett and the other prisoners from the *Derbyshire* were put on an early afternoon train to Sydney. They took their seats in three second-class compartments which had been specially reserved for their transport. Just before their departure, Corporal William Poulston, who was in charge of the military police guarding them, told the prisoners 'if you give us a fair go, I will give you all a fair go'.

Shortly before their train pulled out, a woman appeared on the platform and handed another bottle through the carriage window, saying: 'I want you all to remember Anzac Day.' By this stage, all the prisoners were well on the way. Private Sydney Harold Sheedy, doing five years for desertion, said later: 'We were all pretty well full, some of the boys were drunk.'

The train blew its whistle and chugged out of the station right on 4 pm. The remaining bottles of whisky were immediately opened and cards were produced for the long journey. A court heard later that the refreshments were also allegedly shared with some of the guards.

Not surprisingly, evidence given to the official inquiry by the guards and the prisoners was somewhat convoluted and confusing.

It was after the train had passed Broadford that tensions rose. Jemmett and another prisoner, Francis Edward Ryan, engaged in what their criminal colleagues later described as a friendly tussle in the corridor.

Stationed nearby were escorts Sergeant Job F. Daly, Private Moore and Corporal Poulston, who was closest to the toilets. The sergeant later told authorities his rifle had been resting by his seat.

Prisoner Ryan, however, claimed the weapon was leaning against the toilet door and he had to move it to enter the cubicle. But his evidence did not carry much weight, given his military record.

Ryan had enlisted in early July 1915 under the name of Francis John South and went with the 26th Battalion to Egypt. His rap sheet comprised 14 offences, ranging from theft, desertion, going AWL, resisting arrest, defaulting, escaping from custody, and fraud. In mid-March 1918 he was mysteriously wounded by a rifle bullet. A board of inquiry found it had occurred while he was not on duty, and through no fault of his own. His last AWL offence was on 15 November 1918, four days after the Armistice, for which he was sentenced to one year's detention.

The one fact no one questioned at the inquiry was that a bullet from Poulston's gun had hit Jemmett in the right breast. On 6 May, the corporal appeared before the City Court and was bailed on a charge of murder. Meanwhile, an inquest got under way in Broadford.

The deputy coroner heard that Harold Neville had been in the group playing cards with Jemmett. He later gave evidence that a few minutes after the private left the compartment he heard a shot fired and then someone appeared at the door, shouting: 'Poor Jemmett is shot.'

'I then went into the corridor, and saw Jemmett sitting in the corner with his head on his shoulder. I went to walk up to him, and the corporal said: "Stand back or I'll put a bead through you."'

The noise also alerted West, by then quite drunk, who arrived on the scene just in time to see Poulston and the prisoner Hedley lift the dead man's limp body. According to West, the corporal then pointed his pistol at him, while another guard stood with his rifle at the 'on-guard' position. In the frenzy, West shouted, 'Who shot my mate?'

'I was then hit on the head with a butt end of a rifle [by the escort], and stunned,' he told police.

Confined to his compartment, West said he later spoke to the attending doctor, asking if it was true that Jemmett was dead.

'Too true, lad, he's dead; but keep calm,' the doctor replied.

When the train reached Seymour, West was looking out the window when he saw Jemmett's body being taken away on a stretcher.

'I said to the sergeant, "Let me have one more look at him. He is my mate, and I don't believe he's dead."'

After being refused, West jumped headfirst through the carriage window, landing on the platform. He was immediately pounced on by two guards, who handcuffed him and returned him to the compartment.

The event caused much excitement in the local and interstate press. Had the prisoners been drunk? The *Age* suggested the evidence was overwhelmingly yes. It reported that railway staff had found two whisky bottles and a beer bottle in the compartments after the incident.

The deputy coroner heard that Jemmett's death was not the result of a misunderstanding or prank. Poulston had in fact headed off a planned mass break-out.

Corporal Poulston was a Canadian-born member of the AIF who'd been invalided home from Egypt in 1916. He was in his forties when he signed up for the war, a heavily built man with a no-nonsense manner. He told police he'd placed three prisoners in each of the three compartments, with a military constable and a guard 'armed with ball ammunition' in charge of each compartment. An armed guard was placed in the corridor in front of each compartment.

'About an hour after leaving Spencer Street I was standing in the passageway at the end of the carriage talking to Private [MP, Henry John] Foster and the sergeant of the guard when I heard a commotion in the fourth compartment from where I was standing.

'I went to investigate and saw three men struggle out of the compartment into the corridor. Two of the men were fighting and struggling with the third man.

'I said: "Get back to your places." Someone then said, "There is one of your men," pointing to the man who was being assaulted by the other two.' It was the guard, Private

William John Lennon, that Poulston had deployed at that compartment. 'I caught him by the shoulders and pulled him away from the other two men. He was bleeding from wounds about the mouth and the face caused by blows being struck by the prisoners.'

Several other prisoners had advanced towards Poulston 'in a menacing manner', trying to reach Lennon. One of them said, 'Where is that MP bastard? I want to get him.'

Poulston pulled out his five-chambered, .32-calibre revolver, which was fully loaded. 'I said, "Stand back or I'll fire." They then stood and assumed a threatening and defiant attitude.'

A guard, Private William Charles Moore, then leapt onto the seat at the end of the corridor, raised his rifle to his shoulder and, pointing it in the prisoners' direction, said: 'Stand back or I'll fire.' Jemmett, who had been sitting nearby, jumped up and attempted to wrest the rifle from Moore.

'As he was about to obtain possession I swung my revolver around and fired in the direction of Private Jemmett, who fell onto the seat bleeding from a wound in the right breast,' Poulston said.

Immediately, the group converged on Poulston and Moore, and it wasn't until Moore clubbed one of them with the butt of his rifle and sent him reeling that the melee was controlled. Eventually the prisoners were herded back into their compartments and order restored.

Poulston maintained that he believed Jemmett was going to use Moore's rifle to shoot them. He claimed self-defence, and was then charged with murder.

In his evidence, Moore described the struggle between himself and Jemmett for possession of the rifle. He said the weapon was 'swaying all about' and could have accidentally discharged. The guard had been wounded during the war and was no match for the strongly built young prisoner.

'Jemmett had the best of me in the latter part of the struggle,' Moore said. 'He was a stronger man than me. Taking into consideration all the circumstances, I think Poulston did the proper thing in firing at Jemmett. It was necessary to disable Jemmett. I certainly think that if the deceased got the rifle he would have used it.

'I don't think a punch on the jaw would have disabled him.'

The prisoner Hedley, who had served with the 7th Light Horse, had been a police officer before enlisting, but he had an extensive army rap sheet. A colourful character, he was described in newspaper court reports at the time as a 'well-dressed, respectable-looking young man'. A one-time police officer in Shanghai, he admitted to 'having been charged with hundreds of military offences', though he also said that he could be prone to exaggeration. 'But there are no crimes of violence in my record,' he told the inquest.

In his evidence, he directly accused Poulston of having pulled the trigger just as Jemmett released his grip on the rifle. 'I was present when the shot was fired and saw the whole occurrence. In my opinion the shooting of Jemmett was decidedly not justified,' he said. The prosecution argued the shooting was justified given the charged atmosphere and the likelihood of extreme violence.

Under examination, Moore said the MPs had come under sustained abuse, with one prisoner saying to him: 'You motherless bastards bludging in the government, you'll never take us to Sydney.'

He believed the fracas had been part of a conspiracy: 'From the unity with which the prisoners acted, it looked to me as if it was a prearranged action.'

Lennon, the MP who took a battering, told of being taunted by some of the prisoners as a 'bloody fucking bastard'. He said that while he was guarding one compartment, the men shouted: 'Get out, you black bastard, you fucking MPs.' He exited, hoping the atmosphere would cool, and partially closed the door. But the anger was still palpable, and while standing outside the compartment he heard one prisoner say, 'We will make a break, and we'll get away from this train before we get to Seymour.'

Lennon said he organised a replacement on the door for a brief toilet break. On his return he heard one of the prisoners say to the others: 'Come on, make a bold bid, follow me.'

Just as the prisoner, whom he couldn't identify, made a dash from the compartment, Lennon grabbed hold of him. During the struggle he heard another prisoner urging his cell-mate to 'kill the bastard'. With that he received a solid boot to the ribs, which put him on the floor.

'The man I had, had an arm locked round my neck and gave me a beaut on the nose,' Lennon said. 'I got several also on the jaw. Others rushed in while the blows were being struck and rushed over the top of me yelling, "Kill these bastards. Get out, make a bloody break." It was then that Morrison stepped in.'

The deputy coroner found on the evidence that Corporal William Poulston had feloniously killed Private Harrie Nathan Jemmett, and directed that he be tried for manslaughter.

A lot hung on Hedley's evidence. Was it credible? A handwritten legal opinion presented to the prosecutor's office assessed that it was 'absolutely untrustworthy'. Not only was it in direct opposition to four other witnesses' statements, but the former cop was in his compartment until after the shot was fired. The shooting was justified, it reasoned.

So the prosecution decided not to offer any evidence against Poulston, and the criminal trial did not go ahead. Late in June, the Crown entered a *nolle prosequi*.

The name of Private Harrie Nathan Jemmett, Service number 2927, of the 59th Battalion (Infantry), was listed on the

Australian War Memorial's Roll of Honour. His cause of death was given simply as 'Accidental (Gun shot wound)'.

*

After seeing out the remainder of his sentence at home, John Beaumont West continued on his criminal path. He was a regular at magistrates courts, facing charges ranging from vagrancy, breaking and entering, minor assault and indecent language. But perhaps the most bizarre incident was on the evening of 29 June 1921 when West was found sitting on the footpath outside a Port Macquarie house with blood dripping from his arm. Initially he told the constable he'd had an argument with a Mrs Murphy and had slipped, cutting his arm with his knife.

Then it suddenly became: 'I'm telling lies. I wanted to commit suicide. I wanted to die out on the road.

'I am madly in love with this woman,' he expanded. 'And she won't go with me, so I'll give her a free leg to do as she likes. I am dying slowly and peacefully; if you stop me from dying now I'll do it later on.'

Police went into the house occupied by Selina May Kelly, where they found blood on the floor and a bloodstained knife on the table. There was also a note, written in West's hand and addressed to his brothers, 'especially Charlie'.

> The world is against me. There is only one thing that is stopping me taking the woman I love (I will always be dead or alive), and that is money . . . so please Charlie I want you to promise me, please . . . give my chop of the old man's money to the woman that I love. I have always told you she is my friend and sweetheart, one of the Whitest God ever put breath into.

Separately, he had sent a letter to the family solicitor making a similar request, accompanied by another document described by the lawyer as 'purporting' to be his AIF discharge papers. The makeshift will was witnessed and co-signed by Mrs Kelly; however, in her evidence the widow claimed she was unaware of what she was signing. 'Although I signed it I did not know what the contents of the letter were,' she stated. She also claimed ownership of the bread knife, but said when West picked it up and went to cut himself, she went out into the street for help. By the time she returned, West had cut his arm.

He was fined three pounds and two pounds two shillings in medical costs for attempting to kill himself. That was the closest West would come to dying for the next 29 years. In 1950, he went peacefully surrounded by his family.

In later life, West's friend Harold Neville became a man of letters, keeping up a correspondence with the defence department seeking replacement discharge papers and medals which had been lost and/or somehow destroyed.

His return address was always either Goulburn or Long Bay Gaol. The official replies inevitably told him that he was entitled to nothing more than the British War Medal.

# 8

# A Day in Court

Australia's courts were clogged with returned soldiers in 1919 and 1920. Many of the diggers flooded in through the Western Australian ports and stayed around Perth and Fremantle long enough to get themselves into serious trouble. On one typical day in court in Perth in late October 1919, the sentencing of a group of returned soldiers who had gone on a shooting spree in the brothels around Roe Street was followed by the case of two ex-servicemen charged with violent assault and robbery on the Kalgoorlie–Perth express.

Roe Street continued to be a magnet for servicemen after the war ended. There the French-born madam Josie de Bray continued her reign as Queen of Roe Street. She was known for her striking peroxide-blonde hair and was every inch the grande dame of vice with her expensive wardrobe, elaborate furs and chauffeur-driven car. Her headquarters was a stylish establishment called Josie Villa, better known as Rue de Roe, whose secret entrance was through a service station in close-by James Street.

She had amassed her fortune on the back of the war and the influx of soldiers to Perth and Fremantle. But not every customer who visited Rue de Roe came away happy. Frederick Cooper Bridges paid Josie's establishment a visit around 3 am on 14 August 1919. As the press later phrased it, as genteelly as possible, the drunken ex-soldier made a certain proposal. What he had in mind would certainly not have shocked the brothel madam, and the wad of notes he had in one hand would not have precluded him from a business transaction. But Bridges, stupidly, was waving his service revolver about, so de Bray ended the discussion by closing the front door. As she later told the criminal court hearing, Bridges then snarled: 'I'll settle you some day.'

It would be safe to say Bridges was not a man who impressed the upright men he came into contact with. In early May 1915, under the name of Frederick Charles Seymour, he was severely admonished by the chief justice of Western Australia for character evidence he gave in a case involving an incest charge against one of his friends. Bridges had appeared before the court in the uniform of the Light Horse, although he was actually serving time. He told the court of having once taken the girl out and gave sordid detail of their sexual congress at the end of the day.

His evidence and appearance evidently reduced Sir Robert McMillan to cold fury. He attacked Bridges' character and questioned his lack of gallantry, describing him as a 'shameless blackguard . . . and a disgrace to the uniform, he should have been prevented from wearing it court'. The jury, nonetheless, thought otherwise and Bridges' mate was found not guilty after five hours of deliberation.

The previous year, Bridges had been slotted for two months hard labour for stealing a revolver and pawning it for five shillings, and after the war he would offend repeatedly. So it was that 24 hours after being rebuffed by Madam Josie, Bridges gathered together his reinforcements – war veterans also – Edward Stewart, Leslie Jordan and Henry Ryan.

After a long and sustained drinking session at several pubs, the four men converged on Josie Villa and Bridges knocked on the front door. Josie switched on the light and peered through the peephole, spying the drunken quartet milling together on the verandah. Once again an offer of five pounds was made and Josie once again thought better of admitting the group, telling them, 'Go away, boys, we're all too busy.' She would later tell their criminal court trial the demands were repeated but in 'more forcible and threatening language'. She then spied two of them wink and then nod at Bridges, who crept up to the peephole and peered in.

Josie immediately switched off the verandah light and edged away from the door as Bridges poked his pistol through the slot. It was then she saw a flash.

'A shot was fired without effect,' the court was told. 'And then as she retreated down the passage, a second bullet from the revolver lodged in her arm near the elbow.' The wounded brothel madam, with blood streaming down her arm, made for the safety of the dining room, where she was later treated by Dr Louis Gelle. By this time the group had fled.

It would be an eventful night for their hired driver Humphrey James Hearn, who told the court of having collected the group and taken them on a pub crawl, where they 'indulged fairly liberally'. Hearn told of his alarm when guns were produced by Bridges and Ryan, but the men assured him the bullets were just blanks. On the way to Josie's brothel several shots were fired from the moving vehicle into the sky. Once they'd reached their destination, Hearn said he waited in the car while the four visited the brothel. Shortly after, he heard shots being fired, the group returned to the vehicle and he was redirected to another Roe Street premises. Bridges and another man got out and hurriedly returned a few minutes later, ordering Hearn to 'go for your life'.

The men had roused a lady of the night, Florence Wilson, from her well-earned sleep. Florence occupied the front bedroom, and on hearing a knock on the door went to investigate. She switched on the lights and, peering through the peephole, noticed Bridges and one of his co-accused, Henry Ryan, standing on the verandah. She said one of them was wearing a military uniform. Once again, a 'fiver' was proffered. Sensing danger, Florence declined the offer. Bridges retaliated by pointing the muzzle of his revolver at the edge of the peephole and warning, 'See, we've got this.' Refusing to be intimidated, Florence told him to put the weapon away and leave. To which Ryan exclaimed, 'She's an Aussie, come away.' Bridges added, 'If you are a dinkum Aussie we'll go away. But if you're a Frenchy we would have blown the house up.'

Florence's mistake was to think that she'd sent them on their way. Moments later she slid the cover of the peephole open again and immediately felt a stinging pain in her face and fell back against the bedroom door, unconscious. She'd been shot at point-blank range. Florence was later taken to Perth Public Hospital, where the bullet in her head was extracted. Ryan testified that after this shooting, the group went and had a last drink outside the Imperial Hotel.

The driver said at the conclusion of the group's shooting expedition he was sworn to secrecy. 'Mum's the word,' he told the thugs. But that was until the police came calling.

Stewart and Jordan were hit with three-month terms for unlawful wounding. Ryan, the only one of the four to give evidence, got an extra month, while Bridges copped three years hard labour for unlawful wounding with intent.

There was also another member of the group, James Alexander Allan, a veteran of the 2nd Field Bakery, which had served in France. Allan joined in mid-July 1915, and was sent to Blackboy Hill in Western Australia. The 22-year-old

Methodist's time in France was interrupted by bouts of sickness, including 34 days in isolation in Calais, being treated for venereal disease. He was also admonished for failing to clean the dishes properly. His time with the Army ended on 20 July 1919, less than a month before he caught a ride with the Bridges shooting party.

Allan was fortunate. He avoided any charges simply because he'd been seriously drunk, indeed legless, on the night. Allan told the court he'd consumed between 30 and 40 drinks on the night and remained in the car during both incidents. He couldn't remember a thing, he told the jury, except some shots being fired. His hazy evidence assisted neither the prosecution nor the defence.

Passing sentence, Justice Robert Bruce Burnside looked down on the men with the utmost contempt, taking particular aim at their criminality while still members of the Australian armed forces, and their degradation by drunkenness and visits to brothels at night: 'You bring disgrace upon men who were your comrades in the field, you bring disgrace upon your country and the proud name of Australia, one we all hope to see stand in the Society of Nations [the League of Nations].

'You are all entitled to wear the returned soldiers' badge, which is an emblem of a noble duty nobly done. It carries with it a responsibility which is as great as its reward, and returned men should live up to the traditions of the badge. I have been sitting in the Criminal Court for nearly six weeks, and I have seen a long row of returned soldiers before me, and the guerdon [prize or accolade] which they have gained has been besmirched. It is deplorable this should happen. If the bullet from Bridges' revolver at either of the two houses where the weapon was fired had been deflected ever so little, two women might have been killed, and you men would have found yourselves elevated to a position from which you would only have dropped once.

'By your conduct you have brought disgrace upon the badge you wear and disgraced the name of soldiers generally . . .

'You men know in all probability, and we who stayed behind have heard and read with pride of the conduct of the Australian troops towards the women and children of France. Are we really to believe that such was the case, if this is the way you behave here? We are told that the women and children in France were safe in the hands of the Australian troops, who were models of chivalry as men who regarded a woman's honour as the most precious thing in life. I hope some of you will have good sense and remember that a man's good name is a precious jewel.'

Justice Burnside also told of his concerns that in Kalgoorlie and Perth 'almost every person in the dock has been a returned serviceman'.

This address reflected broader social fears about the behaviour of repatriated Australian servicemen. As early as 1915, the authorities had noted returned soldiers 'lounging about city streets and undermining their strength by excessive drinking'. At the end of the war there were almost 170,000 members of the Australian military overseas and most of them would flood back into the country in the years immediately after the war. Many of them had been permanently changed by their experiences.

Bridges withstood Justice Burnside's fire and brimstone to offend another day . . . and another . . . and another. He regularly appeared before magistrates on burglary and breaking and entering counts, serving sentences ranging from two to four years. In 1926, he was arrested after breaking into a Mounts Bay home where he was found hiding under the owners' bed. The judge sentenced him to 18 months with hard labour. In 1930, he was sent away for four years hard labour for breaking into a Peppermint Grove house and assaulting the family's 15-year-old daughter with a heavy object. His defence counsel often raised his drinking problems in mitigation, but this rarely swayed the judges. One told him: 'In my opinion you are mentally unstable, but not so much as you can be classed as insane. Your disability results from immoderate partaking of liquor.'

Florence Wilson survived her head wound and continued to service her clients, while Josie de Bray eventually headed home, funded by her extensive West Australian property investments, which included a 13-roomed villa at Mount Lawley. But the newspaper headlines would still follow the notorious French brothel keeper. Perth's *Mirror* breathlessly reported in October 1940 she'd been made a prisoner of the Nazis. Maybe they were linking her activities with another scarlet identity, the notorious secret double-agent, Mata Hari, who was executed in 1917 when it was discovered she'd been spying for the Germans during the war. Mata Hari was 41 at the time while Josie was nudging 70.

Whatever the case, the *Mirror* reported: 'For many years the Queen of Perth's Red Light district, more commonly known as Rue de Roe, the strikingly colourful peroxide blonde Princess Josie de Bray has been captured by the Germans in France and is now a prisoner of war in Germany. It is nine months since her last letter from France was received by a Perth accountant, who looks after her affairs here. And in the midst of occupied France word has now come that she is in a concentration camp.

'Though French by birth, she could not enjoy the "privileges" of other French people in occupied territory because she had been naturalised while living in Australia. A Western Australian, who acted as her secretary in France, managed, after many hair-breadth escapes, to elude the Germans. Josie, apparently, was not so fortunate.'

*

Immediately after Bridges' associates were sent down, a soldier named Thomas George Urquhart was brought into the court. Just a month from discharge from the 51st Battalion, he had been charged along with Alexander Leslie Vardy, a seaman gunner in the Royal Australian Navy, of viciously assaulting and robbing a couple of civilians on the Kalgoorlie–Perth express train.

Vardy, 22, had served in HMAS *Australia* in the North Sea campaign, in which British forces kept Germany's main ports blockaded throughout the war. The week before the alleged assault, he had been feted in a homecoming ceremony at the Coolgardie Town Hall. He was the local boy who went to war and came back a man, sporting a blue scar under his left eye and a tattoo on his right forearm. But his six years in the navy was not without blemish. In December 1917, according to his service records, he was convicted for an unidentified civil offence.

As for Urquhart, his assistance in the war effort was also recognised when his enlistment was lauded in the local Kalgoorlie newspaper, the *Western Argus*. He signed up in early July 1917, and was accepted on his second go. The labourer had previously been rejected on medical grounds, but according to his papers an operation had rectified the problem, whatever it was. By that time replenishments for Australia's battle-weary and dwindling forces were in great demand. Every man was needed.

The young man from the goldfields was assigned to the Blackboy Hill military camp, where he not only underwent extensive dental work but was also treated for alcoholism. Urquhart eventually embarked for France, where in May the following year he was wounded in action. He returned to Australia eligible for the standard British War Medal and Victory Medal.

On 22 August 1919, an elderly man from Kalgoorlie caught the train to Perth. Elia Atzel, an Italian-born miner, had just sold his house in the goldfields and planned to relocate to the capital. A widow, Rose Ada May Murray, whom he'd only recently met, had arranged the sale. Atzel had little English, so

Mrs Murray suggested they travel to Perth together. With the 50 pounds given to Atzel as the deposit for his house, and other cash from the sale of his furniture, the two boarded the night train. They were alone in the compartment as the train pulled out of Kalgoorlie, but not for long.

They were soon joined by Urquhart, whom Ada had just met on the platform. The three became four when Vardy took his seat as the train passed Coolgardie, well after sunset. Pleasant conversation was initially exchanged and Ada invited the ex-servicemen to join them in a brandy from the bottle she'd brought for the journey. Elia brought out sandwiches and handed them around. After half an hour or so Urquhart left the carriage and returned with four glasses of beer. They all then retired to the dining car for more drinks. After returning to the compartment, an argument began when the two servicemen asked Ada why she was with 'a black Dago, Greek, or something'. She ordered them to leave, which they did, but they returned soon after.

What happened next was terrifying. 'The door was abruptly opened and the two accused rushed in,' the City Court was later told. 'Vardy took hold of Mrs Murray and tied a handkerchief around her face. Urquhart caught Mr Atzel by the throat with one hand, and with the other punched him violently in the face. He could see the other accused dragging Mrs Murray from the compartment.'

The widow was punched in the face, so hard that the force smashed her false teeth and glasses, and she was knocked unconscious. The 15 pounds commission she'd made from the sale of Mr Atzel's house was stolen from her handbag, which was then thrown from the moving train.

Meanwhile, 'Mr Atzel was punched incessantly until he was rendered unconscious.' The court was told he had been left by the pair 'very near dead', and later spent eight days in hospital.

'Blood was bespattered over his clothes, and upon searching his pockets he found he had been robbed of his money, the proceeds of the house and furniture sale. The two pounds and ten shillings left behind was covered with blood.'

A railway employee standing on the platform between the carriages happened to witness Vardy exit the train. As the express slowed down near the no. 7 pumping station, the sailor jumped off, leaving his partner to complete the journey. When the train reached Southern Cross it was boarded by police, who immediately went to Urquhart's compartment. The uniformed soldier denied any knowledge of the assaults and, when paraded before the two victims, maintained his innocence, to the point of claiming never to have seen them before.

By this time word had also reached police about the strange late-night visit by Vardy to the railway engineer's residence at no. 7 pumping station. 'It's very funny. I hardly know what has happened to me,' Vardy told the engineer, Alfred Philps. 'I either fell or was pushed off the express and, after recovering from the fall, I put my hand in my pocket to get a cigarette and found I had a roll of five-pound notes. I knew they were not mine, nor how they came to be in my possession.'

Vardy would eventually plead guilty to robbery with violence, while Urquhart admitted nothing. He told the court he'd just returned from the war and had met Vardy for the first time on the train. He admitted being in the carriage when an argument arose between the others, but claimed he had left before the situation became too heated. The first he knew of the assaults and robberies was when he was confronted by the conductor in the dining car. When police asked him to turn out his pockets, they found only threepence. He also drew their attention to the absence of blood about his hands and clothes.

Vardy blamed the brandy and beer he'd drunk for his actions on the night. He was sentenced to 12 months jail. Soon after, he moved to New South Wales. Urquhart maintained his denials through the three trials he faced.

At Urquhart's sentencing, the chief justice observed that counsel had pleaded Urquhart's war service in mitigation. It worked with the jury, which recommended mercy, but Sir Robert took a sterner view.

'That the prisoner had done his duty in the past was no justification for breaking the laws of his country, and I'm sorry to say the prisoner is the third returned soldier to come before me in the last few days. In each case the trouble was drink,' he reflected.

With that, Urquhart was escorted down the stairs and into the holding cells beneath the court.

*

Awaiting a date with justice the same day was a recently returned sailor, William Blaize, who would receive two months for threatening police officers with a pistol. The incident occurred on Blaize's first day of civilian life after four years of active service; once again, alcohol was involved.

Blaize was a tough man, powerfully built and of very dark complexion. He was one of the Blaize boys, Fremantle identities well known to the local police, for good reasons as well as bad. His brother Sidney had served with distinction in France, earning the coveted Military Medal for his courage as a stretcher-bearer. But both brothers had street-scrapping reputations.

Young Sidney was central to the fracas that landed his brother behind bars. The brothers and one of their associates, Thomas D. Ross, were seen insulting two constables. Sidney took the matter further and challenged the pair to 'come around the back and fight'.

In police-speak, the constables 'had occasion' to speak to Ross and asked him to move away from the other men. When he ignored the request, he was arrested for disorderly conduct.

As he was being taken away, William Blaize approached the constable and revealed a gun partially covered by his coat. Soon after, Sidney Blaize stepped in and tried to spring Ross. Sidney was promptly arrested, but not before he threatened to sool the gathering mob of onlookers on to the police.

By this time the crowd had swelled to about 400. At one stage it blocked the path of the officers. There was booing and hissing, and some threats directed at the police. William foolishly opted to step in to free his brother. He confronted the officers and, while waving the small nickel-plated revolver in his right hand, snarled: 'Let go my brother or I'll shoot the @#?! pair of you.'

On seeing the gun pointed at his colleague, PC Findlay caught William's arm and forced it up his back, and then whacked him with his baton. By this time the crowd was surging forward and police had to draw their revolvers. In the confusion the Blaize brothers broke free, but were later arrested and taken to the station.

The court heard that when William Blaize was asked to surrender his revolver, he said he'd given it to a mate. They went to collect it in a nearby confectioner's shop. Not surprisingly, when the gun was handed over it was found to be unloaded, and a search failed to turn up any ammunition.

Whether it was the impending anniversary of the end of the Great War, or in acknowledgement of Blaize's naval service, the chief justice said he accepted William's unblemished service record, along with his assurance that there was no intention of inflicting any injury on the constables, who themselves were returned servicemen.

He slotted William for two months on the basis that police officers should always be given protection when carrying out their duty. Sidney was fined three pounds or one month in jail for hindering police, and Ross copped a five-pound fine for having used obscene language and creating a disturbance.

While Sidney had returned from France a decorated hero, his overall war service record would not have passed muster with the judge. His file tells of a young man who answered his country's call, yet couldn't quite leave his former life as a street larrikin, even though he was eighteen months in the naval cadets before signing on with the 44th Battalion in August 1916.

The following March, while at a training camp in Wiltshire, Sidney was disciplined for participating in a disturbance after lights out. A month later he was back on the mat, charged with gambling, again after lights out. Soon he was off to France and by September 1917 was in the thick of battle, acting as a runner, carrying vital messages between positions.

For his repeated bravery, Private Blaize was nominated for the Military Medal. His citation stated:

> This soldier has acted as a Battalion runner since September 1917, and has on many occasions shown conspicuous courage in delivering messages in adverse conditions and under heavy enemy fire. On 4th October 1917, in the operations near Ypres he repeatedly carried messages under heavy shell fire and over open ground to the front line companies, when no other means of communication was available.
>
> At Villers Bretonneux, in May 1918, he carried despatches through an exceptionally heavy gas 'strafe' and in very difficult circumstances. On 4th July, at Hamel, he was engaged for three days continuously in running to the front line companies.
>
> During the whole of the operations from the 8th August to the 2nd October, 1918 he

T. P. Bennett / State Library of Victoria

LEFT: Civilians arriving at Broadmeadows to start their military training. This was the beginning of these ordinary men's journeys to becoming soldiers.

Soldiers on parade at the Broadmeadows camp in 1914 prior to their embarkation for the Middle East. Accommodation at Broadmeadows, like many other camps across the country, was predominantly under canvas and conditions were extremely harsh.

RIGHT: Norman Bruhn racked up one of the worst military records during the war. On his return home he became a major gangster, operating in Melbourne and Sydney.

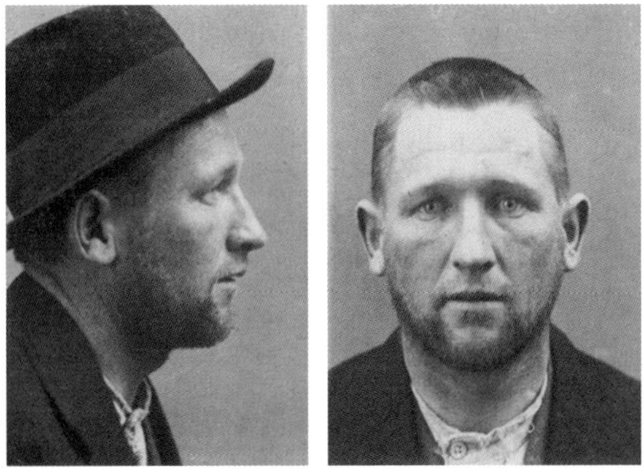

Public Record Office Victoria

Public Record Office Victoria

LEFT: Claude Taylor, one of Leslie 'Squizzy' Taylor's brothers, signed on for service but didn't get past training, going AWL for the duration of the war.

Public Record Office Victoria

RIGHT: William Gruner didn't make it to the front, after he fatally stabbed a former policeman.

Public Record Office Victoria

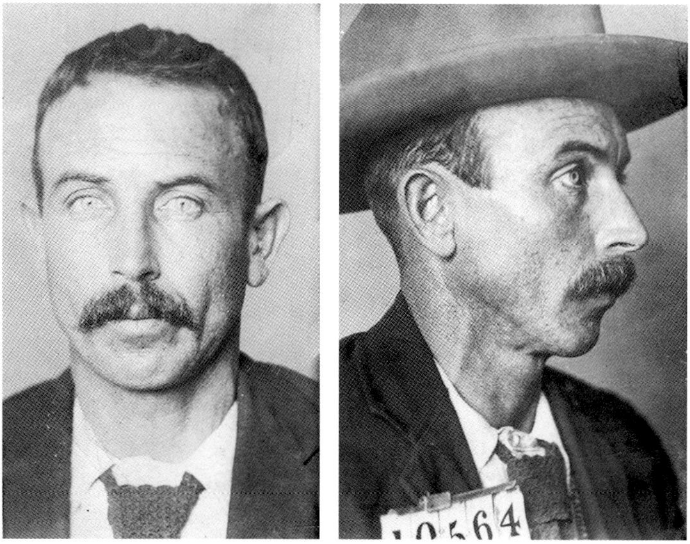


Arthur Geoffrey Oldring hanged for the murders of Margaret Taylor and Rose, her young daughter.

Public Record Office Victoria

Trawool Bridge, the scene of Margaret and Rose Taylor's murders.

State Library of Western Australia 048405PD

Josie Villa, a Perth brothel used by soldiers about to embark for the front; it was also popular with returned soldiers in the 1920s.

AWM P04752.003

In the so-called Battle of the Wazzir, Australian and New Zealand soldiers rampaged through the notorious Cairo red-light district on 2 April 1915. Incited by the large number of prostitutes infecting troops with venereal disease, the men assaulted women, ransacked brothels and set furniture alight.

AWM H00199

The crowded beach at Anzac Cove meant easy pickings for pilferers such as Stanley Bruhn, a member of the well-known Melbourne crime family.

AWM P02282.032

An accused soldier stands between his two escorts during a disciplinary hearing at Gallipoli in 1915. The court martial behind the trenches is conducted by Major A. J. Bennett, second-in-command of the 3rd Battalion; the two soldiers in the foreground are believed to be witnesses.

RIGHT: George Harris, a notorious Sydney gangster and long-serving prisoner, was redeemed on the battlefield.

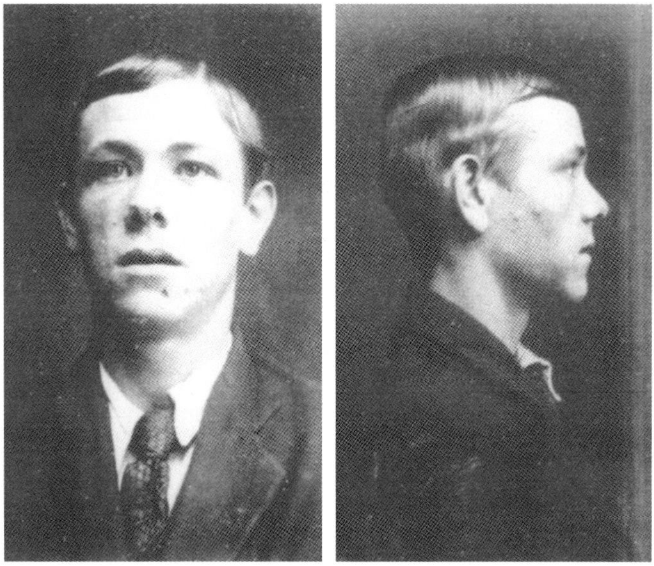

SRSNSW: NRS 2138, Photo No. 8525

The end of the first phase of the Battle of 8 August 1918. George Harris was involved in the crucial second phase.

Sydney International Exhibition of Photography

LEFT: Soldiers up on charges were tried harshly by Judge Ernest Brougham Docker.

BELOW: James Devine, the disgraced soldier, and his brothel-queen wife, Tilly, became leading players in Sydney's postwar underworld.

Fairfax Syndication

George Bickerstaff and Joseph McQueen, close friends, pose for a pre-embarkation photograph.

AWM D00890

Military prisoners exercising at Lewes Detention Barracks in East Sussex.

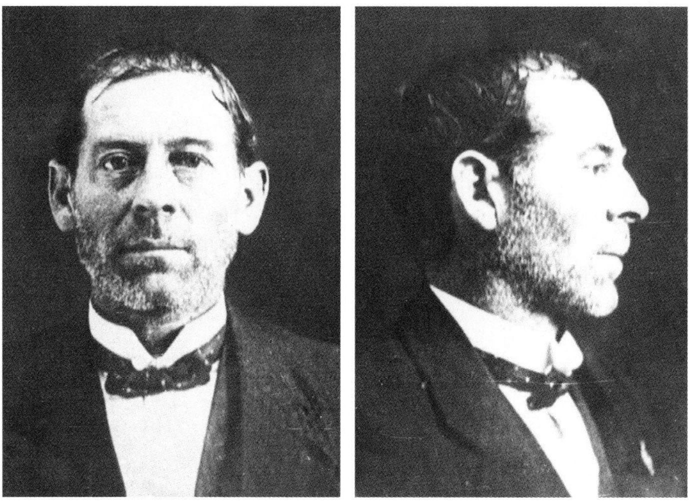

Public Record Office Victoria

Albert Edward Budd was invalided home after being wounded in battle. Blighted by his war injuries and his addiction to drink, Budd brutally slit his sister-in-law's throat.

Sydney gangsters Hampton Hirsham, Cornelius Joseph Keevil and the O'Brien brothers pose for a police picture after their arrests for robbing a prominent bookmaker.

RIGHT: Harry David Graham, a light-fingered jockey and notorious lothario.

Public Record Office Victoria

Public Record Office Victoria

LEFT: Albert McDonald, a decorated soldier, became a trusted gunman in Squizzy Taylor's crime gang.

RIGHT: Joseph Cotter came home from the front and declared war on Squizzy Taylor, firing three shots at him in a street ambush.

Public Record Office Victoria

News Limited / Newspix

After losing its licence, the old Dunolly Hotel became a haven for homeless men and itinerant workers. Returned soldiers Charles Bunney and Robert Gray were brutally axed to death here by Thomas William Johnson.

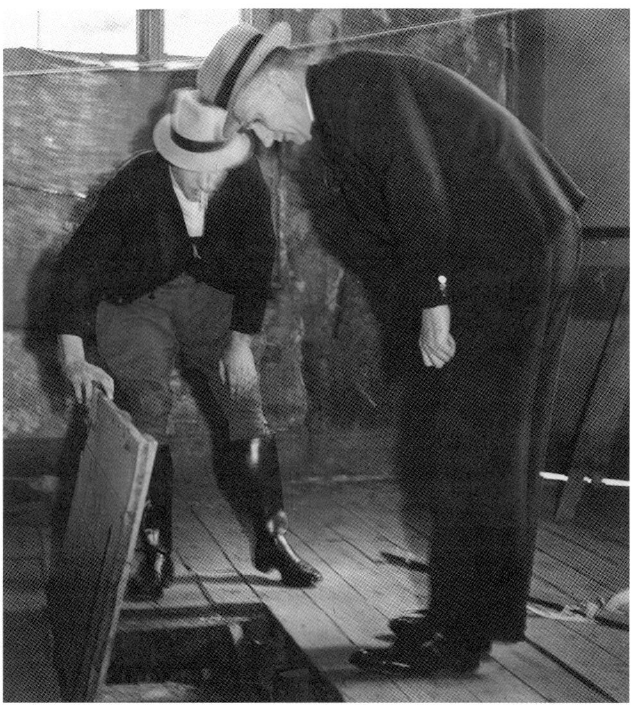

News Limited / Newspix

Melbourne detectives inspect a trapdoor in one of the ground-floor Dunolly Hotel rooms as part of their murder investigation.

News Limited / Newspix

LEFT: The rear of Dunolly Hotel, showing the window through which the bodies of Bunney and Gray could be seen.

News Limited / Newspix

RIGHT: A detective inspects the room where Bunney and Gray were murdered. The killer, Johnson, who had suffered uncontrollable violent rages since childhood, took to the men with an axe after their noise in the room above him disrupted his afternoon nap.

RIGHT: Thomas William Johnson, murderer of Bunney and Gray.

Public Record Office Victoria

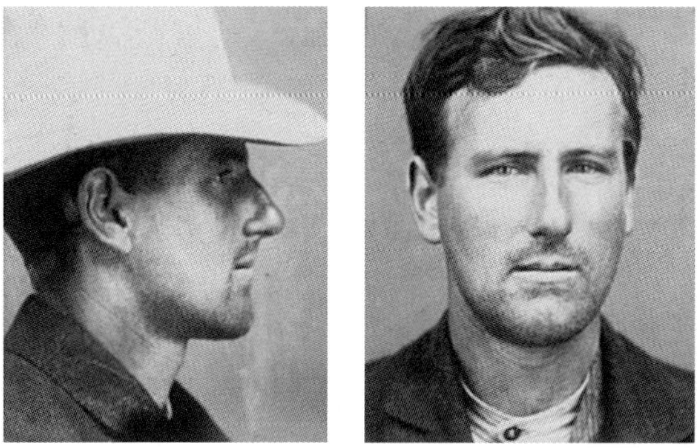

Public Record Office Victoria

LEFT: Michael Cook, a guard at Langwarrin VD camp, raped the daughter of a fellow digger.

RIGHT: Charles Sydney Johnson, a coke-addicted returned soldier, street criminal and pimp, brutally slashed the throat of his lover, Kathleen Price, in an uncontrollable rage.

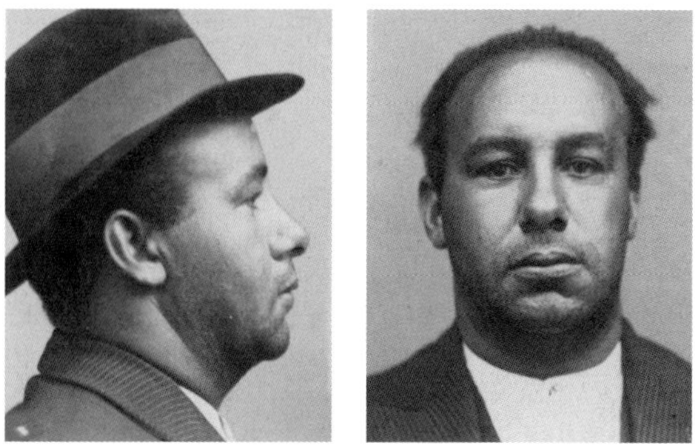

Public Record Office Victoria

Public Record Office Victoria

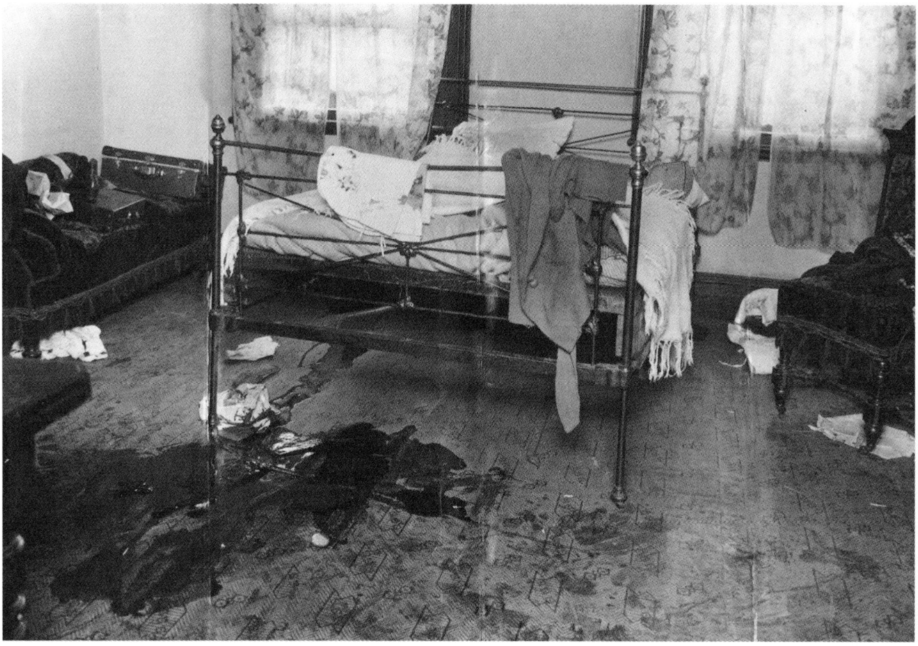

The murder scene in the boarding-house bedroom that Johnson shared with Kathleen Price.

Sydney Living Images

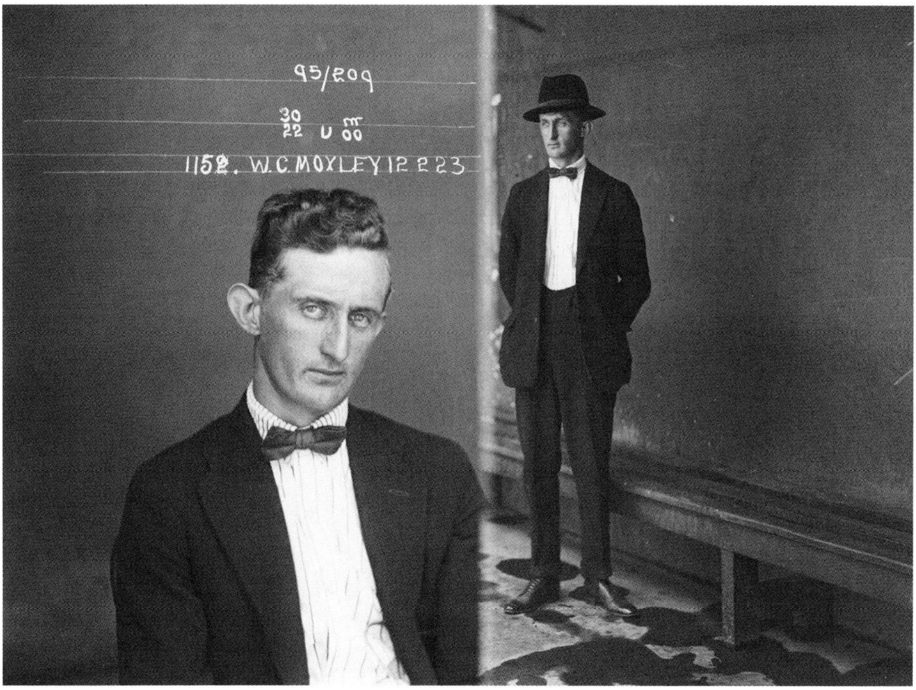


William Cyril Moxley – a police informer and double-murderer.

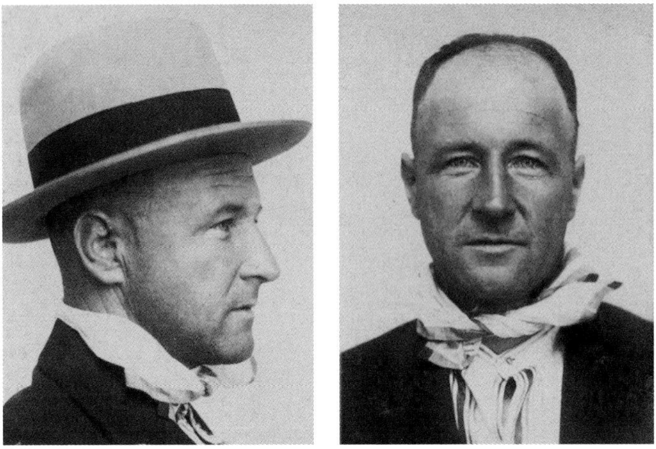

Public Record Office Victoria

Arthur Bazley, a Gallipoli veteran and an ally of Squizzy Taylor's, was shot by Joseph Cotter but refused to identify him as the gunman.

AWM A03662

The Langwarrin VD camp, an enforced home for many infected soldiers who were despatched back to Australia for treatment.

> never failed to deliver his despatches with great expedition, and he has throughout his service shown himself possessed of great courage, determination and resource.

Just three weeks later, on 21 October, Private Blaize was diagnosed with VD and spent the next 33 days in a hospital. The young war hero marked the official end of hostilities in an isolation ward.

Nor was this his last scrape with the dreaded pox. Exactly five months after being given the all-clear, he succumbed to the delights of a prostitute in Belgium. For the next 29 days he would be a resident at Bulford and Parkhouse.

As timing goes, at least when Charles, his father, was officially notified of Sidney's bravery award in January, the hero was between infections.

A year later, after demobilisation, Sidney returned to his favourite battlefield – High Street, Fremantle. In early March 1921 he and Edward Brown had a difference of opinion there which they tried to settle with a bit of biff. Police told the court a crowd of more than 50 had gathered in anticipation of the stoush and had to be dispersed. Half an hour later the combatants were 'fighting fiercely', and charged with breaching the peace.

'Both men had been convicted at the Fremantle court on several other occasions for similar offences and are evidently of a troublesome disposition,' the magistrate heard. After considering the evidence, he said he couldn't split the difference, finding each culpable. Result, a two-pound fine plus court costs.

Six months later he was back again, this time for abusing police officers after a night on the syrup. 'Once a policeman, never a man,' he called to the men in blue after they'd warned him and his mob of late-night revellers to stop battering the front window of a Fremantle fish shop with their boots. Blaize was convicted of disorderly conduct and fined two pounds. The hearing was also told Blaize and his boys would rain stones on the tin roofs of houses on their trek home from the pub.

In 1924, he again made the local newspaper answering a charge of obscene language and resisting arrest in High Street, the location for many of his misdemeanours. No doubt drink was involved.

*

Sidney Blaize had a way of getting in the papers. Almost a decade after the war's end, he publicly revealed his involvement in one of the most dramatic moments of the war in France. Sidney claimed to have been present when Baron Manfred von Richthofen, aka the 'Red Baron', was brought down. The celebrated and feared flying ace was the Imperial German Army Air Service's most decorated pilot, credited with 80 air combat victories. His downing and subsequent death in April 1918 gave a much-needed boost to the Allied campaign, but who killed him has long been a source of contention.

Captain Roy Arthur Brown, a Canadian in the Royal Air Force, was for many years lauded for downing the Baron's distinctive red Fokker triplane during a dogfight over the Somme Valley. Ian Grant in his *Dictionary of Australian Military History* writes that Brown did not initially claim the Fokker. When it was realised Richthofen was involved, he was instructed to write a combat report and the RAF 'officially' awarded the victory to him.

'Controversy raged, with the RAF refusing to admit that Australian ground fire had brought down their leading opponent. However, impartial investigations concluded that Richthofen was hit by one or more of the Australians firing from the ground on the moving Fokker,' Grant wrote.

In January 1928, a former sapper, George Monkhouse, joined in the debate. Monkhouse recalled how he had been taking a swim in the baths on the river that runs into Amiens when he witnessed the downing. He was serving with the 3rd Australian Engineers at the time, in charge of a wireless station in a wood just above Villers Bretonneux. He heard the sound of two planes, one Canadian and the other the red Fokker piloted by the Red Baron. His first reaction, as reported in Perth's *Daily News*, was to fling himself on the ground.

> It appeared to me that the German aviator was involved in the chase and suddenly woke up to his dangerous position. He started to climb steeply. Just then I heard the crackle of machine-gun fire from the wood. Richthofen's plane dipped and I thought it was coming straight for me in the manner he used to sweep down along our trenches.
>
> I don't mind telling you now that I started to run for my life. But I had not gone ten yards when the 'plane crashed. I turned and ran up to the machine. I opened Richthofen's fur coat: but he was dead. The bullets had gone through his back. I took his watch; but I am more than sorry now that I sold it to another Digger. There was no doubt that the machine-gun in the wood 'got' him.
>
> Shortly afterwards a crowd of Diggers from the 44th Battalion ran up and I showed the watch to a man named Blase [*Blaize*], now living in Fremantle, and some others.

Shortly after, Sidney Blaize wrote to the *Daily News* confirming the account, and shooting down other claims to the hit.

I was a battalion runner at the time with the 44th Battalion, and was not more than 200 yards away when Richthofen's 'plane crashed. I don't see how the British 'plane could claim to have brought Richthofen's down when the two planes were flying fully a mile apart from when Richthofen crashed.

The machine-gunners in the small wood right opposite the left wing of the plane when it was brought down were responsible for Richthofen's downfall. I was early on the scene. The first man to reach the plane was G. Monkhouse, who opened Richthofen's fur coat and sounded him to see if he was dead.

# 9

# Addicted to Love

WHAT WILLIAM WALTER PERRY LACKED in height was certainly made up for in his tall tales. Gunner Perry could spin a spell-binding yarn, impressing even his commanding officers. But it was the ladies who were most taken in by the pint-sized Lothario (he was just five foot four and a half inches), from his long-suffering wife to the loyal mistress he kept on the side and the unsuspecting woman he bigamously married.

The delusional Perry's journey through life was signposted by a series of lies, mishaps and criminal pursuits. He was described by his comrades in arms as a malingerer, abusive and foul-mouthed. One branded him 'the biggest liar in creation'. Even his enlistment papers were a hotchpotch of untruths, down to the blatant lie that his birthplace was New Brunswick, Canada, when in fact it was Sydney.

Despite all these shortcomings, Perry was able to impress some formidable politicians that he'd been maligned by the AIF and was truly a rolled-gold digger. An official inquiry was launched in October 1915 at Perry's urging, but the rollcall of witnesses was by and large not supportive of the little digger.

Perry's problems started six months after he signed up at Broadmeadows on 27 August 1914. He was early to answer the nation's call for volunteers, but his enlistment papers should have sounded an alarm for recruiters. Asked if he'd previously served with other armies, he replied yes, 'with the British Forces in China'.

Once in khaki, Perry continued to maintain the lie. His imaginary military experiences grew, as he added the Boer War to his CV and claimed to be present at the retreat from Mons in Flanders. He also claimed the loss of two fingers on his right hand was an injury sustained in the China campaign, though in reality the only fight he'd had was with a moulding machine at a St Kilda timber mill where he was employed before the war. Perry was walking past the machine when his apron got caught. As he tried to pull himself free, his hand was caught by the protruding knives, and his thumb and fingers were badly mutilated. In February 1912, he launched a legal action against his employers for more than 300 pounds in damages. It failed. Strangely, the absent digits are not included in the physical description in his enlistment papers.

Perry was 31 when he signed on, describing himself as an electrician and naming Victoria Rose Perry as his wife and next of kin. Within months he was on board the troopship *Shropshire* bound for the Middle East with the 2nd Field Artillery Brigade. But even before he'd left Australia, Perry's propensity for trouble surfaced again.

According to him, he was walking past a horse being exercised on the deck when it kicked him in the back. Perry landed facedown on the deck. He was taken immediately to the ship's hospital, where he claimed a numbness in his legs that would render him incapable of serving his country on the battlefield. The army doctors diagnosed him as having spinal neurasthenia.

When he reached the AIF camp at Mena near Cairo, an inquiry was held, and he was eventually repatriated to Australia, where physicians could find no physical evidence of a functional nervous disorder. They suspected he was just a malingerer. Their doubts must have been reinforced by Perry's commanding officer, Lieutenant Colonel George Johnston, who had signed his enlistment papers and was well acquainted with the soldier. Writing from Mena, Johnston warned the army that he thought Perry would push for some sort of official inquiry, and so he wanted to place on record his assessment of the man.

> Perry is a great talker and has such a wonderful flow of the language that I was afraid you may be unduly influenced by his version of the story. While on the 'Shropshire' he was kicked by a horse, or at least he asserts that he was kicked, but eye witnesses state that Perry fell while trying to get away from a horse he thought was going to kick him. In any case, the occurrence was thought trifling, and everybody was astonished when Perry reported sick.

Johnston said that from that moment Perry had remained in the ship's hospital, despite efforts to discharge him. It was then that suspicions of malingering first arose.

No doubt referring to Perry's vivid battlefield claims, Johnston continued:

> Perry has always been most theatrical in his attitude, and the general opinion of the officers of this Brigade is that he will endeavour to establish a claim to a pension. I was so impressed with this

> view that I collected all available information about this occurrence, and the only explanation the medical officers can offer is that Perry made such an earnest endeavour to enlist sympathy and prove that he was injured, that this ultimately worked upon his mind. And he afterwards really thought himself disabled, but of one thing I am sure, the actual occurrence was trifling, and could not have any serious effect on him.
>
> I advise you to be prepared for a serious and clever appeal for sympathy and a pension from this man, but I earnestly believe that he is unworthy of any such considerations and hope that any final decision may be left in abeyance until our return from service when the evidence I have collected will be available for consideration by the Minister.

Back in Melbourne, Perry's condition was considered by an army medical board, which in September 1915 ruled that he was suffering from 'hysteria', for which he needed hospital treatment. One of the senior doctors at St Kilda Base Hospital, Dr F.G. Meade, became the gunner's next target. His crude physical tests would be aired at another official inquiry, where Perry would claim Meade had treated him 'like a dog'.

Victoria Perry, his wife since September 1902, told the military authorities of conversations with her husband in which he recounted how he'd been 'knocked about' by the hospital staff. She claimed that in a discussion with Meade, the doctor had told her Perry's trouble was 'all in the imagination', and he would be released in a few weeks. She said he then added: 'Your husband wants firm treatment. There's nothing wrong with your husband. He's as well as you or I.'

Later, she said Meade had advised her: 'I've isolated your husband for punishment. When you go up to him he may tell you he's been harshly treated, but it's all moonshine.'

She said when she eventually saw her husband, he showed her blue bruises on his chest and arms. 'They've been knocking me about,' he told her. 'The doctor got three orderlies to hold me down while they put the battery on my face and tongue. For God's sake get me out of this.'

Meade was convinced that there was nothing wrong with his patient. Consequently, Perry was charged and court-martialled. Perry reacted by complaining he'd been the victim of torture. The court martial proceedings were eventually discontinued, but the hostilities between Perry and Meade continued unabated. Perry told a subsequent inquiry that on his return to the base hospital from the court martial, the medico came up to him, 'livid in the face and white with passion, denouncing the gentlemen of the court martial as a set of blockheads'.

Perry complained to his wife of Meade's behaviour, and after being told that the 'asylum authorities' were keeping a close eye on Perry, his wife decided to spring him.

'I got him out,' she told the inquiry. 'A friend had a motor car and we took him away. He was carried to the car.' In retaliation for his absconding from hospital, his war disability pension was immediately stopped. It was at this point that he sought assistance from the Trades Hall Council and his local Member of Parliament, the ALP's Dr William Maloney.

Maloney referred Perry's case to the Minister for Defence, Senator Sir George Pearce, who advised the Victorian MP that the disgruntled digger would not be arrested following his unauthorised discharge. But Pearce was not fully convinced of Perry's truthfulness. He told a Senate hearing he was at a loss to explain how a man who complained he couldn't walk was able to flee by scaling a seven-foot fence.

Despite Pearce's assurance, Perry was taken by force from his home just before midnight. The balloon went up and the Gunner Perry controversy quickly became public. Sir George had little choice but to instigate a public inquiry, headed by a Victorian police magistrate. The proceedings made great copy for the papers and received widespread coverage. Perry maintained that from his first encounter with Meade, the army physician had called him 'a malingerer, a schemer, an imposter, and a crawler'.

Meade's treatment of the patient – the use of physical aggression, such as kicking, and of electric charges – was not in contention. The issue was whether such therapy was inhumane.

But Perry had a dirty little secret that emerged at the inquiry, and undoubtedly went against him. The court heard from the mistress he had been seeing even while being 'tortured' at the base hospital, in between visits from his wife.

Miss Linda Broadwin entered the witness box to provide what the newspapers described as an 'interesting interlude', in which she described her two-year relationship with a man she believed was single. It was not until she visited him at the hospital that she realised he had a wife.

Asked if the revelation had upset her, she replied: 'I was broken-hearted.'

Did Perry offer any excuse for his conduct, she was asked. 'He told me he had been married only a week before leaving for Egypt.'

After Perry's deception was revealed, he wrote her a rambling love letter which was tendered to the inquiry. It read:

> Dearest Linda, Tonight as I sit here alone my heart feels sick. A letter from dear little Bess at my elbow. The tone of her letter is bright, most encouraging and cheerful – too cheerful in fact,

for a sympathetic way she makes reference to the days that are gone when mother was alive.

I was happy then, but now – oh this cruel fate with cunning treachery, that has condemned me to a woman that I have not seen, whose whole being is enshrouded in mystery. How I hate myself, my life, my very existence! What is my work, my studies, my savings to me now? Simply nothing compared with my state of health. I would be better dead, don't you think so? I LOVE YOU PASSIONATELY.

If I live, I could only live with you and your mother. I feel but for this cruel war you and I might have been happy. But, alas! Sweetheart, another few days of this mental and bodily torture and I will – must end it. My body aches. My head and my heart ache, and for this reason. I did not see you Thursday afternoon, but some of those lady friends were asking about you and your mother.

This week I have shut myself away from everybody. I will come and see you, sweetheart. However I feel, don't blame me, dear, for writing like this, for it is how I feel. Years ago I got myself out to love you and to prove my love. Could I have trusted you then as I trust you now you MIGHT HAVE BEEN MY BRIDE. My head is reeling and my limbs are shaking. I must stop writing or scribbling. I hope this will not make you unhappy or cause you a pang. Good night, sweetheart. Good night, mother – your affectionate though wounded and unhappy soldier boy.

When the betrayed Victoria gave evidence, she was grilled about her husband's dubious war service claims, in particular his story about having fought in Africa.

'You first met Perry about 1901, in Melbourne, and afterwards, he wrote to you from Africa?' it was put to her.

'I first met him just before he went to Africa,' she replied. 'I cannot remember exactly when, but I think it was 12 to 18 months before we were married in September 1902. He was in Africa about eight months.'

'Why did he go to Africa?'

'He went to the war.'

'He told you he was at Magersfontein, Enslin and Elandslaagte?'

'Yes.'

'Are you aware those battles were fought in 1899?'

'I don't know.'

'Your husband has two missing fingers?'

'Yes.'

'He lost them at a sawmill in St Kilda?'

'Yes.'

'It is sworn that he said he lost them in the Boxer rebellion . . . it would not be true?'

'No.'

'Did your husband tell [local justice of the peace] Frederick J. Funston that he had fought in the Battle of Mons?'

'I didn't hear him.'

'Where is Mons?'

'I don't know, somewhere in Africa, I think.'

The court also heard that the medal Perry proudly claimed he'd won for his battlefield bravery had in fact been issued to a G.R. Stewart, a member of the Scottish Horse.

After she stepped down from the witness box, Mrs Perry was overheard telling someone in the public gallery that her husband had instructed her to go to a pawnshop and buy a medal, and then take it to another shop to have it altered.

Mr Funston recounted a conversation in which Perry had told him that he'd been a reservist in the British Royal Artillery, and his injury had been caused by a gun carriage running over his legs during the Battle of Mons; but he had soldiered on and, despite his serious injuries, managed to kill five Germans, one after the other. The public gallery immediately burst into laughter.

Staff Sergeant Berkley of the Australian Army Medical Corps, who was at the base hospital during Perry's time, did not hold back in his evidence: 'Perry was an imposter from start to finish. On one occasion he refused to be shifted from one part of the hospital to another, and struggled vigorously, using his legs freely, though they were supposed to be paralysed.

'He should have been court-martialled dozens of times for his conduct, as he was abusive and foul-mouthed.'

Witness after witness, including his army mates, told under oath of seeing Perry freely walking without the aid of a cane, sometimes even jauntily carrying it under his arm. One impeccable witness, the Reverend William White, told of having seen Perry enjoying a stroll in the city, unaided by a stick. The clergyman said he'd had his suspicions about Perry, but was now convinced he was a 'shammer'. White also told the inquiry: 'He said although he was going to war he would see the Defence Department in hell before he would fire at the Turks.'

Medical witnesses called by Perry's legal team supported his claim that he was suffering from traumatic spinal neurasthenia, but others, particularly those on the military payroll, declared him a malingerer.

When it came time for Perry to take the stand, his answers were unintelligible. He was assisted to the box and at times sobbed, shouting '*Shropshire*' and 'Base hospital'. Eventually counsel gave up and Perry was assisted back to his seat.

When the magistrate handed down his decision a month later, he found none of the accusations made by Perry to be proven. Perry had not been incorrectly charged with malingering, and nor had Meade treated him inhumanely. Meade had reason to suspect his patient was fabricating his disability: 'There were many instances given during the inquiry which, in my opinion, were incompatible with Perry's having an honest belief in his disability. I therefore find that the charge that Perry was incorrectly charged with malingering has not been proved.'

The magistrate cleared Meade of cruelty, but refrained from commenting on Perry's bogus battlefield claims, which were not put to Perry during the hearing. 'It was apparent that Perry was ill at the inquiry. I do not believe that his illness was caused by the treatment he received at the base hospital, or that the treatment there had anything to do with it. It was probably due to the nervous strain and worry caused by the inquiry,' he found.

His illness being established, with the stroke of a pen Perry's pension was restored and he was sent back to the bosom of his faithful wife.

That should have been the end of Perry's infamy. But less than three years later, his army picture was gracing the Wanted pages in police gazettes along the eastern seaboard.

In a prominent official notice published on 13 July 1918, he was referred to as 'Sergeant Walter Kelly, otherwise known as Gunner Perry'. Police sought Perry in relation to the bigamous marriage he had made to a Mrs Gertrude Ann Jane Kelly, nee Spence. Victoria Rose Perry was named as Kelly's lawful wife in the notice, which said that the lovers had last been seen publicly at the home of a Mrs Ogden in Buckingham Street, Sydney.

'They stayed there until the end of February or beginning of March last, and then left, it was believed, for Melbourne. But no trace can be got of the couple there, although Kelly is well known in that city as Gunner Perry,' the notice read.

*

Why do soldiering and bigamy often go together? During World War II, sociologist Samuel Henry Prince noted that marriage was sometimes described as 'a war disease'. The economic ease with which marriages could be contracted in war, without any immediate need to establish a home, let alone commit to a long-term future, meant the real and psychological barriers to marriage were lowered. Some soldiers found it altogether too easy to tie and retie the knot.

Such was the case of George Harold Asquith. When he answered the nation's call to arms in late August 1914 and lined up at the Sydney Showgrounds, he was already a married man. His devoted wife was the former Edith North and they'd wed five years earlier. But on his enlistment papers, when asked if he was married, he categorically answered 'no', and gave his next of kin as a Miss L. Hyland.

Private Asquith completed his basic training at Liverpool before heading off for the Middle East with the Divisional Ammunition Column. But the 24-year-old clerk's time overseas was not without health problems and he was returned home just over six months later with rheumatism. The pains, according to his medical records, were from the hips down, but as subsequent events would show, the disability did not restrict his love life. A month after his disembarking in Sydney, George Asquith was discharged from the AIF as medically unfit.

Between his arrival home and his discharge, George fell in love, and on 24 April 1915, in an understandably quiet ceremony at St Phillip's Church, Sydney, he married Blanche Edith Farran.

The service was subdued for two simple reasons – both bride and groom were already hitched at the time.

Blanche's cuckolded husband, Joseph, whom she'd married in 1905, was in khaki in France. He had been at the front line for two years, and had stayed there even though he had been wounded. All the while, Blanche had been drawing two pounds and two shillings from his weekly allowance, and she kept on receiving it even after she'd tied the knot with Asquith.

It wasn't long before this ruse was revealed. In early November, George, deciding it was a good time to get away, fronted up to the recruiting office for another crack at the army, this time calling himself Harold Asquith Buchanan. This time he nominated his wife as Muriel Edith Buchanan, which was later corrected on his enlistment papers as Muriel Edith Asquith.

But as George counted down the days to his embarkation, the aggrieved parties were busy assisting the police. On 4 December detectives called on Private Buchanan at the Warren Camp in Marrickville. He very quickly coughed up his real name and was escorted back to Sydney.

George and Blanche were both charged with bigamy. She was sent to a female reformatory for six months, while he was slotted for 12 months with hard labour at Goulburn Gaol. It wasn't the first time George had had a brush with the law. In 1910, he was sentenced to a year after pleading guilty to horse-stealing, suspended on a 12-month good-behaviour bond.

This time, the gates of Goulburn were slammed shut on Asquith, but he was not forced to serve his full sentence. Nine months later, he signed a statutory declaration purging his sins and stating that he, George Harold Asquith, was identical with the other recruit, Private Harold Asquith Buchanan. Apparently the army was prepared to forgive if not forget. The khaki Lothario was back in service and, the week before

Christmas 1917, finally embarked in the HMAT *Ulysses* to join the 1st Field Artillery Brigade.

He saw action in France, but was soon back in England, at the training camp at Hurdcott in Wiltshire. On 26 July 1918, he did a runner, and 24 days later he was picked up in Bristol. His not-guilty plea failed to sway the district court martial hearing sitting at Fovant, and he was sentenced to 62 days detention, later remitted by 32 days, the balance to be served at Lewes.

By early the following February, George had made it home to Sydney, and within three weeks he'd been discharged as being medically unfit.

His general health might have been under a cloud, but the demobilised private had not lost his sense of adventure and daring.

By 1923, Muriel had had enough of George and in early November had secured a divorce on the grounds of his repeated adultery. She was given custody of their two small children, leaving George to roam free and for the next 13 years he did just that. In August 1935 he hit the headlines as the 'much married man', with five wives, three of whom were alleged to have been the victims of bigamous ceremonies.

The indefatigable Asquith maintained his reputation as a heart-breaker into old age. As late as November 1953, a woman from Kinglake, a small hamlet north of Melbourne, wrote to military authorities seeking his personal details:

> I am in need of the Army Service number etc of George Harold Herbert Asquith in the 1914–1918 war. I think he joined in Sydney. I do not know his rank for sure. About seven or eight years ago he drew his pension in Bendigo and then later in Footscray. At that time he was a Commonwealth

> Peace Officer. And could I find where he collects his pension now.

The writer signed herself as his wife.

*

As a notorious ladies' man, Herbert Harold Armstrong, aka Harold Anderson Berry and Herbert Horace Armstrong, didn't quite the fit the bill. Florid of complexion and stout of build, the Gallipoli casualty turned soldier-of-fortune quickly discovered his real enemies were the four women he wronged – three of whom he'd married bigamously.

He was first at the altar on 20 December 1905 when, in an Anglican church service in the Victorian town of St Arnaud, he wed Emma Hall, signing his surname as Berry. The couple remained together until he enlisted in late August 1914 in Rockhampton, Queensland, as Herbert Armstrong. He described himself on his recruitment papers as a 31-year-old customs clerk. To question number 7 – Are you married? – he answered 'no'.

Within weeks of enlisting, Armstrong was sent to the Enoggera Camp near Brisbane. He was elevated to corporal and then sent to the Middle East as a member of the 2nd Light Horse regiment. In June the following year he was wounded in the trenches, struck on the head by a piece of shell or a rock or stone.

After this injury, the army sent a communiqué to a Mrs C. Godfrey of Royal Park, Melbourne, advising that Armstrong had been slightly wounded. She had been nominated as his mother and next of kin on his enlistment documents. This brought a feisty reply from the irate Mrs Godfrey, who knew Herbert but obviously didn't care for him. She informed the army that Armstrong 'is not a son but a relative. I have not seen or heard from him for several years and have no knowledge of his whereabouts. His reference to me as his next of kin is entirely unauthorised.'

In the Middle East, promotion came again to Armstrong, who soon rose to acting company sergeant. A former customs agent who had worked in Hong Kong for seven years before the war, Armstrong obviously knew how to socialise in expat circles. An impressionable and unsuspecting young woman named Alice Norton caught the acting sergeant's eye. After a brief fling, they 'married' on 15 November 1916, in a special ceremony at His Britannic Majesty's Consulate at Cairo.

His first wife, Emma Hall, was back in Australia counting the days to her husband's safe return. She'd been receiving 25 shillings a week in maintenance, but that abruptly stopped earlier in the year – possibly the same time Armstrong started courting Alice. Armstrong had put himself down as single on his enlistment form, as many married soldiers did. He did, however, send Emma money until 1916.

Armstrong's union with Alice produced a daughter, but the relationship faltered as his military career hit an obstacle. Shortly after the wedding, he received a temporary commission with the Imperial Army, left the AIF and joined the Egyptian Camel Transport Corp with the rank of second lieutenant. But relationships there soured over a dispute about his pension and commission, or at least that's what he told Alice.

In August 1917, he was discharged from the camel corps and ordered to return to Australia. The following month, the baby arrived.

When it came time for the family to depart for Australia, the baby became seriously ill. Armstrong decided to travel home alone, telling Alice that he would re-enlist in the Australian Army and return to Cairo or, failing that, bring her and the baby out to Australia for a new life together.

He left on 27 October 1917 and sent Alice three letters before disembarking in Australia on 7 January 1918. A week passed before he sent her a telegram from Brisbane to let her know of his safe arrival. After that, Armstrong cut off all contact, leaving mother and child penniless in Egypt.

From her address in Shubra, in northern Cairo, Alice wrote letter after letter to the Australian Defence Department and the 1st Military District in Brisbane, which replied with the news that Armstrong had collected his returned soldier's badge on 22 January 1918, but that was all the department knew.

Alice, a resourceful woman who had probably been a nurse at the AIF infectious disease hospital at Shubra, penned letters to the Superintendent of Police in Queensland; the Red Cross; Registrar of Deaths; Superintendent of the General Post Office, Brisbane; the Registrar-General of Marriages, Commonwealth; the Bank of London, and the major Australian banks, and the census offices in every state.

In a heartfelt letter to the Secretary of the Government of New South Wales in April 1921, she describes her search as being 'absolutely fruitless'.

She even wrote to Warwick Windridge Armstrong, the great Australian Test cricketer who captained the national side in ten matches, winning eight and drawing two. Like Herbert, he was on the large side. As she observed later, 'my husband told me – and I enquired – he is a cousin of my husband; in fact everybody can notice the resemblance. Well, W.W. Armstrong never answered back.'

She wrote to other family members, including Mrs Godfrey, but received no replies.

> I made all the enquiries that were in my
> power but they all have not met with success;
> then myself and child suffered greatly in

> health through my husband's treatment and I feel my position so keenly, as my husband contributed nothing to my support since his departure for Australia in October 1917. I am so fragile now after my husband forsaking me and our child. I don't know if my husband is dead or alive.

Her letter had an immediate effect. The New South Wales Premier's Department immediately referred her concerns to the Officer in Charge of Base Records in Melbourne, who in reply canvassed the possibility of Armstrong being traced through the Brisbane barracks once he applied for his war gratuity. In correspondence, Armstrong had given his address simply as Lennon's Hotel, Brisbane, Queensland. Attempts by the Australian military to trace his movements through the British War Office in London also proved fruitless.

In one official communiqué the Secretary of the Department of Defence, Melbourne, was advised by the Commanding Officer at Australian Headquarters in Egypt that Armstrong was last seen embarking for Australia in the HT *Kyarra*. The commander expressed a personal reservation about Armstrong's behaviour. He concluded: 'It is realised that this is not necessarily a matter regarding the AIF, but it is thought that some steps should be taken in matters such as this, as it is actions such as that taken by Armstrong that bring discredit on members of the AIF serving in this country, and Australians in general.'

Alice wasn't the only one chasing Armstrong. The Queensland Police also had an interest in the elusive soldier, on whom they wanted to serve an arrest warrant over a matter of misrepresentation. The warrant named 'H. Armstrong' as having obtained five pounds from John Morrison, care of Mr Pattison, solicitor, Rockhampton, by falsely pretending that an order drawn on E. F. Broad Limited, Brisbane, would be paid by the said E. F. Broad Limited.

The same notice also referred to the fact that Armstrong was a person of interest to the military authorities, thanks to an overpayment of army wages to the tune of 59 pounds. With so many on his trail, where had the elusive Armstrong got to? Eight months after arriving in Australia, he was back at the altar. The bride this time was Clare Constance Gurr, and the ceremony was brazenly held in the AIF camp at Mitcham, in South Australia. One of the witnesses was Arthur Harper, the camp adjutant.

It wasn't a case of third time lucky, for less than 18 months later the feckless groom dumped Clare for yet another woman. In early April 1920, adopting the name of Herbert Horace Armstrong, he wedded Bertha Rhoda Pollay at Collingwood, in Victoria. The happy couple then relocated to Auckland and a new life.

For three years, Armstrong played the devoted husband. She bore him two children while he provided for his new family by working as a land agent. But it all came crashing down in April 1923, when Australian police came knocking. Armstrong was wanted for making a bigamous marriage to Miss Gurr.

Armstrong was immediately arrested, charged and returned home, leaving behind a tearful Bertha and their two children. But worse lay in store. Waiting for justice back in Adelaide was not only Miss Gurr but also Alice Norton.

According to arresting officers, Armstrong admitted to being the man named in their warrant but refused to answer any questions until he had conferred with his solicitor in Adelaide. Back in Australia and faced with overwhelming evidence, Armstrong stood erect before Magistrate E.M. Sabine and, when asked for his plea, replied in a clear voice: 'I plead guilty.'

The following July, 38-year-old Armstrong began an 18 months jail sentence. In his evidence to the court he had dismissed his relationship with Alice Norton, using the bigamist's best excuse: 'I was not legally married to Miss Norton.' This didn't deter the indefatigable Alice from pursuing him through the courts for maintenance for their daughter. She was unsuccessful. The court found that because the girl had been born in Cairo, the matter was out of the South Australian jurisdiction.

*

Joseph Abraham Cane twice enlisted to fight for his country. But for all his enthusiasm, his military career was overshadowed by serious health issues which would curtail his time in khaki. As well, the grocer's poor judgement in marital matters would feature prominently in his military record.

Short and of sallow complexion, Cane battled with ill health through his war service. The only real enemy he faced in both his tours of duty were the ailments that kept him in army hospitals and sick bays. Both times, he was discharged as being medically unfit.

Cane first enlisted at Brunswick, a working-class inner suburb of Melbourne, in early March 1916. He listed himself as Joseph Alexander Cane, but signed as Joseph *Abraham* Cane. No matter. He was 28 years old, married to Violet, and keen to serve his King on the battlefield. By May that year, Cane was on board HMAT *Port Lincoln,* headed for France with the 60th Battalion.

Three weeks into the voyage, he was in the ship's hospital with a painful swelling in the groin. He lasted until the *Port Lincoln* berthed at Colombo, where the sickly private was returned to Australia. En route, surgeons excised a gland, which according to his medical record was the size of a 'bantam egg'. The pathological report states, 'No organisms found but it appeared Tubercular. Some pus within the gland.' Doctors had also discovered an old head injury, suffered a number of years before, which he had not disclosed at enlistment.

After disembarking at Melbourne, Cane was in and out of the military hospital, before being discharged late in October. Then it was back to Violet, back to the family home in suburban Coburg, and back behind the shop counter.

Obviously his need to see the world was strong, or possibly his need to escape from the one he occupied, because within eight months the restless grocer was back in khaki. In early August 1917 he again embarked, this time as a reinforcement with the 5th Battalion. In November, he was marched into Sutton Veny. But as eager as he was to make his mark on military life, he could not shake off the headaches. Also lurking as a major health issue was his epilepsy. As well, Cane suffered insomnia, periodic fits and bouts of giddiness, and was also an asthmatic.

He was a walking medical casebook, and by mid-January 1918, his war was over, but not before he made lance corporal. He was shipped home in the *Corinthic*, and on April 25 – Anzac Day – was discharged on medical grounds.

Cane evidently had determined not to return to his old life. Two months later he went through a form of marriage with the unsuspecting Mary Elizabeth Lewis, who lived in Peel Street, Windsor, another inner Melbourne suburb. The wedding ceremony took place at Collingwood, a short drive from where Violet was living.

The new bride's family already had their strong suspicions about their daughter's suitor, and on the eve of the wedding, Mary's mother wrote a desperate letter to army command enquiring about the man who had presented himself to her family as 'Corporal Cane':

> Dear Sir, can you tell me if (ex) Corp. J.A. Cane, 5th Battalion, is married or single – he has made several statements to me which I have found out to be false, and as he is engaged to one of my daughters and is to be married this month I thought I would inquire. I am very sorry to trouble you but can you answer this by Wednesday if possible. Mrs M Lewis-Driver.

Two days after receiving her plea, the base records office replied that Private Cane had enlisted as a married man: 'No advice has been received that his wife is deceased.'

By then it was too late. The couple had married and were off to a new life together, first in Richmond and then on to Sydney.

If Mrs Lewis-Driver had taken her concerns to police, the results might well have been different. She was no doubt unaware of a widely publicised and bizarre 'incident' involving Cane which had brought him to police attention some 10 years earlier.

Cane claimed he had been the target of an encounter with a stranger who purported to be his father. He said the man demanded his 'papers of birth' and then physically assaulted him. Even more strangely, Cane told police it wasn't the first time he'd chanced upon the man. It had been happening every quarter for the last year or so, and always when he was walking to Clifton Hill to visit his love interest.

Stretching credulity even further, the 21-year-old grocer's assistant explained that he hadn't previously reported the matter because he initially believed he should bear the punishment, if the aggressor was indeed his father.

But on that summer evening of 19 January 1909, Cane told police he could take no more, according to the *Argus* newspaper.

> On Tuesday evening Cane was going to Clifton Hill to see his young lady. On the way he was reading a book. It was a little towards dusk, and he had to push his face closely into the page. His concentration prevented him from observing the approach of his alleged parent.
>
> The first thing he knew of it was a blow on the side of the head, and the familiar request for the 'papers of birth'. He fell, but getting up again, struck his assailant, who also knocked him down again.
>
> When he got up a second time the older man offered him a drink from a sarsaparilla. He drank, and went on his way. When he arrived at the home of the young lady friend, he was attacked with severe internal pains, and the young lady's mother sent for Dr Bradford, who applied remedies.
>
> The contents of the stomach were kept for analysis, and are now at the Clifton Hill Police station with the report. Cane, when making his statement to the police, seemed to have recovered, except that he appeared a little dazed.

The following day, a sheepish Cane came forward again to confess that the story had been a fabrication, prompted by jealousy and a quarrel with his girlfriend.

Like many bigamists, he was a fantasist.

All this while, Violet Cane pined for her missing husband. She conducted extensive searches and sought the help of the Salvation Army. She feared that the sickly ex-soldier was possibly living a lonely, impoverished life in Melbourne's backstreets.

In a letter to the army's records office, Brigadier (Salvation Army) Arthur Arnott wrote: 'For some time past the relatives and particularly the wife of Private J.A. Cane have been rather distressed owing to the absence of any definite information regarding the whereabouts or the absence of any proof of death.'

The letter, not unexpectedly, failed to elicit any useful information. But several months later the breakthrough came when the Canes were traced to an address in Sydney. Cane was immediately arrested and charged with bigamy.

His arrest entry in the *Victoria Police Gazette* describes him in vivid detail: 'Cane, Joseph Abraham, is charged, on warrant, with bigamy at Melbourne, on the 20th ult. Description: – A discharged soldier, 33 or 34 years, 5 ft. 3 or 4 in., medium build, dark complexion, black hair, clean shaven, Jewish appearance, scar on one side of his head, peculiar turn in one eye; generally wears a dark sack suit and a dark-blue hat . . .'

Wisely, Cane engaged well-known Melbourne barrister Napthali Henry Sonenberg and entered a plea of guilty. The trial at Melbourne's Criminal Court centred on the defendant's two stints in the armed forces and his struggles with poor health. Three or four days before the unlawful wedding (and about the same time the bride's mother was desperately trying to nail Cain), he'd tumbled down a flight of stairs and suffered an epileptic fit. This, Mr Sonenberg suggested, had caused Cane a loss of memory. He added that in May 1920, Cane had been operated on at St Vincent's Hospital, where he'd had a piece of bone removed from his left leg and grafted into his cranium. While his poor medical condition formed the basis of a good defence, it was boosted by Mary's character evidence in which she described him as 'a good husband' and said that she did not feel 'aggrieved against him'.

Mr Justice Schutt said that while he was inclined to deal 'leniently' with the offender, the offence was nonetheless serious and he imposed a six months jail sentence – to be suspended for two years providing Cane behaved himself.

With that Cane walked from court a free man – into whose waiting arms, it remains unknown.

# PART III

# The Professionals

# 10

# The Bruhns Again

When Norman Bruhn and his brothers came home from the war, some of them quickly landed in further trouble. Stanley, who had ended the war as acting sergeant and was the closest thing to a military hero the Bruhns had produced, was in and out of court. In 1920, a year after his honourable discharge, he was before the magistrate charged with a late-night robbery and assault in company. The court was told Bruhn was with a group of men who approached Trevor Montgomery on the corner of King and Lonsdale streets, Melbourne.

The men engaged the motor mechanic in conversation for several minutes before knocking him down and rifling his pockets. They then ran off. It was only later that the victim recognised Bruhn in the city and alerted the police.

Then in September 1928, Bruhn was slotted for three months for having insufficient means of support. It was a simple vagrancy tort often used by police at the time to break up groups they regarded as being criminally aligned.

Bruhn and his brother Eric and their associates were suspected of robbing and intimidating bookmakers, owners and trainers headquartered at the Flemington racetrack. Some had complained to police about being blackmailed.

Police swooped on Bruhn at the Racecourse Hotel, Flemington, and took him back to the watch house. Asked to empty his pockets, Bruhn pulled out just over 60 pounds in cash.

Detective Milne later told the Flemington Court that Bruhn claimed to have won it at the races. 'To which I replied that it represented cash that had recently been stolen from a jockey boy,' the police officer continued. 'When I questioned Stanley Bruhn concerning his means he said he had been employed at the wharf on several occasions recently, but he could not remember the names of the boats on which he had been engaged.'

By this time Bruhn was down for the count, but it wasn't enough for the detective. With his foot metaphorically pinning the young criminal's head to the floor, the detective then accused him of offering him a bribe. 'I will give you 10 pounds if you let me go now,' Bruhn allegedly told Detective Milne. 'I want to go into the country to work.' To which the police officer replied: 'You can make that offer to the court.'

He added: 'I have known Bruhn for a considerable time, but I have never known him to do any work. I have seen him in two-up schools in the company of convicted thieves, suspected persons and reputed thieves. In the last four years I have frequently seen Bruhn loitering about hotels and racecourses.'

It seems that the magistrate was unpersuaded by character evidence from an official of the Port Phillip Foreman Stevedores' Association. At that time the Melbourne waterfront was racked by industrial strife. A controversial new waterside workers' award had come into operation at the start of the month, and wharfies had launched a protracted national strike that would turn violent.

So into jail Stanley Bruhn went.

His next appearance in court was the week before Christmas, again charged with a vagrancy offence, this time in sensational circumstances. On Saturday 1 December 1928, someone had blown up the Greek Club in Lonsdale Street in the city. No one was killed but the explosion was spectacular, and rightly or wrongly it was connected with a series of 'bomb outrages' associated with industrial trouble on the waterfront.

The Victorian police force immediately went into overdrive. Stanley Bruhn and four other men, including Stanley's brother Eric, were rounded up in Ballarat. A butcher's labourer, Eric Bruhn was described by Detective Milne as 'keeping company with known and suspected thieves and has been seen with interstate and international thieves, and practically all the underworld of Melbourne'.

Of Stanley Bruhn, the detective said: 'Bruhn was a companion of known thieves and shop-breakers. It was a practice of the man to demand money from bookmakers and successful horse trainers. There had been complaints that he had robbed jockeys of their earnings.

'He was connected with people who had been in a razor slashing incident,' added the detective, no doubt referring to other brother Norman's key role in the razor gang attacks in Sydney.

Both Bruhns produced evidence supporting their claims that they had meaningful jobs in a slaughterhouse, on the wharves and at a fruit stall at the Victoria Market. Dismissing the charges, the magistrate ruled that while the police character assessments were accurate, the Bruhns had presented plausible evidence as to how they earned their money.

*

William George Bruhn was the brother who had accidentally shot and killed a small boy while he was serving in Belgium.

After the war, he tucked his honourable discharge under his arm and re-enlisted in the family's criminal empire.

His stock in trade was not violence or intimidation. He was a thief by and large and didn't travel far for targets. In mid-September 1928, the engine driver copped 18 months with hard labour for the theft of car tyres and tubes from a train. The court observed that 'some movement from outside' had encouraged the pair.

The heist was an inside job and during his sentencing Judge Woinarski described it as a bold plan which had been perfectly concealed for some time, until the wife of the receiver blew the whistle after a marital tiff.

And not even a strong plea for leniency from Oscar senior, the head of the Bruhn clan, could dissuade the judge from jailing 40-year-old William: 'I am sorry that I cannot accede to the appeal made by the father of Bruhn and that I cannot give that consideration to the appeal for mercy made by the jury which generally I am so anxious to give to a recommendation of that nature.' The jury had undoubtedly taken Bruhn's war service into account when it handed down a guilty verdict but with a strong recommendation for mercy.

The heist took place on 26 March 1927 between Geelong and Ballarat. The tyres were destined for Mile End in South Australia. As the engine driver, Bruhn tinkered with the 'little end' of the engine, causing it to making knocking sounds. He then stopped, as prearranged, close to a crossing at Navigator, near Ballarat. Lying in wait in a truck was Henry James Milner, a train examiner, who removed the tyres from the stationary train while Bruhn 'worked' on the engine. Once Milner was clear, Bruhn rectified the 'malfunction' and the train then continued its journey.

The stolen goods were then driven to Brunswick, an inner Melbourne suburb, and left with their receiver, Euston Murray

Cheers. The plan came unstuck when Cheers' wife exposed the plot to police. Consequently he pleaded guilty to dealing in stolen goods. It is not known if the troubled marriage survived.

Three years later, Bruhn's life was again off the rails when he and three other men were spotted by police loitering near a railway line. The men had alighted from a slow-moving goods train on the Ballarat side of the Lethbridge Station and were on their way to their car parked 200 yards away. Unbeknownst to Bruhn and the others, police had them under surveillance and had already disabled the vehicle. When the officers gave chase the men fled in all directions. Three of them, including Bruhn, were eventually rounded up.

A check of the train revealed the lashings of two of the trucks had been unfastened. And in the pocket of the front door of the stranded car police found gelignite, a wooden rammer and detonating caps.

They were charged with having had gelignite in their possession to enable persons to commit a felony, and with having loitered with intent to commit a felony. They were all found guilty and copped six months in jail.

It seems likely that William Bruhn was despatched to Beechworth Prison, because a few days after New Year his father and mother were stopped by police in Kilmore. They told the detectives who picked them up that they were on their way to Beechworth to see one of their sons.

Police found a box of valuable pipes and cigars in the car in which they were travelling. Oscar Bruhn was charged with possession of items suspected of having been stolen. He pleaded not guilty, saying the pipes had been given to him as a birthday present by an old friend. Senior Detective Carey told the court that there had been numerous robberies of tobacco and cigars recently, and one of Bruhn's sons had been committed for trial for shop-breaking. That was Roy Bruhn, Oscar and Mary

Ann's youngest boy, described by Carey in another hearing that week as 'a dangerous shop and house breaker and gunman'. The *Kilmore Free Press* reported that in a 'dramatic outburst' in court, Oscar 'thumped the witness box and roared out, "I did not know the goods were ill-gotten – before my God, no!"'

Oscar was now 68, and not as sharp as he had been. The magistrate said it was 'deplorable to see a man of Bruhn's age in such a position'. He would not send him to jail, but would inflict a fine of 10 pounds.

It was not the last time the Bruhn boys brought their father grief that year. The very next month, Oscar Bruhn was shot in the groin during a house invasion by two armed intruders looking for Roy.

And then there was Norman Bruhn, who on his return to Australia became a feared gangster, pimp and extortionist.

In early 1921, Victoria's celebrated detective Syd McGuffie led an investigation into a major break-in at a clothing factory in a lane just off Latrobe Street in Melbourne. The impeccably dressed McGuffie would later become the first head of the Victorian Homicide Squad, and would be known for the deep red rose he wore in his buttonhole to signify he was investigating a murder. But for the moment, McGuffie's target was Norman Bruhn.

McGuffie and his team had been keeping surveillance on Bruhn and his West Melbourne home. On February 17, they converged on the house, where they found the stolen materials. Bruhn and wife Irene, a sometime prostitute, were taken into custody and charged.

Out of jail again later that year, Bruhn was charged with having assaulted and robbed a postal worker, Thomas Hogan, of his silver watch and chain, some small change and a stetson hat. In July 1923, he was sentenced to six months jail for indecent behaviour after pursuing three young schoolgirls and behaving in an obscene manner. Then the following month, he was sentenced to 12 months for vagrancy. He was freed on bail, but Bruhn wasn't one for hanging around, as his appalling military record showed. He jumped bail instead.

In late December 1925, Bruhn found himself in 'an exciting incident', as Lismore's *Northern Star* reported it, with four policemen on bicycles.

> Four bicycle patrol policemen, having their suspicions aroused by the actions of three men, proceeded to arrest them. A fight ensued and the police threatened to shoot. After a desperate struggle, during which one of the men escaped, three were handcuffed. Upon examining the locality, parcels of woollen goods valued at 70 pounds were found where they had been thrown over several fences along the street. Later, Norman Bruhn, George Donnelly and John O'Malley were charged with factory breaking and stealing from the Albion knitting mills.

Bruhn had made Melbourne too hot for himself. He departed for Sydney after an unsuccessful blackmail attempt. When a woman refused to pay him 100 pounds, Bruhn took it at gunpoint. During the confrontation a man was wounded, for which Bruhn was charged with the shooting. Again, he skipped bail and headed to Sydney with Irene and their toddler sons. The victim later recovered and thought better of pressing the charge, which was eventually dropped.

Bruhn also thought better of returning to Melbourne. He'd linked up with a razor gang and had bedded the teenage moll, Nellie Cameron, who ran with some of the most dangerous gangsters of the time. In her lifetime, Cameron racked up 73 criminal convictions, mainly for soliciting for prostitution and vagrancy. She was also the first woman to be convicted of consorting with criminals.

Like Bruhn, her father was also a veteran of the Great War, but unlike Bruhn, he had actually done his best. Colin Kelly, Service Number 16280, shipped out to Europe with the 12th Field Company Engineers. There was no doubting 26-year-old Kelly's enthusiasm to answer the call. He tried five times to enlist before finally being finally accepted in October 1916, which tells more about the army's dwindling manpower than the horse driver's suitability as a soldier.

Nonetheless, Kelly was in khaki and was quickly despatched to England. But Private Kelly spent more time in the infirmary than on the battlefield, suffering terribly from the debilitating kidney complaint nephritis. His war service record tells of a constant battle against the disease resulting in painful swelling of his hands and feet, and blood in the urine.

His daughter Nellie was nine when her father embarked for Europe. Four years after his return her parents divorced and Lillian married Robert George Cameron. Nellie took her stepfather's surname.

Known in the press as 'the Kiss of Death Girl', because most of her boyfriends and pimps met violent ends, Nellie had been educated at an exclusive girls' school on Sydney's North Shore. But she was attracted to degradation and violence, and in Bruhn she found a man with no moral scruples, a liar, a razor-wielding thug and someone who made a considerable income as a bludger, feeding off her work as a prostitute. A mean man, especially when drunk, Bruhn was also not averse to inflicting his own form of violence on the teenager.

Cameron was much in demand, turning ten tricks a day, seven days a week. She charged between ten shillings and one pound for each service, and in her spare time taught dancing at Professor Bolot's Academy in Oxford Street.

Bruhn and Cameron were also raking it in with their own form of the 'ginger game', entrapping men then robbing them. Cameron would lure an unsuspecting client to her love nest, and at a pre-coital moment in would dash Bruhn claiming to be the cuckolded husband. The panicked client would be coerced into handing over his wallet and belongings either by extreme force, or in return for Bruhn's silence, or both.

However, it was his role in the razor gang that established Bruhn's fearsome reputation in Sydney. Cut-throat razors became the weapon of choice, thanks to the New South Wales Pistol Licensing Act of 1927 which dealt an automatic jail term to anyone found in possession of a concealed firearm or handgun.

Police struggled to break up the gangs, simply because the victims themselves operated on the fringes of society and were reluctant to reveal what was stolen and by whom. As the *Daily News,* Perth, reported:

> So far the victims of the gang have preserved that silence, synonymous of the underworld, where the person who 'squeaks' for ever afterwards lives in danger. To the average Australian mind the unlawful use of the razor is totally abhorrent, and for that reason the police are inclined to believe that the men who are now terrorising Sydney with their fiendish methods are foreigners. In some Continental countries the knife and the razor are favourite weapons against crooks, and in Italy the slashing of an opponent's face with a razor is regarded as an insult equal in Australia to spitting in another man's face.

Veteran police reporter Hugh Buggy covered the razor wars and thought they were mainly fought over the spoils from the extensive cocaine trafficking. 'Criminals were slashed and maimed and shot down as the feud was fought out with no quarter in the shadowy lanes of Darlinghurst and East Sydney. Hideous face wounds from razor slashes in some cases deprived men of speech, and in others took from them the power to laugh again or even to smile.'

Norman Bruhn quickly staked out his territory in Sydney's underworld with signature acts of fearsome cruelty. In December 1926, a promising professional boxer, Billy Chambers, stepped in to assist a young woman being assaulted by a group of Bruhn's men in a Darlinghurst street. Chambers had effectively disrespected Bruhn's authority and for that he would pay the price. On Christmas morning a group led by Bruhn invaded Chambers' Darlinghurst digs. Once overpowered, the boxer was systematically pistol-whipped before his leg was sliced open, severing the tendons and sinews. Seventy-six stitches saved his leg, but Chambers' fighting career was finished.

By this time the razor war had intensified. Rival criminal gangs were running amok in Darlinghurst and Kings Cross, slashing and stabbing, and robbing each other's sly-grog outlets, brothels and cocaine dens. Tilly Devine, now a leading vice figure with her husband, the AIF veteran James Devine, became a major target of Bruhn and Cutmore.

Bruhn was uncontrollable.

On 22 June 1927, Bruhn was taken down. He'd spent the day drinking in the company of racehorse trainer Robert Miller and a couple of other men. There had been an argument and the group dispersed, leaving Bruhn and Miller to continue at a sly-grog shop called Macks in Charlotte Lane, Darlinghurst. The pair was eventually moved on, but not before Bruhn had typically threatened to shoot the place up.

As they strolled along Charlotte Lane, the busy red-light area was unusually quiet. Two men bumped into Bruhn and Miller, who was quickly advised, 'You're not in this.' In other words, stay out of it. With that, up to five bullets rang out and Bruhn was struck twice in the stomach. 'I'm shot, help I'm shot,' the gangster wailed. He pleaded with a cab driver to take him to hospital, and with the help of a police officer, the wounded Bruhn was lifted into the vehicle.

At Sydney Hospital, with Bruhn struggling to stay conscious, police tried to get him to reveal the hitmen. 'I won't be a copper. I wouldn't shelf anybody. Go away, I'm too sick. I don't want the police to interfere,' mumbled Bruhn to the detectives.

He lasted just a few more hours. His killers were never found. In his evidence at Bruhn's inquest, Miller couldn't – or wouldn't – identify them. He allegedly told detectives, 'If I did know I wouldn't dare tell you.'

Fingers were pointed at John Daniel 'Snowy' Cutmore, the AIF deserter who had walked out of the VD camp at Langwarrin way back in 1916. The Victorian gangster had been a member of Bruhn's gang in Sydney and had been part of the attack on Chambers. Hugh Anderson, in his biography of Squizzy Taylor, *Larrikin Crook*, characterised Bruhn's assassination as payback: Cutmore had killed him in retaliation for robbing a friend.

*

Cutmore's war with society had started well before 1914, by which time he had already notched up 18 convictions. He was known to use a string of aliases, including the names John Harris, John Watson, John Nolan and John McLaughlin. After he was struck off by the army as a deserter in June 1917, he was implicated in the mysterious killing of street identity Charles Cleary. Cleary, who sold race books to punters, was found sitting in a cab in Fitzroy, blood streaming down his face. He had been shot in the head but was reluctant to say how he'd received his injuries. Pressed for information, he initially told police, who were nearby and ran to the crime scene after hearing gunshots, that he'd fallen on the footpath and struck his head. A later medical examination at the Fitzroy watch house located a small bullet wound just above the left ear. In the end, Cleary admitted he'd been shot but because of his failing memory couldn't say who pulled the trigger. The gunman's identity was never revealed – Cleary died in St Vincent's Hospital a fortnight later.

Immediately, the finger was pointed at Cutmore, who was described in police gazettes across Australia as 'an important witness' at Cleary's forthcoming inquest. Cutmore was a feared standover man and violent thug, who was especially vicious when drunk. In 1919, he slowly bludgeoned a rival with an iron bar while the victim was tied up. The mindless brutality only stopped when the target was close to death. In police circles, Cutmore was viewed as a dangerous, but clever, criminal.

His addiction to alcohol once saved him from a stiff jail term when, using the alias John Harris, he was charged with stealing boots from a wagon outside a Richmond factory. Cutmore and his accomplice denied responsibility, claiming they'd been too drunk at the time. The jury found this argument so logical that both men were discharged.

Several months later, Cutmore made mayhem at a circus in the northern Melbourne suburb of Northcote when he and a friend, Herbert Williams, laid into the manager with their fists and boots. The manager had merely asked them to pay for admission tickets.

In his Melbourne days, Cutmore ran with Squizzy Taylor, as well as leading the so-called Safe Prosecution Gang. Similar in philosophy to the Bruhn Razor Gang, it relieved criminals of their booty, relatively safe in the knowledge there would be no complaints to police.

After Bruhn's death, he was out of control and at a loose end. Gravitating back to his home town, he crossed Squizzy Taylor by trashing a small St Kilda brothel that was under Taylor's protection. There was longstanding mistrust between the two, ever since the days of the Fitzroy Vendetta, when Cutmore had been hired to knock Squizzy off.

As the famous story goes, Taylor and Cutmore fought it out in a gun battle in Cutmore's Carlton bedroom in late 1927: both men died of their wounds.

Even after his death, Cutmore's dismal record as a military deserter followed him. The *Hobart Mercury* described him as having once been a member of the AIF who hadn't left Victoria.

Snowy wasn't the only Cutmore to wear khaki. His father, John Samuel Cutmore, enlisted at Blackboy Hill in Western Australia at the end of October 1914. The 38-year-old cook was noticeable for the 'JC-DC' tattooed on his right forearm; 'DC' no doubt being his wife, Delia.

Unlike Snowy, Cutmore made it overseas and was eventually elevated to sergeant. It was a relatively smooth ride in the catering section except for a spot of bother in Mudros when he was severely reprimanded for being drunk while on active service. Cutmore's tour of duty ended in mid-January 1919 when he returned to Australia. A sad notation on his military record states: 'Premature senility'.

James Francis Cutmore, Snowy's younger brother, was just over 18 when he signed on in Melbourne in early July 1915. But it appears he didn't even make it to the training camp. Chances are he was found to be under-age, because birth records show he would have been just 16 at the time. Six months later he returned to the recruitment centre for another crack at khaki, but apparently with no success.

Like Snowy, young James continued to be a person of interest to the police – mainly as a housebreaker and thief.

# 11

# One Enemy and One Friend

CUTMORE WASN'T THE ONLY CRIM who fired a gun at Squizzy Taylor. There was also Joseph Cotter, a onetime member of the AIF. When Cotter signed on to serve his country, there wasn't much the army could teach him about warfare. He had already earned his stripes in the backstreets of Melbourne, running with some of the city's toughest gangs.

He was a thief, a racetrack spiv and an enforcer, who by the war's start had spent time in some of Victoria's worst jails. And by the time of his ignominious discharge, he had racked up one of the worst military records in the AIF. According to one official report, less than three months of his time in the army was spent in the lines. The rest he served under punishment or spent being treated for the pox.

The police and the army were obviously in communication with each other about him. After the war, Cotter's criminal reputation would feature in his military record, which states, 'This man is a notorious gunman and has been on several serious charges since his return from the war.' For their part detectives highlighted his appalling service record in a confidential police report, written the day after the coroner committed him to trial on a murder charge: 'Cotter has been in trouble since he was 14 years of age and his military history shows that he was in trouble all the time he was in the AIF.'

This report recorded that his reputation as a gunman stretched back as far as 1909, when he allegedly shot a rival in the shoulder during an altercation in Bourke Street, Melbourne. By 1913, Cotter was hanging out with the so-called Bourke Street Rats, a motley group of urchins and budding sociopaths. He received a month's jail sentence for his involvement in the gang-bashing of the manager of the American Hotel in Swanston Street. Cotter had been removed from the pub and, while being ushered out, told Robert Watkin Lewis he would 'cut his liver out'. Waiting for them outside were Cotter's Rats, about 14 of them, who laid into the manager with missiles and boots. Cotter landed a glass in Lewis's face.

In late December 1915, Cotter was in a fight with another man outside the Old England Hotel in Bourke Street. Just as a constable on the beat pushed through the gathered crowd to break it up, Cotter drew a small revolver and fired two shots. He was immediately arrested and carted off. In court he was identified by a military policeman as the aggressor. Cotter's defence was provocation. He'd come to the aid of a friend and, in doing so, was assaulted by his opponent, he testified. He said he carried the revolver for protection after being assaulted several months before, and besides, he'd fired the bullets into the ground. Cotter was fined five pounds, in default one month in jail with hard labour.

Joseph Lennox Cotter enlisted in March 1916, just a month before his 24th birthday. He was five foot four inches tall and his distinguishing marks included a scar running from his temple to his right eye. This old wound suggested that the bookmaker's clerk faced his opponents head-on, but when it came time to confront the real enemy, Cotter was found wanting.

By October he was off overseas with the 16th Reinforcements, 24th Battalion, landing at Plymouth six weeks later. By the new year Cotter had incurred the wrath of his superior officers for leaving camp without a pass. For this he was confined to base for a week, with the loss of three days pay.

A month later he was on his way to Le Havre – as a stowaway. Whether this was a show of premature patriotism or because he was doing a runner is unknown. But three days later he was marched back to England under close arrest, and remained there for a month. During this time he was penalised twice for AWL, for in addition to his illegal landing on the beaches of France, he had nicked off again after his return to Larkhill, the major army camp on Salisbury Plain.

The following week he finally made it to France legitimately, and joined his battalion, but only a month later he was out of action, admitted to the 7th Australian Field Ambulance with complications to his left eye. Three days later he was discharged back to the lines – but not for long. The following week he went AWL again, for which he received 28 days of field punishment no. 1.

The 24th Battalion was a seasoned outfit. It had fought at Gallipoli and in France had served at Pozières. In May 1917, on just one day, it would take almost 80 per cent casualties at the second Battle of Bullecourt. Which all goes to put Cotter's need to get away in an even worse light.

It was while he was serving the month of field punishment no. 1 that Cotter broke camp again. Authorities took a particularly dim view of the double disappearance so close to the front line. He was sentenced to two years jail with hard labour and immediately sent to the Australian provost marshal. A week later he was transferred to the military prison at Les Attaques, where he was interned for a year before having his sentence suspended, the reduction assisted no doubt by the manpower shortage at the front.

By late August 1918, Cotter had rejoined his battalion, just in time for major action. But by early March the following year he was before a field general court martial charged with shooting fellow private Donald Alexander Hamilton in the Café des Roses at Charleroi. He went down for 12 months on the charge of negligently using a firearm. Hamilton limped back to England with a gunshot wound in the leg.

Just over a fortnight into his sentence for this shooting, Cotter was back in hospital with a sore penis, and three days later his affliction was upgraded to full-blown VD. After several weeks of treatment, the trigger-happy private was back behind bars in France, where he remained until being transferred to an English military prison in Gloucester.

By late September 1919, the disgraced soldier had boarded the troopship *Port Sydney*, headed for Australia and demobilisation. It would be a notorious voyage, marked by an attempted mutiny, in which Cotter would play his part and, once again, be paraded before the military tribunal.

The *Port Sydney* was not a comfortable ship. The year before, the Australian government had been forced to conduct an inquiry after complaints from troops about the 'bad' food supply and the 'generally disgraceful' accommodation.

This time the passenger manifest comprised an odd assortment of returning diggers, including 70 or so serious offenders from the Lewes Detention Barracks and other jails. Cotter was in good company. At the start of the voyage the men were placed in the ship's cells, but a group of sympathisers stormed the block and released their mates. They then took to the upper decks where, armed with razors, bayonets and revolvers, they planned to take over the running of the ship.

The 'undesirables', as they were later branded by the press, were confronted by officers and men, who eventually restored order. During the melee one of the prisoners, who was serving

12 years for his role in a previous mutiny in Europe, was stabbed with a bayonet and died.

In another incident during the voyage, a soldier who was winning at roulette was attacked by disgruntled losers. Some of them were in the process of throwing him overboard when officers intervened to save his life. Whether Cotter was one of those about to hoist the fellow digger over the side is not known; he was certainly brought before his commanding officers and admonished for gambling.

However, it was his involvement in the attempted mutiny that attracted the biggest sanction. Cotter went before a shipboard court martial for taking an active part in a disturbance on the forward well deck. Cotter was one of seven prisoners charged and convicted over the incident. Their sentences ranged from 28 days to 2 years. His penalty was a year's jail with hard labour.

As for Cotter, the day after Australia celebrated Remembrance Day 1919, he disembarked in Melbourne, and a month later was shunted out of the army – services no longer required. Once he'd finished his military sentence at the Geelong Gaol in February 1920, Cotter easily slipped back into his old life, and his nickname of 'Brownie'.

In a short time, he became a gun for hire, in much demand as rivals shot and clubbed their way to control of the illegal gaming industry flourishing in Melbourne's backstreets and laneways.

Cotter immersed himself in what became known in the underworld as the Fitzroy Vendetta, a protracted feud which began in 1918 over the proceeds of crime, including gambling. It was a vicious campaign, involving shootings, bashings and robberies. It was a fertile battleground for the returned soldier.

Cotter's violent reputation was spreading, particularly his rages when full of drink. One memorable moment was on the night of 17 August 1921 when he was refused entry to a Bourke Street club because he was too drunk. Cotter drew a revolver and the manager, Patrick Boardman, and some of his burly staff quickly jumped on him, then threw him down the stairs.

As the manager later told Cotter's hearing in the City Court, four shots were then fired into the front door. But Cotter wasn't done yet. Later that evening he fired off a few more rounds, this time in the direction of Arthur Bazley, a barman and masseur, who was walking down Bourke Street at the time. Bazley was himself a notorious gunman, a Gallipoli veteran linked to Squizzy Taylor.

Wisely, the crowd scattered, and so did Bazley. He later told the court he knew Cotter. And his strange account under oath goes like this: 'I was walking along Bourke Street, near Russell Street, when I suddenly felt a stinging pain in one of my legs. I did not take much notice of it, and had a few drinks and went to the pictures. Later I found that I had been wounded, and was treated. I did not hear a shot and did not see Cotter.'

Asked by the police prosecutor why he'd run away at the time, he replied: 'Because I saw a lot of other people running.' Pressed on an earlier conversation with one of the police investigators in which he'd pinned it on Cotter, he answered: 'I was in great pain; I cannot remember what I said.'

Cotter was fined 10 pounds for having discharged a firearm.

Six weeks later, Cotter would be a target himself in an episode that would have deadly consequences down the track. During a stroll around Fitzroy one evening, Cotter and his wife, Ethel, and a female friend, May Aumont, were ambushed by four thugs, who had been lying in wait. When the trio passed by one of the gunmen, George Lawson, who was leaning in a doorway, May asked him why he was there. Lawson replied by reaching into his pocket and producing a Colt revolver, then immediately firing two rounds into the air. By this time Cotter was off and nowhere to be seen, deserting the two women.

But Ethel Cotter was no shrinking violet. Married to Joseph, she had a tough life and very quickly learned how to duck a drunken punch, and even how to give one in reply. She was battle-hardened. In one swift movement she rushed at Lawson, brandishing her umbrella. Just as he was trying to evade the swinging brolly, his panicked associate indiscriminately fired a shot – straight into Lawson's backside. In great pain, the hapless gunman was taken to the Alfred Hospital where he later told detectives he'd been held up in South Yarra and after one of his assailants hit him on the head with a stick, he retaliated and took a bullet. No, he couldn't identify the culprit. Lawson was either keeping to the strict underworld code of silence, or disguising the fact that he'd been cowed by a woman.

But it wouldn't be long before detectives learned the truth. A day or so later a well-known criminal called 'Fivo' Olsen took a bullet to the head and died in a lane near the Carlton Club Hotel. The heavy-set Fivo was described by police as a colourful character. He was well known as an offender. John Thomas Olsen was also widely known under the aliases John Harrison and John Thomas. And while the laneway in which he was found was regarded as being of a clean appearance, it did not have a good reputation. It was just the place for an underworld killing. It didn't take police long to follow the trail to Cotter's cottage, a short stagger away. They learned that a group of men had converged on Cotter the previous night, including Fivo. Witnesses told of hearing at least 12 revolver shots, and seeing men sheltering behind trees.

When police came calling, Cotter freely admitted to having killed Olsen, who he accused of 'roughly handling' his wife. But given the treatment Ethel handed out to George Lawson the previous evening, that seems unlikely.

Cotter, nonetheless, stuck to his story and told police: 'I'm waiting. I shot him.'

A search of the house yielded two automatic revolvers, one fully loaded and the other containing two live cartridges. They'd been buried in the garden.

Olsen's widow was then interviewed by police. She claimed that the previous night a man had called at their Fitzroy house and fired three shots at her.

Police later returned to the Cotter home where they found a bullet hole in the front door, and an empty .25-calibre automatic revolver cartridge case in the hallway.

Cotter told police he'd been dressed in his pyjamas and standing in the hall smoking a cigarette, when a bullet pierced the front door. Instinctively he reached for his gun and fired back, hitting Olsen. The victim then staggered off into the distance, mortally wounded.

Charged with Olsen's murder, Cotter pleaded self-defence at his trial. The jury believed his story and without much effort returned a not-guilty verdict.

*

The little gunman would later point his weapon at a much more significant target. Squizzy Taylor was two inches shorter than Cotter, and the two pint-sized gangsters hated each other. In early October 1922, the two men met face to face in crowded Bourke Street. A fortnight before, Taylor had given himself up to police after skipping bail on charges of having broken into a city warehouse.

With his girlfriend, Ida 'Babe' Pender, Squizzy lived a Bonnie and Clyde existence, thumbing their noses at police by sending quirky letters to the press. But on 21 September, Taylor came in from the cold, handing himself in to police at the Russell Street headquarters in a gesture that was widely publicised.

He was immediately put before the court, where he was

committed to trial then released on a substantial bail of 350 pounds and another surety of 350 pounds.

Taylor was free for the moment and eagerly stepped back into the public spotlight. At 8 pm on 3 October he alighted from his chauffeur-driven vehicle near the entrance to the passageway leading to the offices of the Bookmakers' Registered Clerks' Association. Unknown to Taylor, a familiar face was in the gathering crowd. It was Cotter, and he was armed. Drawing a small pistol from his pocket, Cotter walked up to Taylor and fired three shots. One of them struck Squizzy in the right thigh. Squizzy, startled, staggered through the doorway of the building, while Cotter coolly walked away. Fearing the gunman might return, Taylor waited a few minutes before hobbling to his car for the emergency dash to Melbourne Hospital.

Police took little time to track Cotter down to a house in Fitzroy, where the gunman was arrested tucked up in bed. He was promptly charged with having shot at Taylor with the intent to do grievous bodily harm, being found with an unregistered pistol and having carried a pistol without obtaining a permit.

Cotter maintained his silence, so too did his victim. When it came time for Taylor to give evidence at Cotter's trial, the little gangster was at a loss to say who was responsible. He testified: 'I was in Bourke Street, near the Bookmakers' Registered Clerks' Association rooms. I got out of the motor I was in and was about to enter the building when I heard a report. I felt a stinging sensation in my right leg. I came back to the motor and was driven to the Melbourne Hospital. A bullet was extracted from the front of my right thigh.

'I have no idea from what direction the report came. It must have been behind me because the bullet entered the rear of my leg. So far as I know, Cotter and I are on friendly terms. I did not see Cotter that night, and I don't know who fired the shot.'

His driver was equally vague. He saw nothing.

Sub Inspector Thomas Coonan told the hearing of finding two shell cases outside the building. But that's where the police evidence stopped. 'I made enquiries,' he said, 'but no one seemed to know or want to know anything about the matter.'

The case against Cotter collapsed as the police magistrate ruled there was no evidence to prove the accused fired the shots or was in the vicinity when Taylor was ambushed. However, the beak slotted Cotter for two months on the unregistered weapons charge.

After an appeal, the penalty was halved.

Soon after Ethel Cotter clouted George Lawson with her brolly, Cotter legged it from the family home, leaving her with two kids to support.

*

Unlike Cotter, Albert Ronald McDonald, one of Squizzy Taylor's 'soldiers', was a war hero. He received a Belgian Croix de Guerre for his courage during the fierce engagement with the Germans at Herleville Wood in late August 1918. A private with the 2nd Australian Light Trench Mortar Battery, the Gallipoli veteran displayed not just courage, but leadership under intense pressure.

His citation read:

> [He] took charge of a Gun team after the NCO had been killed. He rallied the crew, and throughout the operation did valuable work under extremely difficult circumstances. On the 25th August 1918, when his officer was seriously wounded, Pte McDonald carried on with the operation. Later, he returned to Battalion Headquarters under heavy shell fire with full and valuable information concerning the situation, and then went back and took charge of his team.

McDonald had twice been wounded in earlier campaigns. In that regard, the Gallipoli veteran's military record was exemplary. While his courage could not be questioned, once the smoke had cleared the young Melburnian was out of control.

Official entries in his war record highlight the months he spent AWL; his 60-odd days at the Bulford hospital being treated for VD; being placed in detention for carrying a falsified pass; and the fines he incurred for breaking camp. His crimes and misdemeanours, combined with his bravery, would equip him well for a postwar role as one of Squizzy Taylor's soldiers.

McDonald enlisted at Broadmeadows in late August 1914, and within months had embarked with the 7th Infantry Battalion in HMAT *Horata*. His recruitment papers described him as having grey hair, brown eyes and being physically 'well built'. The lad from working-class Carlton was eager to join the fight.

But at Gallipoli, like many other soldiers, he was struck down with scabies, which forced his evacuation to Lemnos, and then the following week to Malta. He was later transferred to an English medical facility at Hampstead, London. His rehabilitation was interrupted when he went AWL for about seven weeks, managing to spend Christmas Day 1915 on the run. He was given four weeks detention, and lost 78 days pay.

At Perham Downs, he spent a week in detention and forfeited five days pay for being found in possession of a pass belonging to another soldier. Then, on 30 August 1916, the private went missing again, this time staying out until his apprehension on 24 October. A court martial panel sent him down for six months hard labour, which was commuted early the following month to 56 days detention and forfeiture of pay.

Within three weeks, McDonald was in Bulford hospital, reaping what he'd sown on the streets of England. McDonald told doctors the VD he'd contracted was from an 'amateur', in other words not a prostitute, but the strain was nevertheless potent enough to keep him isolated for 64 days.

On his release, McDonald was penalised again for being AWL and breaking camp, but these by and large were minor infractions. The army had a greater need and France beckoned. By 1 March 1917 he'd landed at Étaples.

The 7th Battalion was involved in the advance that followed the German retreat to the Hindenburg Line. It also fought in the third Battle of Ypres, in which McDonald became a casualty, sustaining gunshot wounds to the knee and the head. This put him out of the action for several months, although during this time attempts were made for him to rejoin his unit, but thwarted because of his injuries.

By early in the new year, McDonald was well enough to return to the front, but in mid-April he was injured by a gas attack. He was admitted to hospital and there he remained for several months, being treated for gas poisoning, burns and a recurrence of scabies.

By August, McDonald was fit enough to return to the front once again, this time to Herleville Wood, about 10 kilometres south of the River Somme. Many other soldiers died on their third stint in France, but McDonald came through with flying colours.

Less than two months later, the hero was on his way back to Australia. On 5 April 1919, his award was listed in the *London Gazette*. But how quickly things changed. Less than a fortnight later, the decorated digger was arrested for picking pockets outside the Returned Soldiers Finalisation Depot in South Melbourne. McDonald's status as a war hero helped him to avoid a conviction – his sentence was adjourned and never rescheduled.

It wasn't McDonald's first appearance before the bench. Melbourne's criminal fraternity had put out the welcome mat to McDonald some time earlier. He had already established a close relationship with the two-up tsar, Henry 'Harry' Stokes. Instantly recognisable by his iron-grey hair and bulldog face which gave him the appearance of a permanent scowl, Stokes was a man to be feared. He ran a flourishing backyard gambling operation with the assistance of muscle supplied by Squizzy Taylor. Stokes, it has been said, was the brains behind Taylor. Whatever the case, they were a tight and intimidating combination, and McDonald was a trusted 'soldier'.

One of his first missions was to deal with an opponent of Stokes, the pugilist Edward Whiting. A former Australian middleweight champion, Whiting had a temper that was legendary. In one bout he beat his opponent so savagely that police stepped into the ring to stop him from inflicting further punishment, and in another, Whiting laid into the referee after he'd awarded the fight to his rival on a foul.

Described in police logs simply as a 'dealer', Whiting was a well-known criminal, a sly-grog operator with a string of serious convictions going right back to his teenage years. He had even been refused a hawker's licence because of his criminal record and the poor company he kept.

Whiting had long associated with violent gangs, and was no stranger to attacks on his own life. In late February 1919, he walked into Melbourne's St Vincent's Hospital after six bullets had been fired at him by what he described as an unknown gunman. Just a year or two earlier he dodged a volley of shots fired from a passing car while he was standing on his front verandah. Patched up and back in business, Whiting was picked up several months later by police after a series of raids on known criminal haunts in the Fitzroy area.

Brought before the City Court, he was charged with being the occupier of a house frequented by reputed thieves. One of his housemates was the notorious gunman and lumbering enforcer,

Henry Fitzharding, alias Slater, who was also a known associate of Snowy Cutmore.

The following week, 'Long Harry' Slater and Henry Stokes came together in a celebrated afternoon shoot-out in busy Little Collins Street, just near the town hall. Stokes pumped five bullets in quick succession into Slater, who was rushed to the Melbourne Hospital, and when later questioned by detectives, refused to co-operate. 'I'll say nothing,' was all he said. Stokes was arrested soon after while trying to escape.

At trial, Slater experienced short-term memory loss. Stokes was acquitted of attempted murder, but sent down for six months for discharging a firearm in a public place, the penalty suspended if he left the state. Stokes agreed and packed his bags for a break in Tasmania, while Slater, following his recovery, moved his operations to Sydney, with Cutmore as his travelling companion.

So the enmity between Slater and Stokes was well grounded, and was extended to all their gang affiliates.

Ted Whiting was widely seen as Slater's man and, in more treacherous quarters, as the enemy of Squizzy Taylor. Criminal allegiances aside, Whiting also incurred Taylor's wrath when the little gangster's elaborately dressed moll, Dolly Grey, visited his saloon, drank far too much and collapsed asleep on a couch. By the time she came to, Dolly was half-stripped of her clothes, including a fur coat, and robbed of her expensive jewellery. Whiting and his crew had not only rolled Dolly but, more significantly, disrespected Taylor.

There would be retribution.

Thus it was that Stokes and McDonald took a platoon of reinforcements when they went calling on Whiting at his home early on the evening of 18 July 1921. But it was Whiting's wife, Hilda, a smart woman, who answered the firm knock on their front door.

Stokes asked to speak to Whiting and, when told he wasn't in, asked if his wife was in. Hilda Whiting, who had known Stokes for several years, realised he hadn't recognised her, and to play for time, she told the group she'd go inside and fetch Mrs Whiting.

With that, she closed the door and hurried to the back of the house and collected her child. At the same time her husband came in from the backyard. 'Stokes and his mob are at the front. You had better get out,' she warned him, before heading next door to safety.

Whiting told police he then crept to the front of the house, where he spotted the milling group, and then headed off to raise the alarm at the local nick. In her evidence at McDonald and Stokes's trial, Hilda said that some time later she heard the sound of seven or eight gunshots, but decided not to investigate. She waited until the following morning before returning to her house, where she discovered several cartridge shells on the floor, and bullet holes in the stairs, walls and doors. It seemed someone had shot at the house.

For his part, Edward Whiting said it was only when he was returning with the police that he heard two shots fired. When examined on identification, Whiting's memory had faded. No, he couldn't identify the two gunmen because they were too far away – 16 yards to be exact. Besides, he and Albert McDonald were the best of friends. Furthermore, any suggestion that he'd been intimidated, or approached by the two defendants before or during the trial to fudge his evidence, was also vigorously denied.

Whiting, of course, could have claimed brain impairment after years of punishment in the boxing ring, or the bullet wounds he'd sustained to the head. Whatever the motivation, the veteran fighter adhered to the old rule of the game: a shut mouth catches no flies.

Constable Henry Dunn was more forthcoming in his evidence, identifying McDonald and Stokes as the men he saw come out of Whiting's front gate, turn and fire a shot in the direction of the house. As they walked away, the constable called out: 'We are police. Put up your hands.'

In one movement, Stokes threw his weapon over a fence while raising his arms. But McDonald appeared to be in two minds, until common sense intervened. Another officer, a Constable Holihan, rushed across to McDonald, telling him, 'Hands up!' According to the police officer, McDonald put one hand above his head and the other by his side. He said he heard a click and shouted: 'Put your hands up or I'll blow a hole in you.' It was then that McDonald made a backward motion with his hand as though he were throwing something away – his gun.

Checks on their weapons later revealed the safety catches on both had been released, and the seven-chamber magazines were empty.

Stokes, 39, was charged with the attempted murder of Whiting, loitering with the intent to commit a felony, and with having carried firearms without the permission of the local authorities.

McDonald, 24, also faced the same counts, as well as having attempted to shoot at Constable Holihan with intent to commit murder. For good measure he was charged with possessing a tie pin, a gold watch, a diamond ring, a platinum chain and 56 pounds reasonably suspected of having been stolen.

Both men claimed they'd been drinking all that day and were not in a fit state. McDonald, whose counsel had not failed to brief the bench on his Croix de Guerre, said he wasn't aware that he'd been in Stokes's company, let alone firing bullets into the house of a man he bore no ill feeling towards.

McDonald and Stokes were eventually convicted of discharging their firearms in a public place without permission of the authorities, and being armed with an offensive weapon with intent to commit a felony. Stokes's legal counsel argued his client had been drunk and impulsive on the day, which was quite out of character for a man who, when sober, 'was quiet and inoffensive'. He was fined 20 pounds on the first count, and jailed for 6 months on the other.

McDonald was afforded war-hero status by the bench. He was fined 10 pounds and given a suspended sentence of one month on the second charge. Observed the police magistrate: 'As you come here with a good clean civilian record, and a good war record, I am going to give you an opportunity of becoming an honourable man.'

Their faith in McDonald was shattered when less than a week later he was before the city court charged with being a suspected person. Then in late September he returned to answer a previous count of loitering with intent at South Melbourne, for which he'd been placed on a good behaviour bond, and had breached.

The police prosecutor made a great play of McDonald's association with underworld identities, namely Henry Stokes, along with convicted criminals at Flemington Racecourse. McDonald claimed he'd forsaken the mob and was now cutting wood in Lilydale, outside Melbourne. Police Magistrate Moore sentenced McDonald to three months jail, suspended for twelve months on condition that he be of good behaviour and placed himself under the supervision of a probation officer. He was also warned to stay away from Stokes and his criminal cohorts.

A more astute magistrate would have thrown in Squizzy Taylor and Ida Pender, as McDonald had by this time become a key member of the gang, notably as a safe-breaker and an enforcer. His status as a hard man was given a public boost when he was arrested in an early morning raid by detectives on a flat in the southern Melbourne suburb of Elwood. McDonald had been sharing accommodation with another Taylor cohort,

Alexander Johansen, a career criminal newly released from jail on a bond after serving 4 years of a 10 year stretch for robbery.

When police entered the flat they found McDonald in bed with his companions – two loaded revolvers, one on each side, and a spare on the dressing table. McDonald and Johansen were ready for war. Police also found a revolver in another room, along with crepe and hair for making false whiskers and moustaches, and a pair of goggles.

McDonald and Johansen were immediately charged with the early morning robbery of Rita Moore's frock shop a week earlier, in nearby Elsternwick. A gang member in the heist was Ida Pender, and the 17-year-old flapper would soon afterwards go into hiding with her lover.

Pender, dressed in a distinctive scarlet opera cape which would later form an integral part of the police evidence, had been sitting in a car with one of Taylor's thugs, Percy Speakman, on the morning of the robbery. The pair were spotted by Stanley Valentine Many-Peney, a security patrolman, and David Charles Bennett, a police constable stationed locally, at Elsternwick.

Bennett was in dependable company. Whether the police officer knew it or not, Many-Peney had been in tight situations before as a member of the celebrated 6th Machine Gun Company. In late August 1918, the 23-year-old private had received a gunshot wound to the forehead in France. An actor and theatre usher before enlisting, his flamboyance was on display when just before his wounding, he wrote to his mother from a bombed-out French chateau.

> I am having a ripping time. We are living in the cellars of a lovely chateau which the owner, a French count, left when the retirement came. It would make you cry to see such lovely furniture as this getting knocked about the way it is. Still,

> we salvage as much as we can for the French Mission. I am at present sitting in the reception room, which seems to be all curtains, mirrors, doors and chandeliers. Don't you worry about me, I'm having a fine time, and wouldn't be a civilian in Aussie for anything.

Bennett and Many-Peney kept Speakman's parked vehicle under observation from a distance, unaware that they were about to disrupt a robbery orchestrated by Squizzy Taylor. As they watched and waited, loud noises came from the direction of the frock shop. After a brief discussion, the constable, who'd arrived unarmed, borrowed the watchman's pistol and went to investigate the disturbance, while Many-Peney kept vigil near the car.

Many-Peney later reported seeing three shadowy figures – suspected to have included Taylor – emerge from the gloom and climb into the vehicle as its engine was started. Many-Peney immediately called out to Bennett, who stepped onto the roadway with his gun at the ready.

Bennett would later tell the Caulfield Police Court he'd also heard the car start and had run back up the lane. On reaching the street, he was confronted by the oncoming vehicle. 'I stood in front, pointing a revolver, and called out, "Stop, or I'll fire." But the car came on, the headlights were switched full on my face. I sprang aside and fired, but the car kept on. I fired one or two more shots but without apparent effect.'

Police later found clothing scattered on the road, about 10 paces from where the car had been parked, and the lock on the salon's back door jemmied open.

The getaway vehicle might have slipped police, but the alert constable had got a clear view of Speakman, and soon police were knocking on the thief's door. The watchman had also identified Pender, who was arrested. After giving information implicating McDonald and the others, including Taylor, she was treated as an important witness and packed off to a country town for her own safety. But Ida took flight after being left alone by the town cop while he was having a shave.

It would be several months before she was finally tracked down. Ida Pender had better luck. Following her apprehension in late July, the shop-breaking charges against her were withdrawn by police because of the lack of evidence. McDonald's woes would continue when around the same time he was given a year for obtaining money by menaces.

He'd targeted St Kilda bookmaker Samuel Allen and in a display of public bravado approached him in the crowded bar of a local hotel snarling: 'I want to see you on particular business regarding Squizzy Taylor. He sent me for 10 pounds.'

Allen's response is not recorded. McDonald would not be discouraged. He followed the bookie to the railway station and even boarded the same carriage. When Allen alighted at St Kilda Station, McDonald threatened: 'If you don't give me the tenner, you will be visited.'

Wisely, Allen handed over the cash. It wasn't a 'sure thing' investment for the bookie because he still received an unfriendly follow-up visit. This was too much. He went to the police, who promptly rounded up McDonald. When he was searched, police found a scrap of paper with a St Kilda address, and when detectives visited the house they were greeted by Taylor's elderly mother.

McDonald was charged with demanding money with menace and at his trial Allen refused to give evidence unless he was given protection. This was agreed to by the judge. On Allen's version, the jury found McDonald guilty and he was sentenced to 12 months jail. McDonald immediately lodged an appeal but abandoned it when the appeal judges intimated that they had the power not only to reduce or quash a sentence, but also increase it.

While he was banged up in jail, a letter from McDonald's past would arrive at his Napier Street, Fitzroy, house. It was from the army advising him that his Croix de Guerre citation was available for him to collect. The gangster would have to wait several more months to receive the coveted certificate – as a free man.

12

# More of Squizzy's Soldiers

SQUIZZY TAYLOR NEVER SERVED IN the AIF. His contribution to the war effort was entirely self-interested. The week before Christmas 1917 and in need of some yuletide cash, the gangster targeted an army recruiting gathering outside Flinders Street Station. Penetrating the large crowd, Taylor zeroed in on a railway guard, Hugh Leonard, but just as Squizzy's hand went into his victim's pocket, he was spotted by a railways police officer, who immediately pounced on him.

Taylor panicked and shouted for back-up from his gang. Just as the thugs moved in, a member of the AIF intervened and assisted in the arrest. Taylor was bundled off to the station cloak room for questioning. During a quiet moment, he turned to the soldier, Corporal Herbert Frank Duscher, and demanded: 'What right had you to catch me?'

'Every right,' came the reply. Taylor responded by landing a savage blow on the soldier's nose. He was given three months jail for attempted larceny.

Squizzy left it to his brothers to climb into khaki. Claude Taylor, as we know, signed up but didn't get past camp. Stanley and Albert Taylor both served overseas. They were brothers in arms, marching together into Melbourne's Royal Park recruiting centre on 11 May 1916.

Their father Benjamin's chest would have swelled to see his boys answer the call to arms, had he not died 15 years earlier. This inconvenient fact did not prevent his signature mysteriously appearing on Albert's enlistment application papers, right above that of the boys' mother, Rose.

Albert was the giant of the family – at five foot seven, he towered over his brothers. His enlistment papers show he was a cook, and just a month shy of his 21st birthday, when he signed up. Stanley was almost a year older and a clerk by occupation. The two were inseparable in the army. They trained together and went AWL together. Their flimsy rap sheets were almost a mirror of each other. They shipped off together on 20 October 1916, disembarking early the following January at Plymouth with the 6/2nd Pioneers, later the 4th Australian Pioneer Battalion, which served in some of the very hottest spots of the war in France. And at the war's end they were shipmates in the troopship *Ascanius* on the voyage home, both in line for their war service medals.

The job of the pioneer battalions was logistical support: 'contractor' to the engineers, as a contemporary observer wrote. As combat became more mechanised, the Pioneers laboured to keep strategic roads and rail tracks open, and to build fortifications. The work was by definition dangerous, building and repairing while the enemy took pot shots.

After the war, one commanding officer wrote an entertaining account of the Pioneers' work, in which he suggested that the 4th was a particularly fun-loving bunch in comparison with other units:

> People often smiled at the old 2nd Pioneers – the most respectable, steady, well-conducted battalion

> in the early days of the AIF – but one never could fault them. The 4th Pioneers were about the opposite of the 2nd in some respects, but for fast work, they were unequalled. They specialized in railways – little 21-in. gauge tracks over any country, under any conditions, and broke the hearts of more than one enthusiastic social reformer.

Albert Taylor was one such member of the 4th. In England, he managed to contract the pox, and for eight weeks was banged up in the VD hospitals at Parkhouse and Bulford. But in France, in late September 1917, he suffered a serious shotgun wound to the head, shoulders and right knee. He was evacuated across the Channel to the Queen's Hospital in Birmingham, and four months later returned to his unit in France. By and large he was a well-behaved soldier. Under the heading of character assessment, the notations were always 'good'.

So were the assessments of Stanley Taylor, who had done two years training before the war with his local Citizens Forces unit. He survived the battlefields unscathed and came home a corporal.

In a criminal sense, Albert and Stanley were relatively untarnished, but over the years they remained staunch to their gangster brother. When the police called around to Rose Taylor's East Malvern house to investigate the frock salon break-in, they interviewed Stanley, who was staying there. He showed the detectives his room, where they found a box containing some of the apparel taken in the robbery.

At police headquarters, Stanley denied any involvement in the heist, explaining that he had been standing in Rose's front garden talking to a neighbour when McDonald turned up with a suitcase. The visitor had told Stanley he had been asked to leave the case there. It was placed in the back hall, then McDonald sat down with Stanley and shared a pot of tea.

Stanley initially assisted the police by pointing out McDonald as the man who had handed over the case. Later, however, when he was asked in court to swear positively that McDonald was that man, Stanley, like a true Taylor, simply replied: 'I will not.'

Speakman was charged with robbery and after two trials was acquitted, while McDonald and Johansen were freed after the prosecution entered a *nolle prosequi* because of insufficient evidence.

Several days before his acquittal, McDonald had once again fronted the City Court for breaching the bond he'd entered into the previous September. His past misdemeanours were thoroughly aired with the conclusion, 'McDonald has never been known to follow a lawful occupation'. The seizure of his guns and his close affiliation with known and dangerous criminals, notably Taylor, were also underscored in the prosecution's character assessment.

Added to McDonald's woes was the evidence of his probation officer, who swore that he hadn't seen the gangster for seven months. This time, it was just too much for the magistrate, who ordered him to serve the remainder of his suspended sentence. McDonald's counsel immediately served notice of an appeal, which was dismissed the following month.

*

When Squizzy Taylor was involved in a terrible hit-and-run accident, it was once again Stanley Taylor whose quiet work probably saved his brother from jail.

As Daphne Allcorn, a domestic servant, was alighting from a stationary tram near the corner of Commercial and St Kilda roads just before midnight on 5 May 1924, a Super Six Hudson, which had no lights on, accelerated around the corner and collected her, dragging her for about 15 yards. The speeding car did not stop.

Just before the accident, Albert Radonich, a returned soldier, was helping her down to the road. He ran to her assistance and was soon joined by the tram crew. Using his military training, Radonich instructed the workers to stay with the injured girl while he ran to get an ambulance. But Daphne was placed back on the tram for the short trip to the Alfred Hospital's casualty room. When she was admitted, the 22-year-old was in a delirious condition, in extreme pain, and would survive only a few more hours.

Outside the hospital, a tram passenger named Alwyn Meadows noticed the Hudson car with its mangled mudguard and broken headlamp. He went over and spoke to the driver, and made a mental note of the licence plate number. Two days later, police who had interviewed Meadows took him into the criminal court where Squizzy Taylor was on trial on another matter. Meadows identified him as the driver of the vehicle.

After conveying the dying passenger to hospital, the conductor and tram driver resumed normal service. But the journey was again interrupted, this time by a thickset man who climbed aboard, approached the conductor and told him, 'A chap in the car wants you over there.' The messenger was Charlie Allsop, one of Squizzy Taylor's soldiers.

The conductor and the tram driver accompanied Allsop to the waiting car and conversed with the driver. Back on the tram, conductor Henry McVeigh was observed deep in discussion with Allsop, according to later testimony by fellow passengers.

At the inquest, Meadows once again identified Taylor as the driver who had failed to stop. Taylor denied any knowledge of the event. The coroner committed him to stand trial charged with manslaughter. But at the trial, the conductor, McVeigh, suffered a memory loss. Under examination, he said he could not identify the driver, even though they'd conversed on the night. Citing his war veteran status, he told the court his nerves had suffered because of his 'service over the other side'.

Henry Victor McVeigh's war records suggest that his time in the 57th Infantry Battalion was mostly spent in hospital being treated for diarrhoea and exhaustion. His powers of recollection also appear to have been a casualty. His colleague, driver Bertram Anstey, was just as confused. He couldn't even identify the vehicle, let alone the driver.

Squizzy's brother Stanley was observed outside the coronial inquest, engaging the two witnesses in close conversation. He was in fact a colleague of the pair, a fellow conductor on the Malvern–Prahran tram route. His presence did not go unnoticed by the police and prosecution. Taylor, who initially denied ownership of the suspect vehicle and claimed the damage had been caused by a previous mishap on the return drive from a country race meeting, swore his innocence.

For his part, Allsop, Squizzy's offsider who had spoken so earnestly with McVeigh on the tram, also denied he'd been anywhere near the scene of the accident that night, or at the hospital or on the tram.

*

Charles Edward Allsop and his two brothers had all been in the AIF. But while they were both badly wounded in action, Charlie didn't leave Melbourne, on account of the varicose veins he suffered in both legs. In the end he was discharged from the army, but not before he'd been laid up at the Fairfield Hospital with scarlet fever. The 27-year-old bookie who listed the Royal Hotel, Collingwood, as his home address on his enlistment just wasn't up to military life.

His brother Robert was 36 years old when he enlisted in late May 1916. He and Charlie must have been close because five months later, as Robert was on the point of embarkation with his battalion at Port Melbourne, Charlie masqueraded as a wharfie and infiltrated the unit.

He slipped past the sentries guarding the pier by flashing a forged waterside worker's pass, and mingled with the soldiers, trying to find Robert. When he was eventually challenged, Charlie flashed the bogus pass again, but this time it didn't pass muster. He was charged with having breached the War Precautions Act, and fined forty shillings with four pounds and four shillings in court costs.

Robert boarded the HMAT *Port Lincoln* and headed to war. However, Robert didn't immediately adapt to khaki and was inclined to wander off. His first misdemeanour was at Codford, on Salisbury Plain, on the eve of embarkation for France with the 46th Battalion. He disappeared and was later picked up in Folkestone. On his return he incurred seven days close confinement, and the loss of a day's pay. Then in February 1918, Allsop overstayed his leave in England by 4 days, which earned him 21 days of field punishment no. 2 and the forfeiture of 33 days pay.

Just five months before the war's end, Private Allsop took a serious gunshot wound to the chest and left underarm. He was evacuated to England but, while his life was saved, the wound to his arm failed to respond to the treatment. The limb was amputated, and he was invalided home.

In July 1925, the former soldier was arrested by plain-clothes police who observed him taking bets outside a Prahran pub. The one-armed bookie told them: 'I will go with you. I was going to turn it up before this. Before the war I had a good position but gave it up, and am now not able to follow that occupation. I have only one arm, and my wounds are "all cut up". I have a wife and four children, and will not do it again.'

His war injuries must have weighed in his favour because the magistrate fined him twenty pounds, with two pounds in costs and a stay of seven days to pay.

Robert had long been keen on the racetrack, but 10 years earlier it had almost cost him his life on the flat at Flemington. The incident centred around a defaulting bookmaker, who had been pursued by an angry mob after he accepted bets on horses that got up, and refused to pay out on the winnings. Donald John McLeod repeated this gambit several times, promising he'd settle the bets later in the week. The trouble was, punters were getting wise to him. In the parlance of the day, they knew they'd been 'scaled'.

McLeod was bustled by the crowd, which grew noisier and more violent. They struck McLeod several times and, fearing for his safety, he bolted towards the exit. But in his haste, the wayward bookie stumbled and fell and the mob moved in on him in a free-for-all of whirling fists and kicking feet. Associates of the bookie stepped in and separated him from his attackers. McLeod set off again, but this time he was brought down by the mob and literally beaten to death. Two mounted police constables eventually broke up the crowd, but it was too late. The Carlton bookmaker had been bashed to death for less than 20 pounds.

In a separate but related incident, Robert Allsop was set upon by the murdered bookie's associates, who thought he was one of those who had attacked McLeod. He was struck in the face with a fist and king-hit with a short length of chain.

Samuel Foster Allsop, the third of the Allsop boys, was the first of his clan to enlist; that was in early March 1915 when the colony still swelled with pride at contributing to the mother country's hour of need. Allsop's civilian job as a labourer made him an ideal soldier, but even before he'd made it to Gallipoli, Allsop had been disciplined for twice going AWL and once for being drunk. He did, however, manage to climb at least one rank when he was made a lance corporal with the 6th Infantry Battalion. Then, in late October 1917, he was wounded in action in France. As a result, his left leg was removed from above the knee.

Unlike his brothers, Charlie Allsop's experiences with firearms were not fighting for his country on an overseas battlefield. It was in the back lanes of Melbourne where Charlie carried a gun. He was in a league of his own when it came to criminality. His reputation was outlined in a brief summation by a noted detective, Jeremiah O'Keefe, in a 1925 court hearing: 'I have known Charles Allsop for four years, and he is a reputed shop-breaker, gunman, hold-up man and a constant companion of such men, being one of the worst criminals in this State and a menace to shop-keepers and residents. I have never known him to follow any lawful occupation.'

In the Adelaide Police Court he was described as a 'well-known Victorian criminal', but the prosecution failed to prove that the 25 pounds in notes he was carrying had been obtained illegally. On being discharged, he told the magistrate: 'It is my intention to leave for Victoria.' To which His Honour quickly replied: 'I will not place any obstacle in your way.'

It's possible the magistrate was unaware that Allsop was in Adelaide to escape the heat in Melbourne after a series of high-profile court appearances involving jury-tampering, the brazen robbery of a prominent racing identity at the Bookmakers' Association headquarters, and the armed hold-up of eight men in a suburban card game.

Pressure on Allsop had begun to build when he was arrested loitering around the criminal court in Melbourne on the eve of the much-anticipated trial of his boss, Squizzy Taylor, and four of his gang, who were charged with conspiring to spring the convicted murderer, Angus Murray, from Melbourne Gaol earlier in the year. Murray had been sentenced to death for his role in the botched robbery and brutal slaying of banker Thomas Berriman. Murray had been arrested in a raid on Taylor's rented Middle Park cottage. Taylor was also reputed to have driven the getaway car.

When Allsop fronted the City Court, the prosecution alleged 'he was mixing with men likely to be empanelled upon the jury which will hear the conspiracy charge'. The police informant described Allsop as a reputed 'jury squarer', who had been seen in Taylor's company.

Held once again on a charge of having insufficient lawful means of support, Allsop was remanded for a week and freed on bail of 50 pounds. At the second hearing the police evidence was stiffened: Allsop was reputedly mixing with the men summoned to sit on the Taylor trial jury. When asked by police why he was loitering in the area, Allsop answered: 'I was going to hear Taylor's case.' He was then told the hearing was two days away, but he stuck to his guns. The magistrate decided in Allsop's favour.

Six months later, he was implicated in another incident, one that smacked of standover. Thomas Marriott was in the Bookmakers' Association club rooms in the city when he received a telephone message that 'a lady' wanted to see him downstairs, at the front door. Marriott was by nature a suspicious man, and knew well that bookies were seen as soft targets by criminal gangs.

As a precaution he placed a revolver in his pocket before heading down. On reaching the bottom of the stairs his suspicions were confirmed: there was no woman. The entrance, usually illuminated, was in darkness. Within seconds, he was grabbed from behind and his arms pinned behind his back. But the plucky Marriott, as he was later described in a newspaper report, wrenched himself free in the scuffle and, reaching into his pocket, pulled out the revolver and fired off two shots at close range. The bookie later told police one of the three attackers had clutched at his stomach before 'moving with difficulty' towards the lane.

Marriott set off in hot pursuit, firing two more shots in their direction before returning to the club to alert the police. He'd also got a good look at one of the men, who was of short stature.

Within hours, Allsop was picked up by detectives in his hangout in Prahran and later fronted the City Court on a holding charge of frequenting a public place with intent to commit a felony.

Around the same time, Allsop was booked over a serious armed robbery in which shots were fired. Again, the targets were well-known racing identities. Just before midnight on 15 June 1924, a masked Allsop and three cohorts rang the front doorbell of Rupert Mark Conroy, a Glenhuntly hairdresser and tobacconist. Upstairs eight men were playing a high-stakes card game, and the venue was known only to a select few in the racing industry. The game came to a momentary halt while Harry Bird went downstairs to answer the ring, returning soon after with his hands in the air, followed by the four masked and armed intruders. Pushing Bird into the room, one of the men shouted: 'Hands up! Stand with your faces to the wall.' Another then added: 'You can rest your hands on your head so they won't get tired.'

At first several of the players thought it was a practical joke, until a bullet was fired just above their heads into the wall. By this time the gunmen had their full attention, and with that they started to rummage through the group's pockets while being told to 'look for fawnies', a popular term for diamonds.

Allsop, short and stout and readily identifiable despite the mask, was making his presence felt, brandishing his revolver; at one stage he pressed it firmly into one man's stomach and threatened: 'If you bastards move you'll get plugged.'

Three of the gunmen wore black masks, while the fourth wore a white mask and black hat, and stood watch at the doorway, collecting the spoils. It was widely believed that man was Squizzy Taylor.

Charlie Caylock, a wily horse trainer, had 100 pounds rolled up in his waistcoat pocket. As he turned to face the wall, he surreptitiously placed the cash in his mouth. Another victim slipped a ring from his finger and dropped it down the back of his shirt, while some money intentionally dropped on the floor went unnoticed. Nonetheless, the gunmen made off with more than 100 pounds in cash and more in jewellery, backing out of the room before locking the door and climbing into a waiting car.

Later that morning, by sheer coincidence, Allsop was picked up by detectives and taken to the city watch house where he was charged with vagrancy. Within hours Allsop's charge was upgraded to robbery in company after he was picked out in an identity parade by Charlie Caylock.

'That is Allsop. I think that he was there on Sunday night,' the trainer told Senior-Detective Frederick Piggott. To other senior detectives, Caylock was more emphatic, telling them: 'Yes, that is the man that robbed me. I have absolutely no doubt about it. I have known him for years.'

One of Allsop's associates, tailor's presser Murray Davis, would also be charged in connection with the robbery.

But Caylock's memory would fade by the time it came to the trial. He refused to swear it was Allsop, and claimed that he could pick Allsop among 500 because he saw him every day at the races.

Under examination, it emerged that Caylock had told detectives he'd been threatened by Taylor. The day after he'd identified Allsop he'd been confronted by Taylor and one of his gunmen, Joe Gavey. According to Caylock, the little gangster put to him: 'Have they had you looking at Allsop?'

To which Caylock claims to have said: 'Yes, you won't frighten me. I will fight you or anyone of your friends, any day.'

But Caylock had been rattled by the visit and straight after sought police protection. He was issued with a Colt automatic pistol and given lessons at Russell Street police headquarters on how to use it. His house was also placed under a 24-hour watch.

Meantime, while Caylock remained concerned about his family's welfare, the other victims were expressing concern about the jewellery and keepsakes taken in the robbery. The money was of no consequence, they agreed.

Through a third party, Caylock and Taylor agreed to meet. The arrangement was that both would be alone, but the trainer knew that Taylor wouldn't have the courage to stand on his own. For his own safety, Caylock packed his Colt.

Taylor, of course, wasn't alone. He was accompanied by Ida Pender and two armed enforcers.

Caylock threw caution to the wind and immediately demanded Taylor hand over the jewellery he'd taken in the heist. It was then agreed that if Caylock played dead in his evidence against Allsop and Davis, the booty would be returned to its rightful owners. Caylock was true to his word, but despite the vagueness of his evidence, the magistrate committed the men to trial. In the jury trial, Caylock's memory 'worsened', as did the prosecution's case. In the end, Allsop and his co-accused walked free. But the jewellery was never returned.

When Caylock later approached Allsop, he replied: 'Ida doesn't want to give it back.'

Three months later, police withdrew the armed robbery charges against Allsop involving Thomas Marriott – identity, or the lack of, being the tipping point.

Allsop would be in and out of the courts over the years, always the defendant – except on one occasion. It was in late February 1954, when the 65-year-old bookie went to the Victorian

Supreme Court seeking damages from a disgruntled punter who had openly labelled him a 'thief, a robber, and welsher' at a country Victorian racetrack. In previous court appearances, Allsop had been tight-lipped and unwilling to concede anything except his name, age and address to the prosecution. But this time he was willing to explain his shady past, his former criminal connections and the gangsters he was once allied to.

But not anymore, he protested.

While admitting to have 'done many wrong things in his life' and of being 'very ashamed', Allsop did not disown his friendship with Squizzy Taylor, but he glossed over the gangster's dangerous reputation, telling the court he didn't consider Taylor a notorious gunman. He also said that he had 'hardly known' a man named Henry Slater. Their association, he qualified, was 30 years ago, and besides, 'I did not like Slater.'

Despite this apparent confusion in his evidence, Charlie Allsop once again found himself on the right side of a jury, which awarded him 80 pounds to help soothe his damaged reputation.

Like many of Squizzy's recruits, Allsop remained a loyal soldier right to the very end. He even took a public role in the gangster's funeral service in 1927, assisting the distressed Ida Pender to the official mourning coach.

# 13

# Racetrack Spivs and Shockers

PRIVATE VICTOR ALEXANDER PERRY SPENT most of his years around country racetracks in Western Australia as a jockey and trainer. A man well known to police, Perry was a spiv and an urger. In fact, the police described him as 'the greatest pest on the [racecourse] terrace'. His crimes included passing counterfeit coins to a bookmaker.

But there was also a dangerous edge to Perry.

His career as a jockey and a trainer had effectively ended on 19 March 1906 during the last race at the Bulong meeting, east of Perth. That was the day he steered his mount into the path of Albert John Windsor, riding Umber.

It was a four-horse race.

Young Windsor suffered a broken spinal column and was rushed to the Kalgoorlie Government Hospital. From his deathbed, and in intense agony, the jockey told of how Perry had ridden his horse at him, forcing it into the crowd. The horse then collided with a group before it collapsed, pinning Windsor to the ground. Perry did not hang around; he left the course immediately. In his absence a stewards' inquiry was held and the jockey was banned for two years for 'foul riding'.

But for Perry worse was to come. At the inquiry into Windsor's death it was revealed that Perry had tried to fix the race with the owner of the dead jockey's mount, but was rebuffed. According to John Coen, Perry had asked him what he would give out of the stake if Perry pulled his own horse. In other words, run his mount dead. The jury found Perry had deliberately caused his rival's death by 'wilfully boring' him off the course. He was immediately arrested and charged with manslaughter.

At his trial, the jury took just 90 minutes to find Perry guilty, but with a recommendation to mercy on account of the dangerous nature of the Bulong course, which did not afford any protection to the horses, and also on account of the generally loose methods of running the meeting. The judge heard the jury's plea and sent Perry down for 12 months with hard labour, but not before telling him it could very well have been a life sentence.

It would not be the last time Perry would be behind bars. When he enlisted for the Great War at the start of 1916, he'd just emerged from jail after serving a nine-month sentence for false pretences. At his criminal court trial, Perry was asked by the Chief Justice Sir Robert McMillan for his post-sentence reflections. 'I ought to have gone with one of the expeditionary contingents,' Perry said.

To which the judge sternly replied he was not sorry the defendant did not go, 'because when men like you joined the forces it was not to be wondered at, that complaints were received'.

The previous year, Perry had been warned off tracks operated by the West Australian Trotting Association. Charged with vagrancy in late December 1914, the 40-year-old labourer was described as a 'magsman and tale-teller of a very low order'. In other words, a con man, a swindler and a deceiver. His 'mode of operations was to pick up mugs from the country and men about town, and induce them to back horses for various races. Frequent complaints have reached the detective office regarding the accused's practice of holding back or getting away with the proceeds of the investments,' Detective Sergeant Mann told the police court in Perth. Perry had also ignored previous police warnings.

Robert Young told of being approached by Perry at the Goodwood races four weeks earlier with a 'dead cert' for the last race. Young handed over 10 shillings, never to see it again. As part of the ruse, Perry told the railway employee he'd got four-to-one on the race. Sure enough the dead cert won, but Perry claimed he'd backed a different horse. He also scammed another mug punter on the same day. A Detective Dungey helped seal Perry's fate when he told the judge the defendant earned his living by 'whispering' horses and inducing men to back them. Perry was jailed for two months and told it would have been longer but for his wife and large family depending on him.

The following February, just after being released, Perry was at it again. In company with another grifter, he presented himself to Perth dairyhand, Robert Lawler, as Barber Spencer, the owner of Manicarta, a champion racehorse. The unsuspecting Lawler was told Manicarta was a 'dead certainty' for that Saturday's race, and he could get him eleven-to-one for just a seven-pound stake. But secrecy was paramount, he predictably advised, lest word get out and the generous odds tighten.

Lawler then handed the cash to Perry, who quickly exited. Manicarta was unlucky on the day and failed to run a place. Lawler was equally unlucky and lost his seven pounds, which according to police evidence was never invested anyway. Perry went down for nine months.

Whether the newly released Perry was encouraged by his family to enlist or not, military service gave Bertha Mary Perry and their nine children much-needed financial assistance. Her husband was in uniform and away from racecourses, although he'd registered himself as Victor Alexander Perrie.

Soon after signing up, he was posted to the 11th Battalion and on his way to France. That was in late October 1916, and for the next three or four months the only battles confronting the private were his skirmishes with scabies, for which he was hospitalised twice.

On the night of 14 April 1917 Perry was carrying ammunition from behind the line headquarters to the advanced outposts when he was captured by the enemy.

In his official report to army command, he wrote:

> I was at Headquarters when a runner came from Lieutenant Pope, 11th Battalion, from his advanced outpost to ask for reinforcements as the Germans had launched a heavy attack.
>
> About a dozen of us had left to join Lieutenant Pope whose outpost was the most advanced in the line. The Germans broke through the 4th Battalion on our right and we engaged them on our way up to Lieutenant Pope.

In their scramble the group lost two men, before eventually making it to the post. But that left them at the mercy of the advancing Germans.

> Here we remained until the ammunition was expended and the Germans had surrounded us in masses. Our artillery barrage was also behind us and our Lewis Gun was knocked out of action.

Perry wrote that he watched as his comrades were cut down, including Pope, who took a bullet to the heart. His last order to them was to 'hang on'. Eventually, the dwindling group was overrun and the survivors taken prisoner. Perry was sent to Iwuy, where he was forced to work behind the German lines while they were under constant attack from 'our own shell-fire'.

> During this time we worked hard and starved. I saw many cases of brutal treatment. On one occasion Corporal Chauncey was working hard and 'knocked out' by a German, a Prussian guard, who struck him on the head with a shovel. About the middle of June '17 I saw Private Jenkins, 11th Battalion, reduced to such a low physical condition that he dropped from exhaustion. We carried him home from work and the next day the Germans told us he died.
>
> I saw Private Freeman, so brutally bashed about with rifle butts that he was knocked out several times and had to be carried away. In the middle of August 1917 he was taken away and they told us that he died the next day.

He wrote that by the end of June 1917, he was put on railway work for a period and then on dugouts, moving from town to town. In October 1918 he was about to be relocated to Germany when the Armistice was signed, and he was sent to Belgium, then on to Calais and Dover.

The war was over for Private Perrie, Service Number 336, but for the old confidence trickster in civilian life, there were fresh battlefields. On 25 February 1919 he was sentenced to three months hard labour at Dorchester Prison for false pretences after trying to defraud a civilian patsy of more than four pounds.

Up until his death from natural causes in early May 1945, Perry remained in contact with the minor courts. He lived long enough to see two of his sons, Leslie and John, serve in World War II.

*

Cornelius Joseph Keevil's flirtation with the military lasted just six weeks before he was shunted out for what they called 'riotous behaviour'. In other words, he was out of control and beyond the discipline of the armed services. Keevil, who gave his occupation as a billiard marker, was 23 when he joined B Company 4th Battalion at Cootamundra in New South Wales in November 1915. He didn't get past the training camp.

Once out of khaki, Keevil would see more action as a wannabe gangster. Six years after his ignominious discharge, he was a key figure in the robbery of a well-known Sydney bookmaker, relieving him of almost 350 pounds. Reginald Catton had hidden the stash in the chimney of one of the rooms in his Kensington house, and the hiding place was known only by his family.

With his criminal cohort, 20-year-old Hampton Hirsham, Keevil paid an early evening visit to the bookie's abode, arriving there by taxi. They were joined by two men, the O'Brien brothers, who took up their positions as lookouts on an empty block opposite the house. Hirsham and Keevil then walked to the front door and rang the bell. It was answered by Catton's sister-in-law, Ivy Young, who told them she was alone. Hirsham told her they believed 'there was a lot of money in the house, and we've come to get it'.

'I'm a pretty desperate man,' Hirsham added, to which Keevil contributed: 'Come on, we want the money.' The self-possessed young woman then replied: 'There might be, but I thought Mr Catton had it with him. You are at liberty to look for it.'

With that, the pair walked into the house and began searching one of the rooms. It was there that they eventually went to the fireplace grate and found, secreted behind it, cash in a paper parcel. According to Miss Young, they next asked where Catton kept his betting bags, but the young woman told them she didn't know. The telephone rang and Keevil answered it. Hirsham then cut the wire with a pair of pliers. They left the house and were driven away.

According to police evidence, Hirsham separated from Keevil and headed straight to his boarding house, where he gave the landlady, Gertrude Buckingham, the bag of cash. She asked him how it had gone and Hirsham replied, 'All right.' They counted the money before hiding it in a tin trunk. Over the next few days, Hirsham splurged some of the proceeds on clothing and gifts for Buckingham and her daughter.

Meantime, Keevil was still unaware of the exact amount that was in the bookie's bag. When they next met, Hirsham handed him 90 pounds, claiming they'd netted just 150 pounds from Catton. It didn't take long for Keevil to realise he'd been robbed. He paid Hirsham a visit, demanding the balance of his 'chop' and threatening to shoot him. The landlady gave her caller short shrift, and Keevil departed angrily. Hirsham, who had spent the rest of the proceeds, sensed a payback was coming and decided to head it off.

By this time, a bartender by the name of Roy Frost had been convicted of the robbery. Frost had been identified by Miss Young and in handing down the 18 months sentence on the 23-year-old, the judge declared: 'I have no doubt that the jury's verdict was right.'

A fortnight later, Hirsham arranged to meet a Constable Schmitzer on Newtown Bridge. He told police they'd got the wrong man. Keevil was promptly arrested and charged, along with the O'Brien brothers, who'd kept watch during the robbery.

As it turned out, it was the O'Briens who had provided the inside running about the contents of the grate – they were first cousins of the bookie's wife.

Frost successfully appealed his conviction, and in late August Keevil and Hirsham were sent down for 15 months, 3 months less than the sentence originally given to the innocent man. Judge White sternly told the pair that their crime was too serious to call for leniency, 'but there was a redeeming feature in the fact that the accused had sacrificed their liberty to save an innocent man'. He also went as far as to say that he would recommend a remission on restitution being made.

*

Victor Clarence Ewart, alias Victor Hewitt, ran with some of the hard men of Melbourne's underworld, but his companions were racecourse touts and sly groggers. A Gallipoli veteran, Ewart was demobilised early because of sight problems; despite this affliction, he still kept his eye on the main chance.

Known for his jockey-like proportions, Ewart's early life as a paperboy gave him access to the street gangs and key crime personalities. He kept his ear to the ground and became a valuable source of information. He was also a newspaper runner, and his exuberance for sales landed him in Melbourne's city court charged with making a 'violent outcry' to the 'annoyance of persons using the street'. Describing Ewart as an 'urchin', a beat constable told of how he 'sang out at the top of his voice', thereby disturbing the public peace. Ewart was asked to give the court a demonstration, and did so with gusto. It cost him a five-shilling fine plus two shillings and sixpence in costs.

The following year he was in khaki and about to set off for Gallipoli. But Ewart's war would not last long. A month after the landing at Anzac Cove with the 8th Battalion, he was sent back to hospital in Alexandria with a problem in the sight in one eye. He was discharged and, back in Melbourne, returned to life on the criminal fringe.

The month after the declaration of peace, Ewart and his wife were fined 25 pounds each for sly-grogging in Fitzroy. Then two years later he was charged with loitering at Moonee Valley Racecourse with intent to commit a felony. Track detectives told the court Ewart was observed 'feeling the pockets of several persons' – a wannabe pickpocket.

Early one Saturday morning in April 1924, acting on a tip-off, police raided a major illegal gambling operation in a building opposite the Royal Melbourne Hospital. The bust resulted in the arrests of 46 men, including Squizzy Taylor and his brother, Thomas. They were fined two pounds each. As well as being charged with frequenting a common gaming house without lawful excuse, Ewart, the two Taylors, and Charlie Allsop were booked for being idle and disorderly.

Six months later, Ewart had moved his operations to the racetrack – well, not quite. He was running his own little wagering business outside the course, enticing patrons to participate in a dubious game of chance popularly referred to as a 'barber's pole'. Ewart was spotted by a Constable Makepeace in a paddock just after the last race at Flemington. He had drawn a crowd of about 30 men. The plainclothes cop watched as Ewart took bets and then rolled a block of striped wood on a strip of cloth.

Satisfied he had enough evidence for a prosecution, the constable moved on Ewart, who grabbed the wood and cloth and bolted through the surging crowd. Makepeace's pursuit was momentarily halted by two men who jumped on him. But he quickly broke free by belting one of them with his handcuffs and shoving the other aside. He pursued Ewart, and while drawing his revolver called on him to stop. Ewart kept going, so the constable fired a blank cartridge over his quarry's head.

That stopped him in his tracks.

As well as incurring a 15-pound fine, the prosecution also produced a local police officer known to Ewart. Detective Henry

Carey's character assessment was not good: 'I have known the accused for many years. He is a known cheat and "works" all the metropolitan and country race meetings.'

Six years later Ewart was again prosecuted for operating the 'barber's pole' and again did a runner when police moved in, but was quickly caught. This time it was outside Caulfield Racecourse and in the company of another operator, James Patrick Flack. They had a board on which there were photographs of race-horses. Bystanders were invited to place money on a horse. After the bets were taken, Flack would roll the numbered cylinder on the board. Ewart was in charge of laying the odds.

Not even a vigorous representation by the high-profile criminal barrister Napthali Sonenberg could save Ewart from yet another conviction. Pleaded Sonenberg: 'This game is played in bazaars et cetera, and is the fairest game in the world. It is a fairer game than backing racehorses.'

There was a more sinister side to Ewart's offending. In 1927, he was arrested and charged after a vicious sexual assault on a young Greek woman. The 20-year-old had been found by police wandering about Fitzroy in a dazed state. She later told detectives she'd been in a local sly-grog shop when three men had held her down while another assaulted her. As the newspapers reported it at the time: 'Victor Hewitt [alias Ewart], aged 35, a labourer, was subsequently arrested and a serious charge was preferred against him.'

*

From the moment he arrived at the Morphettville enlistment centre in South Australia and lined up with the hundreds of other willing recruits, Ernest Dyer remained focused on any opportunity that may present itself.

It was late August 1914 and the war was just three weeks old. The 25-year-old gasfitter was quick to answer the call to arms. He became a sapper, attached to the 3rd Field Company Engineers, and before long was in a troopship headed overseas. Dyer showed very early that he wasn't prepared to sit in the shade. Within a year he'd made it to corporal and was focused on progressing further. If it meant spruiking his achievements, so be it.

In a letter to his commanding officer requesting a 21-day furlough in England, Dyer outlines the initial hardships he'd faced during his first year in khaki:

'I left Australia with the 1st Contingent in February and went from there to Gallipoli where I participated in the first landing on April 25, and since then have received two wounds and have had concussion twice. My parents live in England and I have not seen them for six years and I am certain I shall get much better if I could have a complete rest with my people. Hoping you will see your way clear to grant this, my request. I remain your obedient servant.'

The following month, the unmarried Dyer was sprung pumping up his battlefield exploits by claiming to have been awarded a Distinguished Conduct Medal. His exaggerations came to light in a letter from a single woman in Kew, addressed to the 'Minister of Defence Department' in Melbourne.

She wrote: 'Having received a card from a friend at the front today stating that No. 63, Lance Corporal E. Dyer had been awarded the D.C.M., I would be grateful if you will let me know if the same was officially announced, and for what deed the honour was conferred. Lance Corp Dyer is now in hospital in England."

The army's reply to the woman was direct: 'There is no advice that No. 63 Lance Corporal E. Dyer has been awarded the Distinguished Conduct Medal for gallantry in the Field, but should such be received at a later date it will appear in the Commonwealth of Australia Gazette and also in the Press.'

It never happened, of course.

It was true that Dyer had been in hospital. He'd been sent to London, to the Military Hospital at Bethnal Green, suffering a gunshot wound, with pieces of shrapnel lodged in the web of his fingers. He'd also been concussed. And as for his general health, Dyer's records show he'd been quite sickly, battling diarrhoea, tonsillitis, coughing, neurasthenia or fatigue, and nervous exhaustion.

But his health issues appear to have been put aside when the British Forces offered him a commission in the Royal West Surrey Regiment. Dyer, the son of a brewer's drayman, would be a lieutenant.

His bade farewell to the AIF, on 6 October 1915, on the best of terms, so much so that he marched off with an exemplary record; his military conduct was officially stamped: 'Very Good'.

The ambitious young officer rapidly discovered doors were opening for him, particularly in business and social settings. His major interest was horseracing and breeding, and that brought with it a new set of well-heeled friends, including a flamboyant artillery officer, Eric Gordon Tombe, son of a South London clergyman.

Dyer and Tombe's relationship intensified over time, both in a business and personal sense, but it would be doomed. The fallout would result in one of Britain's most bizarre murder investigations.

After the war Dyer did not return to Australia. He remained in England, trying to cash in on the establishment connections he'd made as an officer. His big break came in an unlikely streak of luck. He won 15,000 pounds betting on the champion racehorse, Furious, the winner of the 1920 Lincolnshire Handicap.

It was a massive windfall, and Dyer immediately peeled off 5000 quid and sank it on a racing stable at Kenley, south of

London. Known as the Welcomes, it had a solid reputation in racing circles as a training and stud operation. But that would all change once Dyer took the reins.

In April of the following year, the complex was hit by a major fire. Dyer later told police and insurance investigators he wasn't there at the time. He had been in Brighton and his wife in Scotland. The fire was a real surprise, he insisted.

The other surprise, however, was that he had insured the property for 12,000 pounds, which would have given him 7000 pounds in profit. Not surprisingly, the insurers refused to pay up, leaving the family to live in the loft, the only area not greatly damaged by the fire. For Dyer, it wasn't much of a hardship, given he was spending more nights away from the family on his business interests. Mrs Dyer was often unaware of his precise movements. She later told police it was best not to ask because of his 'violent temper' and his practice of 'always carrying a revolver in his hip pocket'.

By June of 1922, Tombe had stopped visiting the Welcomes. Later that month, in a strange twist, Mrs Dyer was home alone when shortly before midnight she was awoken by stones dropping against the drainpipe. Alarmed, she sent the dog into the yard and the animal headed straight to the cowshed, where it bailed up a figure lurking in the shadows. When he stepped out into the moonlight she saw it was her husband, agitated and dishevelled.

'What are you doing here, Ernest?' she asked him. 'I thought you were miles away.'

Dyer snapped in reply: 'You know the state of my credit. I don't want to be seen here by daylight.'

As she started to take a few steps toward him, he put up his hands and cried out: 'Don't come over here. Don't come out. Get into the house again, for God's sake.'

Dyer later agreed to go inside, where he quickly ate some

food and left. His wife would not appreciate the significance of his bizarre conduct until sometime later.

The following month, Dyer's secret life began to take shape when he announced to his wife that he planned to relocate the business to France. Dyer had been spending freely, particularly in brothels and clubs in London and Paris, and had also borrowed heavily from his partner.

In early June, Eric Tombe met his father at the Strand Palace Hotel in London and told him he was going to Sicily on a trip. That wasn't unusual: Tombe travelled abroad frequently. But his family was none the wiser about his business activities, in particular the partnership with Dyer. The Reverend Tombe told police he'd been unaware of Dyer's existence.

In November 1922, police launched an investigation after advertisements appeared in local newspapers calling for 'men of the highest integrity' to participate in a job scheme. The scheme was in fact a scam, and cash deposits left by the participants disappeared along with the organiser, a man calling himself Fitzsimmons.

Fitzsimmons was tracked down to the Bar Hotel in Scarborough, where he was staying. While police were escorting him to his room to search his belongings, he reached into his pocket and produced a revolver. A detective quickly overpowered him, taking him to the floor in a violent struggle. But as he tried to wrest the gun from him, it accidentally went off, killing the suspect.

Police were unaware of the victim's true identity until they searched his room, where they found just one shilling in money, a ticket for goods that had been pawned that day, a mask, an eyeshade and a quantity of human hair capable of being made into a moustache.

They also located some war service medals, two of them stamped 'Lieut. E. Dyer'. A bag which was initialled 'E.T.'

was also located. Inside were Tombe's passport and other items belonging to him. There were also 180 cheque forms with Eric Gordon Tombe's signature pencilled on them.

Dyer had been engaged in a major fraud, forging his business partner's signatures on cheques, which were turning up across England. Letters bearing Tombe's falsified signature had been sent to their joint bank with instructions to transfer money to Paris, where it would be accessed by Dyer who was to be given power of attorney. The forgeries, according to police, were masterpieces.

In the space of five months, Dyer had drained his partner's bank account of more than 2000 pounds.

By this time, Tombe's parents had not seen their son for months, and they began to fear the worst. Enquiries with his known connections had failed to shed any light on his disappearance, although some had received a telegram purportedly sent by Tombe from overseas. It was all part of an elaborate ruse by Dyer to cover his tracks, and it would have worked had he not widened the fraud.

Almost a year to the day after Dyer was shot dead, police converged on the Kenley stables after a call from the Reverend Tombe whose wife had experienced a vivid dream of their son's body being dumped in one of the three cesspools there.

Mrs Tombe dreamed that her boy lay buried in the garden at Kenley. She told police: 'In my dream I heard Eric say, "Oh, let me out." I felt he was shut in somewhere and could not get free.'

That was all the search party had to go on but, armed with picks and shovels, they dug through the weed-infested bricks and crumbling concrete, working well into the night by the light of hurricane lanterns.

It wasn't until they'd dug into the third cesspool that the secret was revealed. After drawing off several bucketloads of dank water, a pair of feet could be seen. Tombe's body appeared to have been forced through the manhole head-first and then covered in layers of debris. The body was decomposed, with part of the battered skull rotted away, along with the fingers. The body was fully clothed in a brown tweed suit and a dark overcoat. Police also found a gold wristwatch, tiepin and cufflinks – all identified by the Tombes as belonging to their son.

A post-mortem examination revealed that Tombe had been executed – shot in the back of the head at close range, about late April 1922, around the time he had last been seen by his family. Former workers at the complex later recounted to police how they had filled in the first two cesspools, while the third was covered by Dyer himself.

The coronial inquiry into Tombe's death ruled that he died from gunshot wounds at the hand of Ernest Dyer.

*

Harry David Graham liked to claim that he made his living from horseracing. He was, he boasted, an international sportsman, riding mainly on the subcontinent and in Africa and America.

Whatever else, he was certainly a poor speller, because when he enlisted in July 1917, he wrote down his calling as 'jocky'.

A perusal of his military papers reveals a man who for years flew by the seat of his pants, misrepresenting himself from London to Melbourne, where he finally made it into the newspapers, but for all the wrong reasons.

Less than a month after signing up in Toowoomba, Private Graham was off overseas in HMAT *Medic* with the 4th Pioneers Battalion, with which he was mainly engaged as a driver. His war was relatively uneventful. But four months after landing in Liverpool the young soldier was off to the altar with Florence Margaret Tragheim, a bricklayer's daughter, at the Trinity Presbyterian Church in Kensington.

Less than a fortnight later he bade his new bride farewell and headed across the Channel to France. That campaign was marked by several stints in field hospitals suffering nervous stress, until he was invalided to England on 7 August 1918 to convalesce, and back into the arms of his English rose – but not for long.

By December, Graham was agitating for a discharge from the AIF on the grounds that he'd made a new life for himself in the UK. Writing from the Littlemoor Camp in Weymouth, Graham said in his official application that he now had a dependent wife in the UK, and no job or family ties in Australia to 'necessitate my return'. His spouse refused to leave her home in England, and he could earn a living in the UK riding horses. Accompanying the application was a letter in which he stated: 'I have been informed that I have to have guaranteed employment. In actual fact I have this. I am a jockey by profession. I can get a licence from any jockey club to ride. I do not wish to bind myself to one man for a period, which would be necessary if I get one man to guarantee employment.'

By the following March, he had produced a letter from a J. Guppy of Leonard House in Weymouth, guaranteeing him immediate employment once his discharge came through. No job description was included.

With the AIF slow to act, the Grahams decided to deploy the heavy artillery. His wife Florence sent a heartfelt letter to none other than the Australian prime minister, William Hughes, pleading for her husband's discharge. Several weeks later, for good measure, Harry sent off his own letter to the 'Little Digger', appealing for the PM's help. Whether the barrage of correspondence worked or not, by the end of the month Graham was no longer in the army. He was officially discharged on 27 March 1919.

On that day Graham not only bade farewell to the AIF, he also skipped out on Florence – forever.

Some years later, he was called to account for the marital turmoil he had left behind him in England. The base records section at Melbourne's Victoria Barracks contacted Florence, seeking Graham's address in order to forward his war medals.

Florence left the department in no doubt that her husband had not served his uniform well:

> Sir, I am very sorry [I] cannot give you any information concerning my husband's whereabouts. I have not heard from him since 27 March 1919 when he got his discharge. I have made all enquiries to Australia House, London. They did not enlighten me until two years after his discharge that he went back to Australia Nov: 1919 with another young lady. I have not had any support from him, neither have I had any news concerning him. When he used to come home to me on his leave he used to talk about going to Chicago when he had been back to Australia. Whether he has gone there I could not say. Trusting you will get some information of his whereabouts and let me know, I should be grateful to you.

The light-fingered jockey had ridden out of her life and off on his next strange adventure.

On 24 February 1920, Harry David Graham had an appointment with the Port Melbourne Court on serious charges of having stolen from Australian soldiers and their families en route from England to Australia.

Police branded him not only a thief but a stowaway. In the course of his campaign to be discharged from the AIF while in the UK, he had voluntarily relinquished his right to a government-funded passage back to Australia.

The court heard that Graham had been arrested by Constable W.J. Cross as he hovered along the edges of the new Railway Pier at Port Melbourne, peering into the portholes of the steamer *Megantic*. Constable Cross later told the Port Melbourne Court that he observed Graham crawl under a railway truck, while a companion crept onto the ship. When the policeman approached Graham he 'resisted strenuously', but was soon subdued and taken on board to account for himself. On deck, Graham again put up a fight and this time wrenched himself free and bolted. He was quickly apprehended by Lieutenant W.H. Salvator, the ship's provost marshal.

Salvator immediately recognised him as the mysterious soldier he'd seen during the voyage, whose identity he had not been able to establish. The court was told 'it had been a mystery since one day on the high seas, when he appeared on board as suddenly and unexpectedly as if he had fallen from the sky'.

According to the court report in the *Argus*: 'When he was first seen on board he was wearing the uniform of the AIF. He offered no account of who he was and whence he came, and the authorities on board could find nothing out about him.'

On the morning of his arrest Graham was searched, and from his pocket came a silver cigarette case bearing the initials of Private Arthur William Street, one of the returning troops. He also had military papers belonging to Street.

Lieutenant Salvator also shocked the gallery with his account of the wholesale thieving that had been going on during the voyage. While not necessarily pointing the finger at Graham, the officer said the voyage had been the occasion for a veritable maritime crime wave. Thousands of pounds worth of property had been stolen, and hardly any had been recovered.

He detailed thefts ranging from jewellery to washing on makeshift lines: 'An officer who had occasion to leave his cabin for a few minutes returned to find that 50 pounds had been taken from a coat which he left hanging on the wall.

'Only on Sunday, a woman on board was ironing some clothing. As she ironed the things she hung them on a line not 10 yards away, to air. She had ironed and hung up seven garments when she turned her back on them to iron the eighth piece of clothing. A few moments later she picked up the garment to hang it on the line with the other seven, only to find they had disappeared. During the minute or so that she had her eyes off the seven pieces of apparel a thief stole them.'

He then turned his attention to Graham: 'Not only was his sudden appearance aboard a remarkable thing. But it was a notorious fact that men who went ashore with him when the vessel touched land, were brought back to the ship either "doped" or drunk, and minus all their cash.'

Graham was slotted for three months and fined 40 shillings for having resisted arrest.

# PART IV

# Beyond the Reach of Law and Order

# 14

# War's Long Shadow

On the morning of his execution, Albert Edward Budd was given a farewell befitting a brave soldier – an honour guard from his band of brothers, all in uniform with their heads bowed in respectful silence.

To many observers it must have seemed a puzzling gesture, given the woman he had so brutally murdered was the wife of a fellow soldier. But that's how it was in 1918. The number of men returning from the war with psychological traumas, notably shell shock, was growing with every crowded troopship's arrival. The impact of the dreadful physical and mental injuries Private Albert Budd carried from the front line was recognised by his military peers. They understood what he had endured. As historian Michael Cathcart has written in *Defending the National Tuckshop*, a distinctive subculture had formed among diggers, and it persisted on their return home: 'The digger was not a lone individual, he was a member of a brotherhood.'

Some in the brotherhood were 'beyond the reach of law and order'. But in the wider community, the sheer horror and brutality of Albert Budd's crime disqualified him from public compassion.

Albert Budd was among the first Australians to sign on, enlisting three weeks after the war's declaration.

Budd was just a boy when he was adopted by a Melbourne family by the name of Anderson. He quickly became 'Joe' to his extended family and the sobriquet stuck. Even his suicide notes were signed off with simply, 'Joe'. The 36-year-old labourer from Melbourne's Collingwood joined the 5th Battalion, which had only just been raised. Within two months he was on board the requisitioned mail ship, HMAT *Orvieto*, heading first for Egypt and then Gallipoli, where he took part in the first landing.

Budd relished military life. His record was unblemished, aside from a seemingly minor incident in Cairo which earned him an admonishment for allowing a prisoner to escape. However, a serious gunshot wound put paid to Budd's war. A large piece of shrapnel ripped through the gunner's left arm, which left him with a 'useless hand', according to his army medical file. From his hospital bed, Budd wrote to his aunt in Port Melbourne telling her: 'I have done my best.'

After extensive treatment, Budd was shipped home, and then discharged, medically unfit. He also was battling serious but unstated psychological problems. He began working as a wharfie, his meagre income supplemented by his war disability pension.

Budd was not the only member of his extended family to wear khaki. His foster brother, Stephen George Samson, a locomotive driver, was in France with the 15th Australian Light Railway Operating Company. Its role included transporting ammunition and supplies to the front line and returning with the dead and wounded.

Samson was a popular identity in the blue-collar suburb of Port Melbourne, and was well known for his ability with a football. He enlisted in late January 1917, but his overseas campaign almost ended before it began when the troopship he was travelling in, HMT *Ballarat*, was torpedoed by a German U-Boat. It sank at the entrance to the English Channel on the second anniversary of the Gallipoli landing. Those who did not make it into the lifeboats were later collected by a passing destroyer.

Stephen's wife was Annie Elizabeth, and they'd been together five years before he enlisted. Thirty-year-old Annie was described in newspaper reports as being of a 'prepossessing appearance'. She was not a traditional housewife. She devoted much of her time and energy to her Red Cross activities and working for women's rights. She was also politically active as secretary of the Port Melbourne Political Labor Council. And she devoted considerable time as a member of a group formed to greet wounded soldiers on their return to Victoria, appropriately called the Women's Welcome Committee.

Budd was well qualified as a wounded returnee but he wanted more than tea and a kindly word from his sister-in-law, who he would refer to as 'Aggie'. His criminal trial would later be told that Budd wanted a sexual relationship which Annie vigorously refused. He would not be deterred.

In late September 1928, Annie took her complaints to the local police. She told the officers how Budd had been annoying her and how on one occasion he'd broken her window. When confronted with the allegations, Budd told the officers he would stay away from his sister-in-law and pay for the window.

Early the following month, Annie discovered two razors in an outhouse at her residence, and when confronted, Budd admitted ownership of the blades, telling Annie: 'One is for me and one is for you.'

Soon afterwards she received an envelope, signed by Budd, with the scrawled inscription: 'I am going to do something desperate this time. I have got you, so don't give in.'

If Annie Samson feared for her wellbeing, she did not show it. She refused to cower to Budd.

In the week leading up to her murder, the pair clashed on the corner of Graham and Princes streets. It was early evening and Annie and her 12-year-old sister-in-law, Mary Jeanette Samson, had been taking a stroll. According to the young girl, Budd approached them and, referring to a previous incident, said: 'Annie, you closed the door.'

'Yes, I am not going to open the door for you,' she replied.

'I am going to pay you what I owe you,' he declared.

'You said that before.'

As Annie and the young girl walked on, Budd called out: 'All right, Annie. Look out for yourself.'

To which she answered: 'There's a threat for you.'

Within days, Budd would make good his threat. On the morning of 21 October, Annie's sister, Bess Anderson, called at her house with what she believed was some startling news. She'd learned that Budd had slit his own throat in the room he occupied at the home of his foster brother, William Anderson. Budd had then been rushed to the Melbourne Hospital.

At the house, Bess was joined by Harry Pretty, a political colleague of Annie's. The front door was open, so they walked through the hall to the kitchen and out to the back verandah, calling out her name. They eventually went into Annie's bedroom, where they found her body lying in a pool of blood with knife wounds so deep that her head was almost severed. Furniture had also been overturned. Her body was clad in a nightdress. Annie Samson had been dead for some time.

Back at the hospital, Budd was questioned by police. In a chilling exchange, he told the officers: 'I'm all right. I'll soon be ready for the @#$! rope.' The constable then asked Budd what he meant, to which he replied: 'You will soon know all about it.'

Budd asked: 'Did you see Mrs Samson today?'

'Yes, lying on the floor with her throat cut,' the officer replied.

Budd then bared his soul.

'I went to her house at half-past 8 pm yesterday, and got in through a back window. Annie was out so I planted myself inside. She came home, and went to her bedroom.

'I put my coat outside and sneaked up the passage to her bedroom door. I heard a clock strike, I think it was half past nine. I looked in the room. There was a light burning, and Annie was in bed reading. I rushed in and around to the foot of the bed. Annie jumped up and squealed. I pulled her head down to the side of the bed near the bottom and cut her throat.

'She screamed and struggled on the floor. I watched her a good while to make sure she was dead. I shook her, and as she did not move, I went out the front door and went home.'

With blood streaks down his shirt, Budd then sat in his bedroom and penned his confessions. After a short sleep he got up and finished the two notes. By this time the writing paper was also streaked with blood.

At 7 am, Budd calmly washed and dressed in his suit. After placing the note in a drawer, he picked up a razor and drew it across his throat.

When police searched his room they found two bloodstained razors. They also located the notes. The first read: 'I went to the place at 8.30. She was out. I waited till she came in. I done the deed. I am sorry for all relations, her husband and friends. When you read this hurry round to Princes Street as fast as you can.'

The other, to William Anderson, was more forthcoming:

> Dear Bill and Bessie, I cannot stand it any
> longer. I have done the deed. That is the end
> of everything. I went to Aggie's house at 8.30.
> That is the end of me and her. I told everyone
> the police would take me out of the house before

> I was finished. I am sorry I done the deed. I thought I would finish myself. Go around to 127 Princes Street quick. Goodbye – Joe Budd.

Budd later claimed his murderous actions were motivated by loyalty to Stephen, who was serving his country overseas while men were visiting his wife. But it was quickly established that Annie's meetings were in connection with her political and charity activities. He then claimed that on the night of the murder she had rushed at him and he had had no alternative but to slit her throat – and then his own. This was also strongly disputed during his trial.

Nonetheless, Budd attracted much support from returned servicemen, and a petition was presented to the Victorian State Government by the Returned Soldiers' Association opposing the execution, but it failed to save him.

On the day before his execution, Budd received an unprecedented 50 visitors. The following morning a large crowd, comprising returned soldiers in uniform, and even some women, assembled outside the jail gates. At 10 am, the hour of the execution, one of the soldiers gave the order, 'Fall in,' and a minute later many saluted their comrade.

Standing on the scaffold, Budd was asked if he had any final words. He reportedly obliged with: 'If it had not been for drink he [I] would never have committed the crime.'

A day or so later, a newspaper advertisement was placed by some of the men from his battalion. It read: 'In honored memory of our old Anzac comrade, Albert Edward Budd, who died on January 29. He met his death like an Anzac.'

By this time a heartbroken Stephen Samson, the forgotten man, was in a hospital ship returning home. He reached Melbourne in early March, and by the following month he was discharged from the military as medically unfit.

Five years later, two more returned servicemen would face the same fate as Budd, each convicted of brutal and senseless murders, and each battling major psychological issues exacerbated by alcohol and drug abuse.

*

William James Murray was already in the grip of alcohol on his return from overseas. Friends knew that he was merely a shadow of the 30-year-old labourer who had signed up in October 1915 and shipped off to France shortly afterwards.

But as his service record reveals, Murray had difficulties adjusting to military life with the 16th Reinforcements, 3rd Battalion. He was confined to barracks for six days and lost two days pay for overstaying his leave. Later he was given 168 hours detention and forfeited 7 days pay for insubordinate language to an NCO, refusing to obey an order and for having used threatening language to an NCO.

And that wasn't the end of it. Shortly after, he was found guilty of wilful neglect of duty while escorting a prisoner. Later, he would be sanctioned for being AWL.

A little over two years after signing on, Murray signed off. His war ended in December 1917, but not because of insubordination or misconduct. Murray's body and mind could take no more. In the months leading to his discharge, Murray had been wounded on the battlefield in France; he'd suffered trench fever after being buried for three hours during an enemy bombing, experienced painful bouts of myalgia for which he was treated at the London General Hospital, and had been officially diagnosed with severe shell shock.

William James Murray returned from the war a changed man.

After disembarking at Sydney, he was reunited with his wife, Caroline Rhoda Murray, and their children. But Caroline immediately noticed the change in her husband. She described his general behaviour pre-enlistment as 'exemplary', but after his return he took to drink and, when in its grip, would fly into terrible rages. He became so violent during one of his drinking bouts that Caroline had to call the police, who removed him to a reception house where the extent of his brain impairment could be assessed.

After his discharge, the family moved 70 miles south to the New South Wales coastal town of Kiama, but it was far from a new beginning. The Murrays bought a cheap block of land, on which they erected a humpy, but the local council very soon after ordered it be demolished. They were also under the close scrutiny of the Children's Welfare Association, which warned them that if they persisted in staying there, the young children would be taken from them and placed into state care.

Murray was a hard man. Despite his war injuries, he was working as a quarryman, a job that was physically demanding, dirty and unrelenting. The family and financial pressures on the troubled returned soldier were mounting.

On 1 December 1923, it all came to a head after a day of heavy drinking with a workmate, Alfred Hinde, another war veteran with similar health issues. Like Murray, Hinde had sustained a battlefield injury – in his case a slight fracturing of the skull caused by a gunshot wound – and shell shock.

Hinde was a neighbour of Murray's, and on that day the two men travelled the five or so miles from Dunmore to Shellharbour together. On the return journey they sank several bottles of beer. At about 6 pm on the main South Coast road, near the Minnamurra railway station, their lives would change dramatically when they came across 40-year-old George Albert Simpson, who was known to both men. To mark the occasion, another bottle was uncapped and consumed.

Hinde later told police that after he'd left the two men and had gone just a few yards up the road, he heard someone say, 'I'll cut your @#$! throat.'

He turned and saw Simpson on his knees, Murray holding his victim's head back. Hinde watched, apparently frozen, as Murray drew a knife across Simpson's throat. Initially Hinde thought it was a lark and that his friend had applied the back of the knife – until he saw blood gushing out. Hinde said he didn't try to intervene, but simply called out to his friend: 'For God's sake, Bill, come home.'

Murray obliged, leaving Simpson's body partly hidden in a clump of lantana by the side of the road.

According to the forensic evidence, Simpson's throat had been slit with what might be described as military precision. Doctors said Simpson would have been alive for just 20 seconds. As the two men strolled home, Murray said to his mate, 'Don't say anything about this.' To which Hinde replied: 'My oath, not unless I have to.'

That evening, they went to a local dance.

As the two were recovering from their hangovers next morning, Simpson's body was discovered and police took little time to follow the trail to Murray and Hinde, who immediately admitted their involvement. Murray told them he took exception to Simpson, whom he accused of having been rude to his wife, although this was later disputed by the prosecution. Murray's defence was that he'd been in an alcoholic haze at the time, and remembered little of the incident. But during his questioning at the police station, he was able to demonstrate on one of the constables just how he'd sliced his victim's throat.

He told police that before going to the dance he'd gone with Hinde to his parents' house, where he left the murder weapon, telling his father: 'Dad, I went mad. Mind this knife.'

At his trial, Murray, reading from a statement from the dock, cleared his friend Hinde of any responsibility, blaming alcohol for his problems. 'Since my return [from the war] I have taken to drink, and when I am in drink I do not know what I do. I was drinking in the day of the tragedy, and that is why I'm here today.'

His wife told of the times she had had to keep clear of him while he was drinking – 'he goes completely mad' – returning only when he was sober. 'He has complained of his head, and his nerves have got him in such a condition that he trembles all over.'

His Honour, Justice James, told the Central Criminal Court jury that if they thought the accused was in such a state induced by intoxication as not to know what he was doing, they might bring in a verdict of manslaughter, but he advised them not to shirk the issue, not matter how painful it might be.

The members then retired and returned shortly after with a verdict of guilty on the capital charge, but with a strong recommendation for mercy on account of his war service.

The death sentence was duly pronounced. But this was commuted almost three weeks later to imprisonment for the term of his natural life. A short time later Murray's wife and sister personally appealed to the Returned Sailors and Soldiers League to use its influence and push for the sentence to be reduced to life imprisonment, thereby allowing for his eventual release.

The committee declined, stating that it would be 'establishing a dangerous precedent if the league moved for a review of the case by Cabinet'.

*

Charles Sydney Johnson was a Melbourne street criminal and pimp whose reputation for extreme violence was fuelled mainly by his dependence on alcohol and cocaine.

His father was a struggling black American, his mother a white Australian, and his world comprised the grimy backstreets and laneways of Brunswick and Carlton. Not surprisingly, he first became known to local police for minor offences such as illegal gambling, obscene language and unlawful assault. That, however, would change.

In early April 1915, he was implicated in a street murder and charged under his alias of Charles Wilson. A cohort, George Watson, was also charged. According to witnesses, the altercation concerned a racing matter and occurred after much alcohol had been consumed. The victim was George Gregory, a 61-year-old lorry driver.

Jockey Donald McCrae Williamson was a witness to the incident and told police he'd accompanied the pair – who he only knew as Jack and Charlie – from the races on that day. After eating in the city, they went on a pub crawl, first to the International and then to the Builders' Arms, before returning to the International where they joined other drinkers, including Gregory. According to Williamson, a heated argument developed over whether a horse called Tramp had twice won the Onkaparinga Steeplechase in Adelaide. One of the drinkers offered to bet one pound on the outcome, which only intensified the argument. After another round of drinks they dispersed into the street.

Shortly after, more harsh words were exchanged and then a scuffle occurred. Williamson said he then saw Gregory struck from behind by Wilson. The injured man fell to the ground.

After the incident, the jockey walked with Wilson and Watson to Wickham's Coffee Palace in Little Bourke Street, where they slept the night. By the morning, the alcoholic fog was clearing and Williamson recalled saying to Watson: 'The old fellow is pretty bad.' To which came the reply: 'If there is any trouble, you don't want to say anything. Keep quiet and you won't be dragged into it.'

Williamson then retired to Lang's Hotel for a quick heart-starter before going to his own digs. Later in the afternoon he caught up with the pair and was told by Watson: 'The old fellow who was in the brawl last night is dead.'

They then warned Williamson to stay out of town and, if approached by the police, to say nothing. The pair fled Melbourne and later in the week all three assembled at the Wangaratta races, where Williamson was working.

Not long afterwards, Wilson and Watson were picked up by the local constabulary. They were put on a holding charge of vagrancy before being returned to Melbourne, where the charge was upgraded to murder.

Later it would be downgraded to manslaughter, and midway through their trial the Chief Justice, Sir John Madden, directed the jury to return a verdict of not guilty. The reason was not published. The pair walked free.

Six weeks later, in July 1915, the 23-year-old groom walked into the enlistment centre in Melbourne and within a short time was on his way to war with the 7th Battalion.

Johnson found it difficult to shake off his old habits. There was a ready supply of grog and of cocaine for the well-paid Australians, and Johnson took every opportunity. His drug snorting was an open secret among his friends in camp.

Johnson also harboured another addiction – sex. His military records reveal that he contracted VD six times between his enlistment and his discharge and spent 330 days – almost a year – being treated in hospitals on both sides of the English Channel.

And when he wasn't under medical attention, he was banged up in either an English or a French military detention centre. In all, Johnson's sentences totalled 477 days, although he received a number of remissions. His crimes ran the full gamut, from breaking camp and going AWL, to assaulting a fellow digger, to insubordination and drunkenness, escaping from custody and being found in possession of a false pass.

Johnson also had time out after being wounded in France, shot in the left leg on 25 July 1916. Within two days he had been transferred from the 13th General Hospital, Boulogne, to England, where he spent two months convalescing at the Stoke-on-Trent War Hospital in Newcastle.

When he and the army finally parted company in January 1920, Johnson immediately returned to his old haunts in Brunswick and Carlton, working as a hawker. He had also re-established his criminal ties and later took to running a moll, the unfortunate Kathleen Elizabeth Price, who also shared his bed in a Carlton boarding house. They occupied the front bedroom on the second floor, with her daughter, Doris, nine, in a separate room just a few steps away.

It was an impoverished lifestyle and the surrounding houses and boarding places were dilapidated and rat-infested. Then there was the human debris. It was a haven for thieves, prostitutes and vagrants.

It's little wonder that cocaine or 'snow' had reached the slum areas of Melbourne. Historian Chris McConville has described how narcotics were introduced by the 'bright young toughs' who had already done well with illegal liquor trading:

> In the 19th century opiates could easily be bought in city chemists. Opium smokers in Chinatown were discriminated against, but were, at least for several decades, doing little that could be classed as illegal.
>
> With the widespread medicinal use of morphine and other opiates during the First World War, along with experiments in refining cocaine, a new trade appeared. After the Treaty of Versailles Britain had signed off, on behalf of Australia, on laws prohibiting some drugs. These

> laws formed an addendum to global controls to be supervised by the League of Nations. Ex-soldiers and army nurses were by then familiar with refined opiates.
>
> Their demand, along with the new restrictions, allowed some sly groggers to diversify into drugs.

In 1924 a police guide was published for young constables on how to deal with opium smokers, but there was nothing about refined powders or liquids. McConville tells of how police tracked down one trafficker, Henry McEwan, who had moved into narcotics after running a successful sly-grog operation. He was located in Little Lonsdale Street selling packets of the new powder. McEwan told police he was supplying women in the slums, probably in brothels, for two shillings a packet. The drugs were being purchased from chemist shops. Within two years the market had expanded, and so too the number of suppliers. Demand was growing and guns were at the ready to protect operations from standover men.

'Thieves had begun stealing cocaine from chemists' shops, so that limits were placed on dentists using cocaine as an anaesthetic,' McConville writes.

Johnson and Kathleen Price were generally well regarded by the other boarding house residents, who told police they rarely heard a voice raised in anger. But in the wider community Johnson's dependence on cocaine and alcohol, and his associated rages, were well known.

On the night of 1 December 1923, Doris was alone and had crawled into her mother's bed, where she eventually dropped off to sleep. Kathleen had been out working and eventually returned with Johnson about 11 pm. Johnson was high on drugs and alcohol, and quarrelsome. Fearing a confrontation, Kathleen told Doris to go to her own room.

At about 2 am, Doris was awoken by her mother's loud screams, so she climbed out of bed and ran into the room. 'He had my mother by the hair and the bread knife in his hand,' the young schoolgirl recalled.

Johnson ran the knife across her mother's throat and then smacked it across the Doris's face and shouted at her to go away, before discarding it under a sofa, complaining, 'This knife is not sharp enough.'

'He then threw my mother to the floor and put his foot on her. Then he opened a drawer and took out a table knife. I ran screaming down the stairs. My mother was screaming out, "Help, Topsy! He is going to cut my throat."' Topsy was the boarding-house keeper, Clara Aumont.

While Johnson was rummaging in the drawer, Kathleen, covered in blood, rolled under the bed. But that gave her no protection. He reached under the bed and seized one of her legs and dragged her onto the side of the bed. As she struggled to get away, he kicked her in the head and about the face.

He then cut her throat.

In the meantime, Doris had run in to Mrs Aumont and shouted to her: 'Quick, my father is cutting my mother's throat.'

Mrs Aumont took Doris into the front downstairs bedroom, which was occupied by a disabled resident, while Johnson rampaged upstairs. It wasn't long before he ventured down and entered the room, smeared in blood. While he was distracted, Mrs Aumont sent the terrified Doris, still in her nightdress, to fetch the police.

He acted like a madman and did not appear to know what he was doing, Mrs Aumont later told investigators. 'He was like a lunatic and was singing out and was mad. He was not sober, he was drunk, he did not seem to know what he was doing.'

Asked by Clara Aumont what he had done, Johnson just gabbled: 'She is as dead as Julius Caesar. I love that woman, I would go to the gallows for her.'

Doris, dishevelled and her feet badly cut, made it to the Carlton Police Station where, according to a report in the *Argus*, she rushed in and cried: 'A man has Mother by the hair and is cutting her neck with a table knife.'

Two constables immediately ran to the house, one of them carrying the hysterical Doris in his arms. They found the front door open and Johnson standing on the doorstep, dripping blood.

'What is the matter here, Johnson?' one of them asked.

'Nothing,' answered the killer.

'We will go upstairs and see.'

'Yes,' replied Johnson, 'come upstairs and see.'

As they approached the murder scene, the bloodied body of Kathleen Price came into view. 'Did you do this?' Johnson was asked.

'There she is dead, she is dead all right. I will say nothing,' came the reply.

Johnson was handcuffed and taken to the station for charging, but not without a struggle.

At his trial Johnson pleaded not guilty to murder. In a statement from the dock, he said: 'I remember nothing of the affair. The first I knew of it was when I awakened in the cell next morning. I then expressed my horror. I had always been on friendly terms with this woman. All I can say is I am sorry from the bottom of my heart for what has happened.'

There was no question that Johnson had slit her throat, but his defence team argued that he had been in no fit mental state to have formed the intention to kill Kathleen, his brain being so addled by drugs and alcohol. Clara Aumont had given evidence of earlier that night seeing Johnson 'sniffing something up his nose. It was white.'

Johnson's legal counsel told the jury that the evidence showed his client was what was known as a 'cocaine fiend'. 'He cultivated the habit at the war, and he has kept it up ever since,' the lawyer said.

The jury returned with a guilty verdict, but a strong recommendation for mercy.

Johnson showed little emotion when the death penalty was imposed. Asked if he had anything to say, he simply replied: 'No.' The sentence was later commuted to life imprisonment. He died in the Geelong Gaol on 1 July 1939.

*

Johnson's murder trial shone a light on the behaviour of Australian soldiers overseas. Henry Gaw, who fought alongside Johnson in France, told of the extensive use of cocaine among some of the soldiers. Gaw said that when the 'snow' was combined with booze, Johnson would fly into a rage. He told of one incident at the Sutton Veney base in England when the killer assaulted three soldiers in the canteen.

'He had this stuff. I did not know what it was at the time. He had one drink with me and finished up punching three of us,' recalled Gaw.

In an address to the court, his own counsel spoke of the drug's grip on Johnson: 'A man under its influence was without memory, will or the power of forming an intention. He was not merely a lunatic, but was worse in that he had no understanding on what he was doing.'

John Andrew, a childhood friend who later served with Johnson in Sutton Veney, testified that the defendant started sniffing coke while in the military. He boldly asserted that most soldiers who took cocaine did so 'to make them a bit game to go into the trenches'. They did not foresee that tragic after-effects would be felt years later.

# 15

# The Thirties

FOR MANY RETURNED MEN, THE late twenties and early thirties were cruel years. Even VC winners like Joe Maxwell were not immune. After the war, Maxwell married, worked as a journalist on the famous Sydney *Sun* and wrote his popular memoir, *Hell's Bells and Mademoiselles*. But at times the battle of the booze temporarily defeated him. His marriage failed, and he lived in one place then another, even spending time in a psychiatric hospital in Goulburn. Fortunately, he made it through the challenging postwar period, and consolidated his life on the other side of World War II.

Many others never settled. One soldier called Charles Adam Bunney came home from the front line with major psychological issues. He endured regular nightmares and uncontrollable shaking, and became a serious alcoholic.

A capable horseman, Bunney first saw action as a member of the 5th Victorian Mounted Rifles contingent against the Boers in South Africa. The Dutch-Afrikaner settlers had formed themselves into well-organised commando units, and to counter their campaign the British called upon Australian and New Zealand mounted troops. The Frankston carpenter sailed from

Melbourne in early March 1901 with the Left Wing, comprising four squadrons of horsemen.

Private Bunney survived the Boers, returning to Australia wearing the Queen's South Africa Medal with five bars.

In 1914, Bunney, by then aged 40, took the first possible opportunity to get back into uniform, heading off with the 5th Battalion in the first convoy that shipped overseas. His unit landed in Egypt and then it was on to Gallipoli and straight into the action, defending the beachhead at Lone Pine and the Valley of Despair.

Bunney was also deployed at his civilian trade of carpentry and it was while installing beams in a dugout that he was buried after a bomb attack. The panicked private was trapped by heavy timbers and soil. He screamed loudly for help as his mates frantically tried to dig him free. Eventually the debris was cleared and Bunney was lifted out, but much the worse for wear. He had not suffered any major physical injuries, but he was struggling psychologically. As noted in his medical records, he would be afflicted with associated nightmares and constant shaking. Alcohol would take over his life.

After the cave-in, Bunney was not evacuated from Gallipoli. The following March he was elevated to lance corporal, and in the same month was shipped to France, to another killing field. He got some respite after taking a bullet to the left forearm and being transported to Boulogne. But the convalescence would not be without incident.

In one particular episode, Bunney lost control and had an altercation with a Frenchwoman and was arrested. Bunney was accused of entering the woman's home against her will. Madame Bescorp had told his court martial of how Bunney had followed her sister to Madame Bescorp's home at 20 rue Bomarsund, Boulogne, late on the evening of 19 June 1916.

'My sister had shut the door as soon as she entered the house, but the soldier opened it again and walked in,' Madame Bescorp told the inquiry. 'My children began to be afraid, because he looked very cross. I pushed him gently out trying to make him understand that he had to leave.

'When he got in front of my door, in the courtyard, he struck me violently in the face, causing my cheek to swell. A set of false teeth was broken in my mouth. I then hurried away to fetch the police.'

Madame Berthe Waulle described Bunney as being 'drunk', and said that after he'd struck her sister 'violently', he fled the house. But the soldier would not be discouraged. The witness continued: 'He went away, but in the same street he tried to enter different houses.'

He was apprehended a short time later by two British soldiers. Bunney pleaded guilty to having been drunk while on active service, but not guilty to assaulting the Frenchwoman. The tribunal agreed, and gave Bunney the maximum 28 days of the dreaded field punishment no. 1. Having served his sentence, Bunney was sent back into action, working as a stretcher-bearer at Passchendaele, Broodseinde Ridge and the Hindenburg Line, scenes of some of the bloodiest conflicts of the war. By this time, his mental state was deteriorating and his alcohol consumption increasing. His medical records reveal that he often trembled uncontrollably, and suffered lower back pain, erratic heartbeat and irregular breathing. In July 1918 he was repatriated back to Australia.

Once home, he was discharged as medically unfit, and from there he was on a downward spiral. His alcoholism worsened, as did his general health. He was in and out of hospital, and the subject of police attention during some of his drunken episodes. In early November 1927, he tried to kill himself.

According to a report in the *Argus*:

> Charles Bunney, aged 49 years, married of Upwey, was admitted to the Alfred Hospital yesterday morning suffering from a bullet wound in the body. In a statement to hospital authorities he said that he was cleaning a rifle at his home, believing it to be unloaded, when it suddenly discharged, and the bullet penetrated his abdomen. Attracted by the noise, Bunney's wife entered the room and saw her husband lying on the bed with the rifle beside him.

It was clearly a suicide attempt, and after he left hospital Bunney was placed in an institution where his alcoholism could be treated.

But by 1937 he was alone, a widower of limited financial means. He moved from town to town in search of any form of work, before arriving in Dunolly, in central Victoria. With his meagre serviceman's pension, he needed a cheap place to stay and became one of a group of fringe-dwellers rooming in the rundown Windsor Castle, a de-licensed hotel. He struck up a friendship with a fellow resident, a prospector and returned soldier, Robert McCourt Gray, who was also a heavy drinker.

Staying on the floor below was the stockily built Thomas William Johnson, a deranged veteran who had served in the Royal Australian Navy after the war. From early in life, Johnson had suffered uncontrollable violent rages. As a child – one of thirteen growing up in a poor family in Hobart – he had once attacked his father and bedridden mother with a knife, his sister would testify.

Johnson had started work as a farmhand, but a childhood fascination with ships soon led him to the navy, where he signed on for the standard seven years just before he turned eighteen. He became a stoker, and served both at HMAS *Cerberus*, the training depot at Westernport, and in HMAS *Sydney*. At first, his commanding officers signed his character as good, but by late 1922, he was in trouble. He copped 60 days civil imprisonment in Melbourne and was then discharged, services no longer required. Rudely ejected onto civvy street, he returned to labouring but built an extensive criminal rap sheet that ranged from robbery, through to assault and wounding, to larceny.

Johnson also had an addiction to booze, and on the afternoon of 3 October 1938 he was trying to sleep off a hangover when constant banging from Gray's room above sent him into a rage. Grabbing an axe, he stormed up the stairs and thumped his fists on the door. He later confessed to detectives that as soon as Gray opened the door he clouted him with the axe.

The former stoker was 40 years of age, not tall but powerfully built. Gray, a 73-year-old man, didn't stand a chance. Hearing the commotion, Bunney went to Gray's room and saw his friend's bloodied body lying on the floor. He was stunned and didn't say a word. As he looked across at Johnson, the killer launched a series of axe blows. 'I think that I hit Bunney twice, and Gray twice, with the axe,' Johnson said in his statement. 'I gave them a couple of hits while they were lying on the floor, just to make sure. I then locked Gray's door with a small padlock and key. I then went outside and threw the key away.' He added that if anybody else had come along at that moment they would have met the same fate.

Four days later police were contacted by a friend of the two men concerned about their welfare. Police found a bloodstain in the passage, about three feet from the padlocked door. There was also blood on the skirting and panels of the door. The air was thick with an overpowering stench seeping out from under the door of Gray's room.

The dead men were lying on their backs with their heads towards the door. The murder weapon was neatly leaning against a wall, covered in blood.

Strangely, Johnson didn't flee the murder scene. He stayed another two nights before hitching a ride on a transport truck to Melbourne, where four days after the murders he handed himself in to police.

Unshaven, wearing a faded blue overcoat and a shirt open at the neck, Johnson appeared before the court undefended at his trial. He answered sharply, 'Nothing,' when the magistrate asked him if he had anything to say about the charges.

The confession he made to police was chilling in its simplicity: 'I knew that I had killed both of the men with the axe, my only excuse is that Gray was making a noise upstairs when I was trying to have a sleep. I did not want Bunney to be a witness, and that was the reason that I killed him. I was sober when I killed both men. I often get into a bad temper, and I was in a bad temper when I killed Gray.'

The court heard that Johnson had considered 'burning the place down – but it is different burning them cold and burning them hot. Only for the two old fellows [other residents] living there it would have gone up.

'I thought of carrying the bodies to an old mine shaft, but the mess in the room was too great, so I cleared out instead.'

The court heard from a mental health specialist, who concluded Johnson was suffering from a hereditary disease that made him periodically unsound mentally. But another doctor appointed to Pentridge Prison concluded the killer was not insane, nor was he an imbecile – he was just abnormal.

In a statement from the dock, Johnson told the judge: 'I don't know what came over me. These men were my friends. I would never injure them in any way. It is just like a bad dream to me now, but it is coming back to me bit by bit. I am sorry for the deaths of these two old chaps. I leave it in your hands. That is all.'

There were public protests against the hanging of a man who many thought insane. Even the trades and labour council appealed for a stay. But the state was adamant that Johnson should die. And he was prepared to do so. On the morning of 23 January 1939, Johnson declined the spiritual comfort of a chaplain, and when asked on the gallows if he had any last words, brusquely answered: 'Get on with the business.'

*

Sidney George Paul's early start in life was more remarkable than his war record. English-born, Paul was orphaned at 10 and came to Australia as a ship's steward searching for adventure. But after enlisting at Liverpool in February 1915, the 23-year-old clerk and motor driver was off overseas again.

Paul served in France as a member of the 5th Field Ambulance, and his misdemeanours there were petty: once talking on parade, another time being absent for 15 minutes while on picquet duty. All in all a military record that reveals a man focused on his role.

When he disembarked in Sydney in early April 1919, and officially discarded his khaki uniform two months later, Sidney Paul could have counted himself as being among the fortunate.

But his wanderlust returned and by the following year he found himself in Belgium, married to a local girl, Claire Paulon. There he helped his in-laws run a brewery which had been almost destroyed by the Germans during the war. He later travelled to the Congo, where he worked for five years, before returning to Belgium in 1930, starting a small pottery business and a small farm.

The pottery enterprise was short-lived thanks to a landslide, so he and his wife sold the farm and their share of the brewery and headed for England. The aim was to start a sack importing business. But like many of the commercial enterprises associated with the former digger, it failed. That was in 1938, and Paul was forced to get a sales job in London, but he lost that as well. However, instead of telling his wife, Paul would rise every morning, dress in his best suit and head off to his nonexistent workplace. At the end of each week he brought home a 'pay packet', which was actually funded by a secret loan of 150 pounds from his sister.

When Claire Paul became pregnant again, her husband grew desperate. The couple already had four children.

By the October of that year, Paul was deep in debt and depression. In a deranged state, he decided the only way out of the predicament was to kill his wife. On 3 October, he waited until their children had left for church, then went out to the garden shed, where he found a hatchet.

He returned to the house and, in a frenzied attack, beat Claire over the head 15 times. It was a brutal and senseless killing. To try to cover his tracks, the bloodied Paul slashed himself with a razor before running from the house screaming that the couple had been attacked by an intruder. He told police that the man, who had a heavily scarred face, had also stolen 160 pounds from a wardrobe.

To add weight to his story, Paul was clutching a button he claimed he'd wrenched from the 'horrible' attacker's clothing during the struggle in which he was 'knocked out'. But police would later discover the button was common to four others found in a tin in the house. The thread also matched that found on some of the buttons. Detectives carefully examined the garden at Paul's house and found no footprints. The hedge gap had also been blocked with barbed wire.

Police also located the bloodstained hatchet hidden under the verandah.

Paul's story disintegrated entirely after a neighbour told of hearing a scream. Looking through his bedroom window, the neighbour noticed a woman stooping at the window of the sun parlour of Paul's home. He then saw Paul enter the room and bend down, and then pick up an object and begin striking at something on the floor.

Paul was charged with his wife's murder. At his first court appearance, wearing a bandage around his head, he denied any responsibility. 'I had no motive and no desire to kill my wife or injure myself. I did not object to my wife having another child,' he pleaded.

He was found guilty of his wife's murder and sentenced to death. A week later the British Home Secretary, Sir Samuel Hoare, recommended a reprieve.

*

Another returned man, William Cyril Moxley, was in a different category of murderer altogether. In the annals of Australian crime, he was a monster. He suffered severe migraines, and blackouts which doctors attributed to the bullet fragments embedded in his skull. He had acquired this wound not in the service of Empire but as a 'soldier' in the backstreets of Sydney after the war.

Moxley was described as good-looking. His army papers paint the 19-year-old driver as having fair hair and complexion, and grey eyes. But in his police mug shots those eyes have a dull, soulless quality.

He enlisted in Sydney very late in the war, on 13 May 1918. Within two months he was en route to England with the 3rd Battalion. Along the way, he went AWL for two days while stationed at Blackboy Hill camp just out of Perth, and while at sea spent ninety-six hours in detention and forfeited four days pay for making an improper reply to an NCO.

He disembarked in England when the war had just two months to run. He developed a romantic association with young Ada Murphy, a waitress, and married her.

Six weeks after he'd returned to barracks as a married man, Moxley was off on his own adventure, and remained on the run until he was picked up as a deserter and shipped back to Australia. As a khaki criminal, Moxley's ranking is not that high. His wartime offences were not of great significance. He would earn his evil notoriety later, in civilian ranks.

In mid November 1930, he ran into a spot of trouble, up against the violent underworld identity Ernest Edward 'Dicky' Devine. Moxley had been working as a taxi driver when he collected Devine and another man, named Kello, who asked him to take them to some hotels. The group finished up at a local watering hole at Auburn, where the car was parked on a nearby vacant block of land. There they were joined by one of Devine's cohorts, a labourer, Robert Duncan.

Moxley claimed the pair had then tried to induce him into participating in a plan to rob the hotel after closing time. Moxley baulked.

'I don't want to be in this,' Moxley said he told the pair. To which Devine replied: 'Well Snowy, I am going to shoot you.'

'I thought he was joking,' Moxley told police. But Devine then referred to Moxley's reputation as a dog – a police informer. 'You are a friend of Detective Bowie,' Devine put to Moxley, who not surprisingly denied any association.

Unconvinced, Devine leapt out of the car and charged straight to the driver's side window, where he pointed the revolver at his target and pulled the trigger.

'I heard a crash in my ear, and it knocked me across the seat,' Moxley said. The bullet had fragmented on impact, which most probably saved his life.

After recovering his senses, Moxley said he sat up and asked them why he'd been shot, and once again they accused him of being an informer. Moxley again protested his innocence, but not enough to convince his attackers.

Recalled Moxley: 'Devine then said, "I'm going to shoot you again. I'm going to put this bullet right down your neck."' Moxley was pinned to the seat as Devine levelled his revolver at his head, just a few inches from his skull.

'Then he pulled the trigger, but the gun misfired. Devine said, "I can't get this gun to go." I kicked myself free . . . and jumped out of the car and ran away. I met a car, and the driver took me to hospital.'

Moxley didn't stick around for medical treatment. Instead he fled the hospital with pieces of shrapnel still in his skull, where they remained. Devine was arrested later that night still wearing his bloodstained shirt. Moxley's reputation, however, didn't assist in the prosecution's case. The gunmen were acquitted after Moxley, from the witness box, agreed with their legal counsel that he'd been officially declared an habitual criminal.

A few years later, at the Darlinghurst Sessions in March 1923, he pleaded guilty to 20 charges, including house breaking, receiving and stealing in a dwelling. Moxley was not above invoking his very ordinary military record whenever he was in a legal jam. Throwing himself on the mercy of the court, the onetime private pleaded: 'When I got back from the war I was not in good health, and it was a case of "steal or starve". I would rather work than steal.'

The magistrate, no doubt aware of his extensive rap sheet, sent him down for three years with the observation: 'You don't deserve any leniency.'

Moxley soon added blackmail and extortion to his criminal pursuits. Armed and wearing a mask, he would frequent public parks after dark, preying on couples locked in embraces in their parked cars. The surprised lovers would then have to pay for his silence. This was often referred to as 'foxing'.

On the night of 5 April 1932, the scam took on a more sinister tone. Frank Barnaby Wilkinson, 25, and his sweetheart,

Dorothy Ruth Denzel, 21, crossed paths with Moxley at the Strathfield golf links. The couple would be brutally bashed and murdered for just seven shillings.

Medical evidence given at their coronial hearing was stomach-turning, as the government medical officer detailed the severity of the blows Moxley inflicted on his victims. Frank Wilkinson's skull and the upper bones of his neck were shattered. There were black marks evidently caused by gunpowder. Seventy-two pellets of shot and a wad were found in his head. His jaw was broken and there were facial wounds. His wrists had been tied together with a string of brown rug, a stocking and a piece of twine. Death was caused by the shotgun wounds.

Dorothy Denzel was found with her lower undergarments tied around her neck. She had been killed in much the same way as her boyfriend. Her lower jaw was broken in two and her upper jaw was torn away. According to the newspaper accounts of the time 'there had been revolting injuries to the lower part of the body and the young woman had been nearly choked'. It almost goes without saying that she had also been brutally raped.

By the following morning, when the couple had failed to return to their anxious families, police were notified. Their fate remained unknown until almost a week later when a police officer, searching in thick bush near the Holsworthy Military Camp, came across a grassy patch of earth caked with blood. Using a stick, he scraped away some of the soil to reveal a human hand. Assistance was quickly summoned and further digging revealed the body of Frank Wilkinson, who had been buried face down.

The hunt for Dorothy intensified, with police reinforcements and about 100 local farmers combing the area nearby. A breakthrough came the following day when a police officer spotted a black beret on the road at Milperra, not far from

Frank's body. It didn't take long for Dorothy's remains to be located, placed face down in grassy mud about a mile away. Forensic examinations revealed they had both been shot at close range.

The police investigation by this time was tracking well. Moxley was the prime suspect. A manhunt was launched. The day after Dorothy's remains were discovered, the killer knocked on the door of a house in Lakemba. He found a woman called Maria Harding there, alone with her two children, aged three and five.

With the gun in his hand, Moxley told her: 'I want you to give me somewhere to hide. I am in trouble and a man fired at me.' Concerned at what he might do if she refused, Mrs Harding let him inside the house and the two went into the kitchen, where she was made to make him tea. All the while, the agitated fugitive walked nervously about the room, peering through the window blinds for any movement outside.

Later that day when the local butcher made his usual call, Moxley warned her: 'If you tell him I'm here, I'll hurt you.' Moxley hid in the house until the butcher left. After that she cooked him two chops and made him more tea, before he finally left the house about four o'clock in the afternoon.

The search for Moxley intensified.

He remained on the run for another week, during which time he grabbed a bicycle and brazenly rode it across the Sydney Harbour Bridge, which had been officially opened just the previous month and was still something of a novelty even to locals.

Then, on 17 April, searchers discovered a rough camp close to Sydney's outskirts, with newspapers gathered together as a makeshift bed and the remnants of a fire. Police concluded that Moxley must have panicked and fled the area, because he'd left behind a chaff bag stuffed with old clothes. They also found his shotgun, which turned out to be the murder weapon.

The extensive hunt for Moxley ended when two patrolling police officers nabbed him at French's Forest. The arrest was not without its drama when Moxley, alerted to their presence by the sound of a twig snapping underfoot, made a desperate dash for freedom down a rock-strewn hillside. But he was eventually overpowered by the pursuing constables, who leapt onto his back and cuffed him.

In custody, Moxley denied killing the couple, at first blaming a man he knew only as 'Snowy'. The truth eventually emerged and in a statement to police he revealed how he'd encountered the young couple after parking his truck near the golf links. Moxley said he was short of cash and saw a chance of filling his wallet. He went over to the two, who were sitting in the grass, and demanded money.

'The man said he had only seven shillings. The girl took it from his pocket and gave it to me,' Moxley told detectives. 'I walked round the motor car, and then the man rushed at me. We came to grips but I must have hit the man first. I had nothing in my hand when I hit him.

'The girl did not cry out; she seemed terrified. I then told the girl that if she cried out I would hurt her. I tied the man's hands, and put him in the back of the motor car. I told the girl to sit beside me.'

Moxley claimed he then drove his terrified captives to Liverpool, where he took them into an empty house and left them trussed up while he got some petrol. Moxley said after he returned and untied them, the man had attacked him.

'We had another fight. I don't remember what really happened. I cannot remember anything being said or done. All I know is that we were both fighting and struggling on the ground.

'From then on my memory is blank.'

Moxley's memory loss left the jury unconvinced, and they returned a verdict of guilty. Justice Sir Percival Halse Rogers passed sentence of death: 'You have been found guilty of one of the most foul crimes that has ever been known in this state. Everything that could be done on behalf of the defence was done by your counsel, and in my opinion, the jury has come to the only conclusion that was open to it.'

Moxley, in mitigation, expressed remorse over his actions and revealed the violent circumstance of his childhood. His father had been shot to death. Then, when Moxley was just 10, he accidentally shot his brother dead, and was discharged by the coroner at the inquest.

His head wounds, he said, were the consequence of 'doing a service for the police', which had caused him memory loss and contributed to uncontrollable rages.

It was later revealed that during his trial Moxley had tried to take his own life by smothering himself under his blankets, but was stopped by the duty warder. He was then placed under a special watch with a guard stationed outside his open cell during the day, and another at night when the door was locked. A warder was also posted between Moxley and any visitors.

But the double murderer and rapist ultimately embraced his sentence, even writing to the New South Wales Minister for Justice urging him to apply the death penalty. He was duly hanged on 18 August 1932.

His last hours were spent in the company of his Salvation Army chaplain, Colonel Pennell, to whom he entrusted his personal diary. On his last night, just before he was transferred from the observation ward to the death cell, Moxley apparently wrote:

> Colonel Pennell and I have spent a happy night together. We looked for my star. It appeared at 5.25 am. We gazed at it together. It is my guiding light.

> I shall leave here at 7.45 am to go to B cell. It does not worry me as death is sweet to me. I have said goodbye to my friends and relatives on this earth. I know I shall be with my mother by 9 o'clock today. I shall know the great secret. My mind is at rest and I have put my trust in God. He has led me for 12 days. This morning I shall have no breakfast but Holy Communion.
>
> If I cannot get help from that then nothing will help me.

With the rope around his neck, Moxley turned to his confidant and asked: 'You will bury me, won't you, Colonel?'

'I will, Bill,' replied the chaplain.

With that, the trapdoor opened and William Cyril Moxley dropped through the gap.

# 16

# Two Brothers

WHEN WORLD WAR I BROKE OUT, the Hopkins boys from Melbourne were among the first to answer the call to arms, enlisting on the same day at Broadmeadows. They joined the 7th Battalion led by Lieutenant Colonel 'Pompey' Elliott, one of the boldest Australian officers the war produced.

Though they were assigned to different companies, for a time the military career of these brothers, former grammar school boys, followed similar paths. Both of them would very quickly become commissioned officers, and both would be wounded in action a number of times and cited for courage. But while one would be awarded the Military Cross and bar, the other would have his medal disallowed, along with all the standard service decorations.

The older brother, Joseph Walton Hopkins, came home from the war as Major Hopkins, a decorated hero who had been wounded on three occasions. His Military Cross and bar underscored a fine military record. It was near Ypres in early October 1917 that the then Captain Hopkins impressed his superior officers with his courage and leadership, rallying the men of his company when four of their platoon commanders were hit and leading them to the battalion's objective. He also exposed himself to enemy fire through his personal reconnaissance. 'His courage and coolness inspired not only his own Company but the other Companies of the Battalion under circumstances of great danger and difficulty,' his citation read.

The following month Captain Hopkins added a bar to his medal for his actions during a similar encounter with the enemy. Around the same time as he was presented at Buckingham Palace and lauded for his dedication to duty, his younger brother Ernest stood before a court martial and was stripped of his rank. It was a cruel blow to the boys' parents, Mary and Joseph, a hard-working and respectable couple from Moonee Ponds.

Even before the war, Ernest had found himself in trouble. In 1912, the young clerk fell foul of the law after a series of strange incidents at Albury, on the Victoria–New South Wales border, where he was working. He came under strong suspicion over a fire which had been deliberately lit in one of the rooms of the Albury Hotel.

Hopkins had been a guest and it was the second blaze at the old pub within a week. In the second fire, the blinds and bedclothes had caught alight in room 1. Police had found the window slightly open at the top and the bottom, which would have given the arsonist an opportunity to throw a match through the window from the balcony.

When an inquiry into the fire was held at the Albury Courthouse, Hopkins was required to give evidence. Standing before the coroner, he denied setting fire to the hotel room. He said that on the night of the second blaze he'd been drinking with a fellow named Gibson, and just before midnight he'd passed room 1 and 'there was nothing wrong'. Back in his own accommodation in room 9 he slept soundly, he said, until he was roused by the fire alarm.

Asked by the coroner to give his current address, he answered 'Albury Gaol'. Since the fire, he had been on remand over two theft charges, which had yet to be heard. The Albury Police Court was told that a constable had been called to the hotel after a complaint from one of the guests about five stolen shirt collars, valued at two shillings and six pence. Police found new collars in Hopkins's drawer, and the victim claimed them as his own. Hopkins vigorously denied they were stolen, saying he had bought the items in Melbourne where 'there were hundreds of such collars sold'. There was a second charge against him for having refused to pay three pounds owing on his hotel meals and accommodation.

The case was held over for a week to allow Hopkins an opportunity to arrange his defence. A week later, police told the police magistrate 'they had made enquiries as to the character of the accused and had received satisfactory replies from Melbourne'. His Melbourne connections, no doubt his parents, must have also stumped up the cash for his hotel bill, because the hotel keeper asked that Hopkins be excused after the three-pound debt had been paid.

Hopkins was only 19, an inexperienced young man from a decent family, who had got himself into trouble while away from home. The magistrate told Ernest he would give him the benefit of the doubt, and sent him on his way. Soon after, Ernest joined the Royal Australian Navy, and made it to acting able seaman, but in late 1913 was discharged, 'services no longer required'. Although his last assessment there was officially 'satisfactory', his naval records also reveal that he served his last two months under sentence of imprisonment.

That was that, until the following year, when Ernest and Joseph signed up, and were handed over to Pompey Elliott's tender care; known for his stern discipline of the 7th Battalion, Elliott was just the right man for the job.

The 7th was part of the first AIF convoy, embarking in mid-October for the Middle East. From there it went on to Gallipoli, and participated in the landing on 25 April 1915. Five days later, Ernest was made up to lance corporal. He took part in the Krithia charge, four miles north of Cape Helles, and received a gunshot wound to the foot. He was evacuated on a hospital ship to Malta, where he was treated at the military hospital at Mtarfa. Two months later he was discharged as fit for service, but his progression was halted when the lance corporal was busted for AWL and drunkenness. Not for the first time, he showed he had no head for alcohol.

The demoted private was also dogged by a series of highly personal ailments, including orchitis and epididymitis, painful inflammations of the testicles. By January 1916, Ernest was well enough to rejoin the 7th Battalion; two months later he was elevated to second lieutenant and was on his way to Marseilles. It would prove to be a memorable tour of duty.

In August 1916 he was severely reprimanded by a court martial for being drunk, then several weeks later he was wounded in action with gunshot wounds in the wrist and back. After spending almost three weeks at the 2nd Field Ambulance in France, Hopkins packed his gear and headed back into combat.

On the night of 30 September, Hopkins earned a citation for his 'gallantry, initiative and his leadership' in a raid against the Germans at the Ypres Salient. According to his CO, Hopkins, in charge of one group of men, had 'on four different occasions personally protected his bayonet men by using his revolver. (As well), he kept his men well in hand during the raid, and withdrew them successfully'.

Ernest Hopkins was the 7th Battalion's intelligence officer, and a month or so later he travelled from France to England on military business. There, he experienced a meltdown, going

AWL and staying on the run for 57 days. Finally apprehended in London, he was packed off to the dermatological hospital at Bulford, where he remained for three months with a particularly angry strain of VD.

Brought before a court martial, Hopkins claimed amnesia, giving evidence he'd been in a fog during much of his illegal absence. From his halting recollections, Hopkins was able to scramble together an explanation of sorts. He told the presiding officers he recalled travelling from France to England, and going from Liverpool to London to purchase some kit in preparation for his return to the front. But from that time the curtain had descended; his head was in no-man's-land for the next 55 days.

'From that moment I have no recollection of anything that happened,' he testified. 'On the 30th January I was walking along Southampton Row and I saw an officer at a distance whom I had known intimately on Gallipoli. I did not speak to him.

'When I saw him I suddenly realised who I was and where I was. A little while after I looked at my Pay Book. From my Pay Book I found I had drawn money during the time my mind was a blank. I found I had a little money.'

He then went to AIF Headquarters in Horseferry Road, central London – not to hand himself in, but to pick up some cash from the pay office. He was apprehended when one of the clerks there cross-referenced his name against an official list of absentees.

Hopkins told the court martial that he'd had bad nerves a month or two before going missing. This he attributed to the encounter on 30 September that resulted in his mention in orders. After the raid he and his unit were sent into action again at Gueudecourt, on the Somme battlefield. Though traumatised, he went through another battle there: 'I used to suffer from dreams and nightmares.'

Under cross-examination, Hopkins said he could recall visiting his brother, who was convalescing from wounds at an Australian Auxiliary Hospital in South Kensington. But he had no memory at all of going to the AIF pay office.

The prosecution described Hopkins's account as a 'remarkable story' in which he appeared to be rational up to a certain period of his leave.

'(But) from a certain date he remembers nothing further, nothing from the time he got into the taxi, after he bought the articles of the kit, until about seven weeks afterwards when walking along Southampton Row he sees a friend from the 7th Battalion. The court will consider that story. It undoubtedly appears the accused is in a low state of health.

'It seems strange that if this is true, as the accused alleges, that he remembers nothing. It seems strange that no one can say that he looked after him or took care of him during this time. He had been taken care of; London is not a place of philanthropists. He was in somebody's care. It is strange nobody has come forward.'

What the prosecution failed to say was by that stage of the war medical specialists knew that shell shock was not only associated with concussion from a direct blast. Thousands of men serving at the front also reported symptoms including amnesia, recurring nightmares and pain in the head. As a contemporary study examining brain trauma occurring in the period from World War I to Afghanistan observes, 'when it had become clear that many cases of shell shock were not directly related to a head injury, military medical authorities attempted to restrict use of the diagnosis. Servicemen invalided from the front were given a preliminary label of "not yet diagnosed, nervous", and those who failed to recover but had no visible cerebral injury were then classified as "neurasthenic".'

In other words, someone like Ernest Hopkins could not expect much sympathy from the presiding officers at his court martial, especially as he had gone AWL a second time, while awaiting his hearing. After his discharge from the VD hospital, Hopkins was placed in close arrest at the Bhurtpore Barracks in Tidworth. In mid-May 1917, he slipped his guard and scarpered to nearby Salisbury, where he remained for a couple of days, until his arrest in the bar of the Crown Hotel.

'Anxiety and worry made me fed up, and longing for a few hours' freedom, I went to Salisbury not realising the enormity of my offence or the very serious injury I was doing my escort,' he told the disciplinary hearing.

Things looked very bad for Hopkins. But from out of the gloom came a glowing character assessment by his superior officer, who praised the lieutenant's courage and dedication, and was able to pinpoint all the major engagements in which he'd served. It was an impressive list.

'I know the second officer before the court,' the captain began. 'He left Australia with the original 7th Battalion, as a private. He gained all his promotion through distinction in the field. He has been present at the defence of the Suez Canal in 1915; landing on Anzac with the 2nd Brigade at Cape Helles; left two days before the evacuation. He was at the defence of the Canal in 1916; he came to France with the 1st Division; was present at Fleurbaix, Messines; at the first and second Pozières; at the Bluff at Ypres; at first Gueudecourt.

'He took part in a raid in conjunction with me at Ypres Salient on the night of 30 September to 1 October 1916; he was mentioned in orders for his part in that raid; it was in Battalion orders. He was recommended for a Military Cross. I know of no other orders. I left the Battalion shortly afterwards.

'In the fighting line he is an excellent soldier. I do not know a better one in the battalion. To the personal bravery of this Officer was mainly due to the success of that raid.'

On 23 July 1917, Ernest Hopkins was cashiered, and shipped back to Australia. But it seems he could not stay away from the army. In Melbourne on 20 December he signed up again and was sent to the Broadmeadows camp, where he was elevated to corporal.

Hopkins would see out the war in camp, while the doctors again wrestled with his claims of amnesia. According to his official medical history, he claimed to have lost his memory for up to five days in May 1918. A memo from three of his senior officers stated: 'Eight days ago he again had loss of memory extending over four or five days. Has had pain in the head . . . also subject to nightmares . . . otherwise health good.'

Another entry noted that Hopkins suffered lapses of memory. 'These are either genuine or not genuine. If genuine, he is unfit for the A.I.F. – if not genuine, he should be dismissed.' It recommended his case be brought before a specialist medical board.

By the end of October, repeated examinations of Hopkins were unable to detect any 'abnormal' features associated with memory loss. There was a strong recommendation that he should be discharged from the hospital and immediately returned to the AIF. Within two days, Ernest Hopkins was discharged from the military as 'Medically unfit – disability amnesia'. Ten days later the war in Europe ended.

*

Out of khaki, Ernest Hopkins became Ernest Andrew Loughrey or James Grayly, depending on the charges or which judges he was facing.

By April 1920, Ernest James Hopkins was known to police as a petty thief. At Melbourne's City Court, police told how he'd been apprehended after pilfering an overcoat and a razor from a bedroom in Parer's Hotel, Bourke Street. The bench applied some leniency and gave him a bond after telling him they saw a chance of him reforming. But no sooner had he signed the papers and walked out through the courthouse's heavy wooden doors than he was collared by a detective who frogmarched him to the nearby watch house to be charged with two further counts of larceny from the same hotel, and another of illegal possession.

A year later he was back in court pleading guilty to housebreaking. This time he was luckier: the Chief Justice, Sir William Irvine, deferred sentence, releasing him on a two-year good behaviour bond. In September, Hopkins was charged, as Ernest Andrew Loughrey, with having been found in a dwelling house without lawful excuse. For that he was given 18 months jail.

After he had served his sentence, Hopkins seems to have tried to make a normal life for himself, even finding himself a job. But he couldn't manage.

At a court hearing in the following June, prosecutors applied to have his original good behaviour bond struck out and an immediate sentence imposed. Hopkins pleaded for leniency claiming his workplace had become 'intolerable' after colleagues learned he was on a court-imposed bond for theft. As well, the club at which he was a member was also informed of his criminal status, and the executive summoned him to a meeting at which he was given the ultimatum of resignation or expulsion.

'That night I took to drink,' he told the chief justice. 'I know it is a pitiful excuse, but it is the only one I have to offer.'

Sir William said that 'wisely or unwisely' he had extended Hopkins an indulgence mainly because of his guilty plea, even though he had several previous convictions for larceny against his name.

'As far as I know you are the first man to whom such an indulgence has been extended, to be brought back for sentence,' the judge told Hopkins. 'It is essential that, if this merciful practice which is sometimes adopted, should be continued, the conditions under which men are allowed their liberty should not in any case be broken. I cannot give any weight to what you had to say.'

With that, 'Iceberg' Irvine, as he was known, slotted Hopkins for the original 12 months, to be served concurrently with his present sentence.

In Pentridge, Hopkins was detailed to help load hay onto a horse-drawn wagon. He could not fight temptation. Choosing the right moment, he crawled into the hay and remained there until the wagon departed. Near Royal Park, Carlton, he carefully climbed down, leaving behind some of his prison uniform. Then he headed straight to Moonee Ponds, where he changed into street clothes.

By this time, his absence from Pentridge had been noticed and the alarm raised, but the escapee was well and truly gone. Hopkins stayed free for about three weeks until he was arrested at a Salvation Army home in Newcastle, New South Wales. For local police it was a two-for-one result, for they found another former inmate of Pentridge sleeping in the same room. The pair was undoubtedly up to no good: a search of the lodging uncovered two pairs of leather gloves, a tin of pepper, and a short iron bar that had been hidden under a pillow.

Hopkins's partner in crime was William Westley Higgins, who had been serving a two-and-half-year stretch for house-breaking and illegally using a motor car. He and two others had broken into a warehouse near Toorak railway station and made off with cloth, ribbons and other material valued at 100 pounds. They had been arrested driving along Glenferrie Road in the leafy Melbourne suburbs of Hawthorn. When they were pulled up by patrolling police, a search of their car revealed a jemmy. Higgins, according to the evidence, took police to a house in nearby East Kew where the stolen materials were handed over. Slotted for two years, Higgins had managed to escape from incarceration while undergoing treatment for an eye injury sustained in the jail's machinery shop.

Like Hopkins, Higgins had served in khaki, but he was a late recruit to the war, enlisting in Rockhampton, central Queensland, in August 1918. He remained in Australia until his discharge at the end of December, yet that didn't discourage him over the years from pursuing war medals in letters which had the official return addresses of His Majesty's penal establishments at Pentridge and at Bathurst.

After their capture, Higgins and Hopkins were back in the Supreme Court, before Judge Woinarski. He handed them additional two-year sentences. They immediately appealed the penalties. Hopkins, under one of his assumed names, Loughrey, argued that he wasn't given the opportunity during the trial to put his plea before the court, claiming he'd been sentenced without being heard. The Chief Justice invited him to explain his actions to the court. Hopkins told of how he had climbed onto the wagon when the warder's view was blocked, and didn't alight until his transport reached Royal Park. But when the prosecution asked how he'd managed to change out of his prison clothes, Hopkins made no reply. Nonetheless, both he and Higgins had a year lopped off their additional sentences.

In 1940, Higgins, then in khaki again, hit rock-bottom when he was convicted of stealing petty cash collected for Australia's 'Patriotic Fund'. The 42-year-old soldier pleaded guilty in Brisbane to taking a collection tin from a 13-year-old schoolgirl on the pretext of assisting her. He then collected cash from bystanders and pub patrons before fleeing with 30 shillings or so.

As for Ernest Hopkins, after he served his time he disappeared from public view, a victim of his weakness for booze but also of his traumatic experiences of war. His brother, Joseph, became a successful and long-lived fruit grower along the Murray River.

# 17

# Three Lives

THOMAS GROGAN DIDN'T HESITATE WHEN he heard that his captain was stranded in no-man's-land during a particularly nasty exchange with the enemy at the Battle of Fromelles. After all, this young digger from outback New South Wales had already covered the ground several times that day and made it back safely each time.

'Has anyone seen the captain?' the colonel of the 30th Battalion asked the assembled group of men.

It transpired that the Germans had shot Captain Blair Anderson Wark in both legs, and the wounded man remained where he fell, in a trench belonging to the enemy.

Informed of his officer's predicament, the colonel said, 'God help him! I can't ask any man to go out into that hell after him.' But from the crowd came the call 'Hell for me!', and Tommy Grogan, the horseman from Bourke, stepped forward, saluted and volunteered to crawl back out.

Grogan eventually came across Captain Wark trapped in heavy mud up to his waist, with three wounded Germans close by. The *Bathurst Times* later recounted the legendary episode:

> Everything but his braces had gone and the liquid fire was gradually creeping up. The captain was in great pain and fading, but Grogan extricated him from the bog, and dragged him up an 18-foot parapet to the safety of the Australian trenches.
>
> Tommy managed to get him to the top, and had to throw him over – broken legs and all – to the other side. The machine guns were hailing bullets, and the captain told his soldier to put him in a shell-hole and save himself. But Tommy said, 'We will live or die together.'

In the scramble back to their lines, Captain Wark was hit again, but his rescuer copped not a scratch. Once they'd made it, Grogan collapsed from exhaustion and remained unconscious for five hours. Within a fortnight of his brave deed, the private was promoted to corporal. He also won the Military Medal. In the citation, the battalion's commander lauded his courage 'alone and in the face of very heavy artillery fire'.

On paper at least, Grogan and Wark had quite a bit in common: they were both country boys and just 22 when the rescue took place. But from then on, their lives took very different paths.

Wark recovered from his wounds. In November 1916, he joined the 32nd Battalion and soon distinguished himself as a brave leader. Promoted to major, he became one of Australia's highest decorated soldiers with a Victoria Cross and a Distinguished Service Order.

His entry in the *Australian Dictionary of Biography* tells the story:

> Experienced and self-reliant, careless of his own safety, yet solicitous for his men, at the age of 24

> Wark was given temporary command of the 32nd Battalion in operations against the Hindenberg line that began on 29 September 1918. Often moving ahead of his troops in the face of heavy fire, he secured the help of a passing tank near Bellicourt and attached 200 leaderless Americans to his command before rushing a battery of 77mm guns which were firing at his rear companies: he captured four guns and two of their crews. With two non-commissioned officers, he surprised and captured fifty Germans near Magny-la-Fosse. On 1 October he dashed forward and silenced machine-guns which were causing heavy casualties. For his bravery he was awarded the Victoria Cross.

Grogan was wounded in the knee in 1917, and after treatment returned to the front line. Then his number came up. In mid-March 1918, he sustained a serious gunshot wound in the left leg and was sent to England to recuperate. He would not be fit for front-line service again.

His war service papers show that he had a fine record overall. His young wife, Nellie, had reason to be proud of him. So did the people of Cobar, where Thomas and Nellie were living when he signed up. They obviously had an investment in him, for before he went off to war they formally presented him with a set of military brushes.

But something went badly wrong with Grogan's life after the war. Perhaps it was thanks to his bung leg, which evidently was never the same again, though he returned to work as a labourer. In 1919, the *Western Age* newspaper, Dubbo, reported that Grogan, who was still undergoing treatment for his injuries, had been granted a service pension of eleven shillings threepence weekly: 'How he is to live on this inadequate allowance until such time as he is able to work, is . . . not stated.' The Cobar Soldiers' Red Cross Committee referred his case to the local member of parliament, apparently without success.

In May 1920, Grogan was charged in Brisbane with having stolen in company a bag containing more than 400 pounds from a leading local businessman. Norman Edgar Bayard, a family member of Bayards Pty Ltd, a major Brisbane retailer, had been carrying the day's takings to the bank. He was travelling on a tramcar, sitting with the bag between his feet. When he alighted at his stop, the bag and money were missing. It was a daring heist, but it didn't take long for police to round up the gang of four, and within a short time they were all informing on one another.

When confronted with the evidence that he'd received 70 pounds from the heist, Grogan allegedly spat out: 'I was only the tool in this matter, and was taken over to do any stoushing that may have been necessary. If they got 400 pounds, I am the mug again, as I did not get my whack.'

Grogan, alas, got his 'whack' in the District Court when he was slotted for nine months.

*

Grogan had always kept bad company, even before he enlisted. Before the war, his circle included a youth named Cyril Emanuel White who had been out of control from an early age. When White was just 16, he was convicted of assault in company.

In 1912, White was in trouble again, this time charged, along with another man named Robert Hagar, of robbery under arms. Both men went armed with revolvers, and on a single day, in separate incidents, they held up two Chinese vegetable growers near Cobar.

According to the police evidence, the pair first went to the gardens of Goo Leong on the pretence of buying melons. They produced a revolver and aimed it at the gardener's head. A bullet was fired, just missing the man's ear. Then while one of the robbers held him at gunpoint, the other searched the house and took about five pounds and some jewellery. Before fleeing, they threatened that if Goo Leong gave them any trouble they would kill him once they were released from jail.

An hour or so later they confronted Goo Leong's business partner, Luey Ah Long, as he was returning in his horse-drawn cart to the garden. He later told police he'd been accosted at gunpoint. He said Hagar had been wearing a handkerchief or calico round his top lip at first, but it later slipped down revealing his face.

Both men were waving their revolvers about when White demanded his cash. 'I haven't much money,' the market gardener told them. To which White replied: 'I want money, you yellow @#$!.' Then he added: 'Go on, we want money quick; me bushranger.'

Luey Ah Long told the pair: 'All right, you want money, I give it to you.' He handed them about a pound, in silver and copper. But it wasn't enough; they ordered him from the cart while they searched for any cash or valuables that might be there. Coming away empty-handed, they sent him on his way with White's warning: 'Don't come back to Cobar,' adding that if he made trouble he would kill him.

For the police, it was not a hard case to crack. Luey Ah Long gave detailed descriptions of the pair. He'd known them since they were youngsters, and White had often been to the garden.

The suspects were arrested at their respective family homes and charged. A gun was found in White's bed, but he had no idea how it got there. Both pleaded not guilty, claiming they were nowhere near the scenes of the robberies, and nor had they seen each other for several days.

Family members provided alibis, but these were shaky at best. Not for the last time, Thomas Grogan stepped forward to testify that he'd been playing billiards with White at the very time he was alleged to have held up the two men.

Grogan was then a labourer at the Fort Bourke gold mine. He testified under oath that he was known to White, and on the day in question had 'seen him in the front of the Commercial billiard room, and had a game of billiards with him' which took between 30 minutes and an hour. White and Hagar's lawyers argued that the Crown had not established guilt beyond all reasonable doubt, and asked for an acquittal.

The prosecution pointed to glaring contradictions in the accounts of witnesses called by the defence. The case wasn't assisted by the open displays of chortling by young friends of the accused during some of the police evidence.

The jury found both men guilty. Sentencing the pair, Judge Gibson said it was a 'great pity' that he hadn't the power to order them both a flogging. With that he slotted Hagar for 18 months with hard labour at Goulburn, and White for three years.

White was not long out of jail when he assaulted a woman in Nyngan, in central New South Wales. He was convicted on two charges. It was his third serious conviction, yet when he later fronted a Queensland recruiting centre to enlist, it was as if he had spent the previous three years in a recreation camp. To question nine on the attestation, 'Have you ever been convicted by a civil power?', the ex-con answered, 'No'.

This was not an ideal beginning to White's military career, and within the fortnight he was on the lam, wanted as a deserter. Two months later he would be given another chance when he signed up again, this time at the Enoggera Barracks near Brisbane. He was sent to the killing fields of France with the 9th Battalion in March 1916.

At Étaples, White cooled his heels for about six months at the 1st Australian Divisional Base Depot before heading off, remaining on the run for just over three months before he was picked up by military authorities. He was sent directly to the field punishment compound at Étaples while the paperwork was being completed for his court martial. But White wasn't for hanging around. After two days he broke out of the compound, and this time he put a distance between himself and his pursuers, crossing the English Channel. He later maintained he'd travelled freely after obtaining a leave pass and boat warrant from an Australian soldier attached to the 1st Division Headquarters. White couldn't recall the soldier's name but remembered handing him 30 francs.

Four months later he was arrested in London by an alert English bobby, William Pell. The constable asked White for his pass and was handed a combined leave and railway ticket, which immediately raised his suspicions.

'I arrested him,' Pell wrote in his statement, 'and escorted him to the police station where I searched him and found three rubber stamps. The accused gave his name as No. 4203 Private William John Greenwood, 1st Pioneer Battalion AIF.' William Greenwood did in fact exist, and was at that moment where he should have been, with his unit in France.

Meantime, White was also found to have picked up something else on his travels – a bad case of venereal disease. The authorities packed him off to Bulford, where on 10 August the management received an official communiqué from the AIF's assistant provost marshal, alerting them to their new patient and urging them to keep a close eye on him.

'The above named soldier was this day admitted to your hospital for treatment. I beg to inform you that this man is a prisoner awaiting trial on very serious charges and I shall be glad if you will have kept him under strict surveillance. Kindly notify me twenty-four hours prior to discharge in order that I can make the necessary arrangements for escort.'

But within days White had escaped.

By this time it also appears that White had taken a wife, Georgina Jessie, who resided at Old Swan, an inner area of Liverpool. In August 1917, at the height of her husband's war with the army, she told investigators she had not laid eyes on him for the past two months, although she had received a letter from him the previous week. It was postmarked Bulford Hospital, Salisbury Plain.

The missing prisoner was eventually apprehended on 3 September in Liverpool, where police caught him in the act of casing a bicycle shop. A local detective sergeant, Alfred William Roberts, spotted the fugitive digger, even though White was wearing civvies: 'I asked him for his registration papers and he said he belonged to Ireland and did not require any. I was not satisfied with his answers and arrested him.'

The suspect was taken immediately to the police station, where he was searched. The arresting officers found a handcuff key and a blank travelling warrant in the lining of his trousers. He was charged with being in unlawful possession of a bicycle and with being a deserter. White had told the arresting officer that he'd fled from the 2nd Manchester Regiment, but it was only a matter of time before his real identity was discovered, and on 15 September White was handed over to the AIF.

A fortnight later he was on the run again, albeit for just a few hours. White was with eight other prisoners in Rochester Row Police Station when he and two cellmates broke out, shortly after the 10 am check. Their cell door had been unlocked for another prisoner who was in a lavatory. According to the official police report: 'The accused escaped by cutting and bending an iron bar of the grid iron of the cell passage window, which had been severed by a fretwork saw.'

White's freedom was fleeting. By 7.30 pm he'd been recaptured and frogmarched back to the lock-up. Three weeks later he was away again, and that was the last the army would see of the runaway soldier. Almost two and a half years later, in an internal memorandum from AIF headquarters in London, White was discharged from the Australian Imperial Force on account of his desertion.

'He therefore forfeits all claim on the Government of the Commonwealth of Australia to any Service leave which may be granted in respect of military service, also all monies which may be decided upon as gratuities in respect of War Service, and furthermore, forfeits all claim on the A.I.F, or Australian Commonwealth Government to provide, for him or his dependants a free passage to Australia,' the memo stated.

*

The year after he finished serving his time for the Bayard robbery, Grogan crossed the border into New South Wales. There he chose a less energetic means of relieving victims of their cash – the old three-card trick.

The Darlinghurst Sessions was told of how Grogan had engaged a 'mad man' to cheat and defraud one Algernon George Keen of 28 pounds. It was on the morning before Armistice Day 1921 when the Granville builder bumped into Grogan, who told him he was a stranger from the west. Together they visited a hotel in George Street. There they were joined by a third man and, perhaps unwisely, Keen accompanied them to nearby Moore Park.

While there, the trio were approached by the so-called mad man, who told them he had just broken out of a hospital and, producing three cards from his pocket, said: 'I lost 50 pounds yesterday to a doctor who taught me this game.'

The sting then began in earnest. The mad man shuffled the cards about and the nominated card was 'selected' several times.

The mad man said he would bet anything up to 30 pounds. Grogan and his partner invested one pound each, and Keen removed his wallet from his coat. Just as he opened the wallet, Grogan reached across and plucked 28 pounds in notes, much to Keen's surprise, and put them into the pot. The card-sharp quickly shuffled the three cards and spread them on the ground, face down. The wrong card, not unexpectedly, was turned up, and when Keen protested that he had not intended to bet such a large amount of cash, the mad man immediately snapped up the notes telling him: 'You've lost.'

Keen then walked away, but was joined shortly afterwards by Grogan, who told him: 'I knocked the man and grabbed all the money I could get, which was two pounds. We will split it up.'

The victim reported the incident to police, along with detailed physical descriptions. Grogan and the others were rounded up and later charged with conspiracy to cheat and defraud. In a statement from the dock, Grogan denied any association with the mad man, but admitted playing the game, adding, 'I did nothing dishonest.'

The jury was unimpressed and returned a guilty verdict. Grogan's front-line experiences were again aired, and well received by the judge, who said: 'I intended to impose a sentence of three years imprisonment, but I have taken into consideration the prisoner's military service, and the bravery he displayed. I will therefore halve the sentence, which will be 18 months hard labour in Bathurst Gaol.'

After his release Grogan returned to Queensland and to his old ways, lifting almost 10 pounds from a country visitor he encountered in Brisbane. Grogan and the genial Albert Keith Hill struck up a friendship during which the swindler, now calling himself Delaney, told his mark he knew just the man who could give him a job. Not surprisingly, Hill was happy to meet this man, who purported to be a wealthy squatter from Longreach.

Grogan's methods were the same as before. A quick trip to Victoria Park was suggested. There they rested on the grass and discussed Albert Hill's exciting future. Within no time a 'weird individual' approached with bank notes protruding from his pockets. As the police court in Brisbane was later told, this 'mad man' asked the trio: 'Where is he? Where is he?'

'Where is who?' asked the purported squatter.

The mad man told the story of how he had lost 100 pounds, but how he had discovered a new trick by which he was going to win the money back. Three cards were produced and the squatter accepted the mad man's challenge to try to pick out the queen, for which he offered five pounds for a wager of just ten shillings. Not surprisingly, the squatter won.

With that, Hill excitedly threw down his 12 pounds and before he could nominate his card, a blue started between the others – no doubt a strategic distraction. The mad man was last seen scampering away with the cash and the cards.

Grogan and the squatter chased after him and returned shortly after, claiming to have headed him off. They handed Hill two pounds, advising him to go 'while the going was good'. But Hill stood his ground, demanding more money. He was given an extra five shillings.

Hill might have been from the back blocks, but he knew he'd been had, and he went straight to the police, who went straight to Grogan. As the Brisbane *Courier* reported at the time, the decorated soldier and the detectives were 'old acquaintances'.

Grogan was ordered to make restitution or risk two months jail.

*

By 1920, White had returned to Australia, where he was soon back in court, facing charges of inflicting grievous bodily harm. This time his victim was war hero Charles Raison. The Lismore farmer had served at Gallipoli, then won a Military Medal on the Western Front while White was hiding from military police in the backstreets of Liverpool and London.

Sergeant Raison of the 25th Battalion had shown great courage during an attack on the enemy trenches south of Morlancourt, near Albert, on the nights of 10 and 11 June 1918. According to his citation, his platoon was held up by a machine-gun firing directly at them from a trench about 50 yards away. Together with Lieutenant George Lendrum Cromie, Raison bombed and killed a number of the enemy in the trench, undoubtedly saving many Australian casualties. Cromie was awarded the Distinguished Service Order.

On 25 July 1920, White, who had been drinking heavily, went to the stables at Lismore's Imperial Hotel, where Raison was working as a groom. According to the police evidence, White tried to draw Raison into a fight. Neither man knew the other; they were complete strangers.

White drew a revolver and fired three shots, two of the bullets striking his victim. According to witnesses, he had gone 'completely off his head'. Raison was rushed to the local hospital where he remained for several days before being released.

The wanted man was arrested shortly afterwards. He told police that he could remember nothing about the incident. He was charged with maliciously wounding Raison with intent to do grievous bodily harm.

At trial in Lismore, White was keen to give his version of how he had served his King and country during the war. He played the traumatised soldier, and in a statement from the dock detailed what the local newspaper described as 'his extensive war service'. He claimed he'd received a shrapnel wound in the head in France in 1917. This evidence wasn't challenged.

Indeed, a Lismore doctor gave evidence that the effect of even a small quantity of drink taken by a man who suffered in the war as the accused had would have the effect of making him irresponsible for his actions. With that, the jury returned a verdict of not guilty on the grounds of insanity, and the judge directed that White be detained at the Governor's pleasure.

Within a few years he was back on the streets and back before the courts. In 1928, he was charged with assaulting one Leslie Butler in an alcohol-fuelled altercation over a woman in the victim's South Brisbane flat. White and Butler were being entertained by two women, and when one of them collapsed on the couch, Butler tried to relocate her to a bedroom. White, well lubricated, flew at Butler, claiming he was taking liberties with the woman, and smashed him in the face with a bottle, breaking his nose.

White denied he'd used a bottle, claiming it was a sharp punch. He was originally charged with grievous bodily harm, which was later reduced to common assault with a guilty plea. He was fined five pounds, in default one month's jail.

White's life continued to spiral downwards. He not only had an alias known to the courts – Kenneth Kennedy – but had two warrants from the New South Wales Children's Court hanging over him for disobeying a magistrate's order for the support of his wife.

The police gazette described him as:

> Thirty four years of age, 6 feet high, thin build, fair complexion, dark hair turning grey, blue eyes, thin drawn features, scar on right side of forehead, birth mark on chest, small mouth, artificial teeth, tooth on one side of upper gold plate capped, usually dressed in grey clothes, may be employed as a photographer at side shows, and is said to be travelling in a Ford car bearing Queensland number plate Q118–300.

There we must leave White, driving off into the distance, a carnie worker in an old Ford at the start of the Great Depression.

*

Grogan could never settle to a life of domesticity. His wife, Nellie, had divorced him in 1925 for desertion. By then he had well and truly gone down the track of becoming a robber, fraudster and drug user.

In 1928, he was back before the bench charged with possession of opium. In and out of trouble, he eventually died in obscurity in North Sydney in 1956 at the age of 62.

Life turned out very differently for the man that Grogan had saved in the Great War. Blair Wark, the son of an engineer, and a trained quantity surveyor, had returned home to set up his own successful firm. He also took up public roles, including life governor of the Benevolent Society of New South Wales. His first marriage failed, his second lasted.

In 1940, Wark was appointed commander of the 1st Battalion of the Australian Military Forces, the volunteer forces that would eventually fight on the Kokoda Track. But he did not see action again, dying suddenly of heart disease on 13 June 1941 at training at Puckapunyal, in Victoria.

His *Australian Dictionary of Biography* entry noted that Wark was given a military funeral at which it was said that he had 'lived the life of three men'. The same might be said of his rescuer Grogan, who had been a respected young mine worker and husband, a conspicuously brave warrior, and then a low crook.

Of the soldiers in this chapter, two are easy to understand: Wark was of solid middle-class Scottish stock, well educated, professional and public minded. White was a bad 'un, and quite possibly a mad 'un. But Grogan – what sort of man he actually was, and what he might have become if he had returned home able-bodied – remains unknowable.

In August 1918, a few months after he received the wound that led to his discharge as an invalid, a pal of his named Sergeant E.J. Dunkley sent a photo of Grogan to the *Western Age*, Dubbo, with the following note:

> I am sending you a photo of a pal who is lying wounded in hospital, having been knocked out at Messines last March. His name is Corporal Thomas Cyril Grogan, better known as Honest Jim, and he enlisted in Newcastle at the beginning of the war.
>
> He is one of the original 30th Battalion, and was one of the first Australians to win a Military Medal in France. That was at the battle of Fromelles, on 19–20 July, 1916, when, under heavy shell and machine-gun fire, he carried his severely wounded captain from the German front line to a place of safety. He is one of the gamest soldiers that ever left Australia. He is known in Cobar, Newcastle and Sydney.

Whatever had happened to the man we can catch a glimpse of in this letter, the digger who had earned the warm regard of his mates, a soldier known to his unit as Honest Jim?

On the morning of 11 November 1918, when the Armistice was signed and the guns finally fell silent, a new task was presented to tens of thousands of diggers. Their job now was to return home and put behind them the horrors of the past four years. For all these men life had changed dramatically, and many found the challenges of returning to civilian life daunting.

Some, hopelessly damaged by their wartime experiences, staggered into lives afflicted by violence. Others took the opportunity to apply what they'd learned at war on a civilian battlefront.

For a third group it was a straightforward matter of resuming their criminal ways. They were the khaki criminals.

## Corporal T. C. Grogan, M. M.

Sergeant B. J. Dunkley, A.I.F., writes from 'somewhere in France'—'I am sending you a photo (which, unfortunately, is too indistinct for reproduction) of a pal who is lying wounded in hospital, having been knocked out at Messines last March. His name is Corporal Thomas Cyril Grogan, better known as "Honest Jim", and he enlisted in Newcastle at the beginning of the war. He is one of the original 30th Battalion, and was one of the first Australians to win a Military Medal in France. That was at the battle of Fromelles, on 19–20 July, 1916, when, under heavy shell and machine-gun fire, he carried his severely wounded captain from the German front line to a place of safety. He is one of the gamest soldiers that ever left Australia. He is known in Cobar, Newcastle and Sydney.'

# Acknowledgements

My thanks go to Pan Macmillan for their confidence in this project, in particular to my publishers Tom Gilliatt and Claire Craig, but also to editors Jo Lyons and Julia Stiles, and to Alex Lloyd and Deborah Parry. A top team.

Thanks also to the staff of the Public Record Office Victoria, in particular Ali Webb, Rebecca Young, Charlie Spiteri, Christine O'Donnell and Pam Sheers, and the public archives of Queensland, South Australia and New South Wales.

As ever, thanks to Rosalie Bray for sharing her memories, April Robinson for her valuable contributions, and Tyson and Evie for keeping me on track.

For their perceptive feedback, I'm indebted to Sibylle Noras, Peter Clarke and Aaron Robinson. Thanks as ever to James Morton.

And to Sybil Nolan, my never-ending gratitude for her unstinting advice and encouragement, wise counsel, technical assistance, professional input and perceptive suggestions. The book would not have been possible without her.

# Bibliography

**Books**

Anderson, H., *Larrikin Crook: The Rise and Fall of Squizzy Taylor*, Jacaranda Press, Melbourne, 1971.

Austin, R., *As Rough as Bags: The History of the 6th Battalion, 1st AIF, 1914–1919*, R.J. and S.P. Austin, McCrae, Victoria, 1992.

—— *Cobbers in Khaki: The History of the 8th Battalion 1914–1919*, Slouch Hat Publications, Rosebud, Victoria, 1997.

—— *Black and Gold: The History of the 29th Battalion, 1915–1918*, Slouch Hat Publications, Rosebud, Victoria, 1997.

Bean, C.E.W. *The Story of Anzac: From the Outbreak of War to the End of the First Phase of the Gallipoli Campaign, May 4, 1915,* Angus & Robertson, Sydney, 1921.

—— *The Story of Anzac: From 4 May, 1915, to the Evacuation of the Gallipoli Peninsula*, Angus & Robertson, Sydney, 1924.

Beaumont, J., *Broken Nation: Australians in the Great War*, Allen & Unwin, Sydney, 2013.

Begg, P., *Geelong: The First 150 Years*, Geelong Advertiser Pty Ltd, Geelong, 1990.

Belford, Walter, *'Legs-Eleven': Being the Story of the 11th Battalion (A.I.F) in the Great War of 1914–1918*, Imperial Printing Company, Perth, 1940.

Blair, D., *Dinkum Diggers: An Australian Battalion at War*, Melbourne University Press, Melbourne, 2001.

Bollard, R., *In the Shadow of Gallipoli: The Hidden Story of Australia in World War I*, New South Publishing, Sydney, 2013.
Carlyon, L., *Gallipoli*, Pan Macmillan, Sydney, 2001.
—— *The Great War*, Pan Macmillan, Sydney, 2006.
Cathcart, M., *Defending the National Tuckshop: Australia's Secret Army Intrigue of 1931*, Penguin Books, Melbourne, 1988.
Challinger, M., *Anzacs in Arkhangel: The Untold Story of Australia and the Invasion of Russia 1918–19*, Hardie Grant Books, Melbourne, 2013.
Davies, W., *In the Footsteps of Private Lynch: Retracing the Experiences of a Private Soldier in the Great War*, Transworld Publishers, London, 2009.
Deayton, C., *Battle Scarred: the 47th Battalion in the First World War*, Big Sky Publishing, Newport, NSW, 2011.
Facey, A.B., *A Fortunate Life*, Penguin, Melbourne, 2005.
Frances, R., *The History of Female Prostitution in Australia*, in Perkins, R., Prestage G., et al. (eds), *Sex Work and Sex Workers in Australia*, University of New South Wales Press, Sydney, 1994.
Gerster, R., and Pierce, P., *On the Warpath: An Anthology of Australian Military Travel*, Melbourne University Press, Melbourne, 2004.
Grant, I., *A Dictionary of Australian Military History: From Colonial Times to the Gulf War*, Random House, Sydney, 1992.
Keneally, T., *Australians: Volume 2—Eureka to the Diggers*, Allen & Unwin, Sydney, 2011.
Laffin, J., *Western Front 1916–1917: The Price of Honour,* Time-Life Books, South Pacific Books Division, 1987.
Lynch, E.P.F., *Somme Mud: The Experiences of an Infantryman in France, 1916–1919*, Transworld Publishers, London, 2008.
Maxwell, J., *Hell's Bells and Mademoiselles: A True Love Story of Life, Love and Larrikinism on the Western Front*, HarperCollins, Sydney, 2002 (1932).
Mitchell, G.D., *Backs to the Wall: A Larrikin on the Western Front*, Robert Macklin (ed.), Allen & Unwin, Sydney, 2007 (1937).
Monash, J., *The Australian Victories in France in 1918*, Hutchinson & Co., London, 1920.
Morton, J. and Lobez, S., *Dangerous to Know: An Australian Crime Compendium*, Victory Books, Melbourne, 2009.

—— *Gangland Australia*, Victory Books, Melbourne, 2010.

Morton, J. and Robinson, R., *Shotgun and Standover: The Story of the Painters and Dockers*, Pan Macmillan, Sydney, 2010.

Oliver, B., *War and Peace in Western Australia: The Social and Political Impact of the Great War, 1914–1926*, University of Western Australia Press, Perth, 1995.

Pedersen, P., *The Anzacs: Gallipoli to the Western Front*, Penguin, Melbourne, 2010.

Serle, G., *John Monash: A Biography*, Melbourne University Press, Carlton, Victoria, 1982.

Stanley, P., *Bad Characters: Sex, Crime, Mutiny, Murder and the Australian Imperial Force*, Murdoch Books, Sydney, 2010.

Straw, L., *Drunks, Pests and Harlots: Criminal Women in Perth and Fremantle, 1900–1939*, Humming Earth, Scotland, 2013.

Thomson, A., *Anzac Memories: Living with the Legend*, Oxford University Press, Melbourne, 1994.

Travers, R., *Diggers in France: Australian Soldiers on the Western Front*, ABC Books, Sydney, 2008.

Tregarthen, G., *Sea Transport of the AIF*, Australian Naval Transport Board, Melbourne, c. 1925

Wilson, G., *Bully Beef and Balderdash: Some Myths of the AIF Examined and Debunked*, Big Sky Publishing, Newport, NSW, 2012.

—— *Dust, Donkey and Delusions: The Myth of Simpson and his Donkey*, Big Sky Publishing, Newport, NSW, 2012.

Writer, L., *Underbelly: Razor*, Pan Macmillan, Sydney, 2011.

**Journals and gazettes**

Close, K., 'The Demise of Bicycle George: A Life of Crime', *The Journal of Public Record Office Victoria*, September 2010.

Frances, R., *White Slaves and White Australia: Prostitution and Australian Society*, History Council Lecture, History Council of New South Wales, 2004.

Harrison, M., 'The British Army and the Problem of Venereal Disease in France and Egypt During the First World War', *Medical History*, vol. 39, no. 2, 1995.

Jones, E. and Fear, N., 'Shell Shock and Traumatic Brain Injury:

A Historical Review', *American Journal of Psychiatry*, vol. 164, no. 11, 2007.

Mulder, A., 'The Camp Hospital for Venereal Diseases, Langwarrin, Victoria', *Australian Society of the History of Medicine*, Perth, 1991.

Nelson, E., 'Victims of War – The First World War, Returned Soldiers and Understandings of Domestic Violence in Australia', *Journal of Women's History*, vol. 19, no. 4, 2007.

*Police Gazette,* Victoria, New South Wales, South Australia and Queensland.

Prince, S.H., 'The Canadian Family in Wartime', *Marriage and Family Living*, vol. 4, no. 2, Spring, May 1942.

Smart, J., 'Sex, the State and the "Scarlet Scourge": Gender, Citizenship and Venereal Diseases Regulation in Australia During the Great War', *RMIT Women's History Review*, vol. 7, no. 1, 1998.

Stagnitti, J., 'Criminals, Prostitutes, Vagrants and Drunkards: 1920s Carlton', *The Journal of the Public Record Office Victoria*, September 2006, no. 5.

Straw, L., 'The Worst Female Character: Criminal Underclass Women in Perth and Fremantle, 1900–1939', *Journal of Australian Studies*, vol. 37, no. 2, 2013.

Wilson, G., 'A Prison of our Own: The AIF Detention Barracks 1917–1919', *Sabretache*, vol. 46, no. 2, June 2005.

**Online publications**

Biancani, F., 'Let Down the Curtains Around Us; Sex Work in Colonial Cairo, 1882–1952', The London School of Economics and Political Science, 2012, http://etheses.lse.ac.uk/486/

Garstang, E.J., 'Crime and Punishment on the Western Front, the Australian Imperial Force and British Army Discipline', Murdoch University, WA, http://researchrepository.murdoch.edu.au/728/2/02Whole.pdf

Kibble Education and Childcare Centre, *Kibble—A Lasting Legacy: Child Migration 1859–2009*, January 2014, www.kibble.org/history/booklets/child-migration.pdf

McConville, C., 'Melbourne Crime: From War to Depression, 1919–1929', Obituaries Australia, National Centre of Biography, March 2014, http:// adb.anu.edu.au/essay/6/text28416

# Bibliography


**Online resources**

Australian Dictionary of Biography: www.adb.edu.au
Ancestry.com.au
Australian War Memorial: www.awm.gov.au
National Archives of Australia: www.naa.gov.au
The Long, Long Trail: www.1914-1918.net/
Trove (digitised newspaper reports and images), National Library of Australia: www. trove.nla.gov.au

**Archive resources**

Mitchell Library, State Library of New South Wales
Public Record Office Victoria
Queensland State Archives

**Newspapers**

*Adelaide News*
*Advertiser*, Adelaide
*Advertiser*, Euroa
*Advocate*, Burnie
*Age*
*Albany Advertiser*
*Albury Banner and Wodonga Express*
*Argus*
*Arrow*, Sydney
*Bacchus Marsh Express*
*Ballarat Courier*
*Barrier Miner*, Broken Hill
*Bathurst Times*
*Bendigo Advertiser*
*Border Morning Mail and Berrima Times*, Albury
*Border Watch*, Mount Gambier
*Brisbane Courier*
*Canberra Times*
*Chronicle*, Adelaide
*Clarence River Advocate*
*Courier*, Hobart

*Cumberland Argus and Fruitgrowers Advocate*, Parramatta
*Daily Herald*, Adelaide
*Daily News*, Perth
*Euroa Advertiser*
*Evening News*, Sydney
*Examiner*, Launceston
*Farmer and Settler*, NSW
*Flemington Spectator*
*Geelong Advertiser*
*Geraldton Guardian*
*Gippsland Mercury*, Sale
*Goulburn Evening Penny Post*
*Herald*, Melbourne
*Kalgoorlie Western Argus*
*Kilmore Free Press*
*Leader*, Orange
*Maitland Weekly Mercury*, NSW
*Maffra Spectator*
*Mirror*, Perth
*Mirror*, Sydney
*Morning Bulletin*, Rockhampton
*Muswellbrook Chronicle*, NSW
*North Eastern Ensign*, Benalla
*Northern Star*, Lismore
*Queensland Times*, Ipswich
*Recorder*, Port Pirie
*Register*, Adelaide
*Richmond River Express and Casino Kyogle Advertiser*
*Singleton Argus*
*Spectator*, Maffra
*St Arnaud Mercury*
*Sunday Times*, Perth
*Sunday Times*, Sydney
*Sydney Morning Herald*
*Tamworth Daily Observer*
*Townsville Daily Bulletin*

*Truth*, Melbourne Edition
*West Australian*
*Western Age*, Dubbo
*Western Champion*
*Western Star and Roma Advertiser*, Toowoomba
*Williamstown Chronicle*
*Windsor and Richmond Gazette*, NSW

# Notes on Images

**Public Record Office Victoria**

- Norman Bruhn. PROV, VPRS 515, P0001, Prisoner No. 36147, Item Number 71.
- Claude Taylor. PROV, VPRS 515, P0001, Prisoner No. 32905, Item Number 63.
- William Gruner. PROV, VPRS 515, P0001, Prisoner No. 34611, Item Number 67.
- George Blunderfield, who changed his name to Arthur Geoffrey Oldring. PROV, VPRS 264, P0001. Capital Case Files Unit 7. George Blunderfield/Arthur Oldring December 1917.
- Trawool Bridge. PROV, VPRS 264, P0001. Capital Case Files Unit 7. George Blunderfield/Arthur Oldring December 1917.
- Albert Edward Budd. PROV, VPRS 5900/P, Unit 1 – Photographs of Prisoners Sentenced to Death.
- Harry David Graham. PROV, *Victoria Police Gazette*, June 1920. Discharged Prisoners List 27/2/20, page 19. Prisoner No. 35615.
- Albert McDonald. PROV, VPRS 515, P0001, Prisoner No. 36457, Item Number 72.
- Joseph Cotter. PROV, *Victoria Police Gazette*, 1924, page 7 of the Supplement to the *Victoria Police Gazette* – Prisoners discharged as shown in group photos.
- Thomas William Johnson. PROV, VPRS 515, P0001, Prisoner No. 37646, Item Number 74.
- Michael Cook. PROV, VPRS 515, P0001, Prisoner No. 34483, Item Number 67.
- Charles Sydney Johnson. PROV, VPRS 515, P0001, Prisoner No. 37059, Item Number 73.
- CSJ/KP murder scene. PROV, VA 667 Office of the Victorian Government Solicitor, VPRS 30/P, Unit 2029. Melbourne Supreme Court, case number 5 of 15, February 1924.
- Arthur Bazley. PROV, VPRS 515, P0001, Prisoner No. 38440, Item Number 76.

**Sydney Living Images**

- Mug shot of Hampton Hirsham, Cornelius Joseph Keevil, William Thomas O'Brien and James O'Brien, Special Photograph number 446, 20 July 1921, Central Police Station, Sydney. New South Wales Forensic Photography Archive, Justice & Police Museum, Sydney Living Museums.
- William Cyril Moxley, Special Photograph number 1152, 12 February 1923, Central Police Station, Sydney. New South Wales Police Forensic Photography Archive, Justice & Police Museum, Sydney Living Museums.

# Index

Ah Long, Luey 288
Albany convoy 38–41
Allan, James Alexander 129–30
Allcorn, Daphne 206–7
Allen, Samuel 201–2
Allsop, Charles Edward 207, 208–16, 225
Allsop, Robert 208–10
Allsop, Samuel Foster 210–11
Anderson, Beth 242
Anderson, Hugh 179
Anderson, William 243
Andrew, John 255
Armistice 15, 18, 53, 97, 103, 104, 107, 119, 221, 292, 298
Armstrong, Herbert Harold (Horace) 156–61
Armstrong, Warwick Windridge 158
Arnott, Brigadier (Salvation Army) Arthur 165
Asquith, Edith 153
Asquith, George Harold 153–6
Atzel, Elia 133–6
Aumont, Clara 253–4
Aumont, May 187
Bathurst Gaol 89, 239
Battle of the Wazzir 48–50
Bayard, Norman Edgar 287, 292
Bazley, Arthur 187
Bean, Charles 2, 3, 10, 45
Beaumont, Joan 47
Bennett, David Charles 199–200
Bennett, Esther 79, 81, 84
Bennett, Fred 79
Bennie, Dr 57
Berkley, Staff Sergeant 151
Berriman, Thomas 212
Berry, Harry Anderson, *see* Armstrong, Herbert Harold (Horace)
Bescorp, Madame 257–8
Bickerstaff, George 50–2
bigamy 143–66
Bird, Harry 213
Birdwood, General Sir William 12–13
Blaize, Charles 139
Blaize, Sidney 136–42
Blaize, William 136–7
Blunderfield, Charles Farrow 36
Blunderfield, George Farrow, *see* Oldring, Arthur Geoffrey

Boardman, Patrick 187
Bourke Street Rats 183
Brakespeare, Arthur 35
Brennan, Richard 101
brideships 106
Bridges, Frederick Cooper 127–32
Broadwin, Linda 148–9
brothels (Perth) 42, 126–8
Brown, Captain Roy Arthur 140
Brown, Jessie Ward Farrow 36–7
Bruhn, Eric 169–71
Bruhn, Irene 9, 174
Bruhn, Mary Ann 173–4
Bruhn, Norman 4, 7–16, 17, 19, 23, 169, 174–9
Bruhn, Oscar Charles (Jnr) 20–1
Bruhn, Oscar Snr 7–8, 172, 173–4
Bruhn, Roy 173–4
Bruhn, Stanley 16–19, 169–71
Bruhn, William George 19–20, 171–4
Buchanan, Harold Asquith, *see* Asquith, George Harold
Buchanan, Muriel Edith 154–5
Buckley, Trooper Maurice 58–9
Budd, Albert Edward 239–45
Buggy, Hugh 177–9
Bulford VD hospital, *see* venereal disease
Bunney, Charles Adam 256–62
Burnside, Justice Robert Bruce 40, 130–2
Butler, Leslie 296

Cameron, Nellie 175–7
Cameron, Robert George 176–7
Cane, Joseph Abraham 161–6
Cane, Violet 161–2, 164
Carey, Detective Henry 225–6
Carey, Senior Detective 173
Carley, Sarah 71
Cathcart, Michael 239
Caylock, Charlie 214–15
Challinger, Michael 107
Chambers, Billy 178
Cheers, Euston Murray 172
Clark, David Quinton 23
Cleary, Charles 179–80
Coen, John 218
Conroy, Rupert Mark 213
conscription 29, 89, 95
Cook, Michael 61–4
Cook, Minnie 63
Coonan, Sub Inspector Thomas 191
Cotter, Ethel 187–8, 191
Cotter, Joseph Lennox 182–9, 190–1
Cozzie, Charles 43
Cromie, Lieutenant George Lendrum 295
Cross, Constable W.J. 235
Cutmore, James Francis 181
Cutmore, John Daniel 'Snowy' 44, 55, 178, 179–81, 182, 195
  aliases 179, 180
Cutmore, John Samuel 181

D'Haenens, Charles 20
Daly, Sergeant Job F. 118
Davis, James, *see* Devine, James Edward
Davis, Murray 214
de Bray, Josie 42, 126–8, 132
Denzel, Dorothy Ruth 267–8
Devine, Alice Teresa 97
Devine, Ernest Edward 'Dicky' 265–6
Devine, Frank 92, 98
Devine, Frederick James 97
Devine, James Edward 92–8, 178
Devine, Matilda 'Tilly' 92, 94–5, 97–8, 106, 178
Docker, Alfred Brougham 91–2
Docker, Sir Ernest Brougham 4, 90–2
drugs 251–5
Dunkley, Sergeant E.J. 298
Dunn, Constable Henry 196
Duscher, Corporal Herbert Frank 203
Dyer, Ernest 226–32
Dyer, Mrs 229–30

# Index

Edwards, Harold 40–1
Edwards, John, *see* Cook, Michael 63
Efford, Charles 30–1
Elliott, Lieutenant Colonel 'Pompey' 272, 274
Elliott, Nellie 41–2
Ewart, Victor Clarence 224–6

Facey, A.B. 25
Farran, Blanche Edith 153–4
Farran, Joseph 154
Findlay, Constable 137
Fitzharding, Henry *see* Henry Slater
Fitzroy Vendetta 181, 186
Flack, James Patrick 226
Fraser, Albert James 103–6
Frost, Roy 223–4
Funston, Frederick 150–1

Garstang, Edward 2–3, 65
Gavey, Joe 214
Gaw, Henry 255
Gelle, Dr Louis 128
Gibson, Judge 289
Godfrey, Mrs C. 156, 158
Graham, Harry David 232–6
Grant, Ian 140
Gray, Charles 23
Gray, Robert McCourt 259–62
Grayly, James, *see* Hopkins, Ernest
Grogan, Nellie 286, 297
Grogan, Thomas 284–9, 292–4, 297–9
Gruner, Hubert 27–8
Gruner, William Edward 27–9
Guidotti, Marie 42–3
Gurr, Clare Constance 160

Hagar, Robert 287–8
Hall, David 75–8, 81, 83–4
Hamilton, Donald Alexander 185
Harper, Arthur 160
Harper, Sapper David 19
Harris, George 70–85
Harrison, Private Richard Thomas 28
Hearn, Humphrey James 128
Heath, John 60–1
Hedley, prisoner 119–23
Hewitt, Victor, *see* Ewart, Victor Clarence
Higgins, William Westley 281–2
Hill, Albert Keith 293–4
Hinde, Alfred 246–7
Hirsham, Hampton 222–4
Hoare, Sir Samuel 264
Hodges, Justice Henry Edward Agincourt 64
Hogan, Thomas 174
Holihan, Constable 197
Hopkins, Ernest 272, 273–83
  aliases, 279
Hopkins, Joseph Walton 272–3, 274, 283
Hughes, Billy 29, 233
Humphries, Phillip James 47
Hutton, William Ness 65–6
Hyland, Frank Thomas, *see* Neville, Harold John
Hyland, Miss L. 153

Imlay, Oliver 99–101
Irvine, Chief Justice Sir William 280–1

James, Justice 248
Jemmett, Harrie Nathan 116–24
Johansen, Alexander 199, 206
Johnson, Charles Sydney 248–55
Johnson, Thomas William 259–62
Johnstone, George 53, 145–6
Jones, Joseph 98–101
Jordan, Leslie 127, 129

Keen, Algernon George 292
Keevil, Cornelius Joseph 222–4
Kelly, Colin 176
Kelly, Gertrude Ann Jane 152

Kelly, Selina May 124
Kennedy, Kenneth, *see* White, Cyril Emanuel
Kibble boys 50–1
Knox, Kitty 107–8

Lane, Harry 16
Langwarrin military camp, *see* venereal disease
Lawler, Robert 219
Lawson, George 187–8, 191
Lennon, William John 120–23
Leonard, Hugh 203
Leong, Goo 287–8
Leroy, Mme Gabrielle Smeets 17–18
Lewes detention barracks 97, 110, 112, 185
Lewis, Mary Elizabeth 162–3
Lewis, Robert Watkin 183
Lewis-Driver, Mrs M. 163
Linklater, Ada 71
Linnane, Martin 102–3
Loughrey, Ernest, *see* Hopkins, Ernest

Madden, Sir John 250
Maguire, Thomas Vincent 98–101
Makepeace, Constable 225
Maloney, Dr William 147
Mannix, Archbishop Daniel 59
Many-Peney, Stanley Valentine 199–200
Marriott, Thomas 212, 215
Maxwell, Joe 26, 46–7, 111, 256
McConville, Chris 251
McDonald, Albert Ronald 191–202, 205–6
McEwan, Henry 252
McKinley, John 99
McLeod, Donald John 210
McMillan, Chief Justice Sir Robert 127, 218
McPhail, George 51
McQueen, Joseph 51–3
McVeigh, Henry Victor 207–8
Meade, Dr F.G. 146–8, 152
Meadows, Alwyn 207
Miller, Robert 178–9
Milne, Detective 170
Monash, John 3, 81, 82
Monkhouse, George 141–2
Monnier, Marie Louis, *see* de Bray, Josie
Montgomery, Trevor 169
Moore, Police Magistrate 198
Moore, William Charles 118, 121–2
Morrison, John 159
Moxley, William Cyril 264–71
Mudros tent hospitals 11, 181
Mulder, Audrey 54
Murchison, Archibald 59–61
Murphy, Ada 264
Murphy, Mrs 124–5
Murray, Angus 211–12
Murray, Caroline Rhoda 245–6
Murray, Rose Ada May 133–6
Murray, William James 245–8

narcotics, *see* drugs
Neville, Harold John 113–16, 125
Norton, Alice 157–9, 161

O'Brien brothers 222–4
O'Keefe, Jeremiah 211
Oldring, Arthur Geoffrey 29–36, 36
Olsen, John Thomas 'Fivo' 188–9

Page, William 113, 116
Paul, Claire 262–4
Paul, Sidney George 262–4
Paulon, Claire, *see* Paul, Claire
Pearce, Senator Sir George 3, 147–8
Pearse, Samuel 106–8
Pearse, Victoria Catherine Sarah 107
Pell, William 290
Pender, Ida 'Babe' 189, 198, 199–201, 215, 216

Pennell, Colonel 270–1
Pennicott, Sergeant Richard George 112
Perry, Bertha Mary 219
Perry, Victor Alexander 217–22
Perry, Victoria Rose 144, 146–7, 150, 152
Perry, William Walter 143–53
Piggott, Senior Detective Frederick 214
Pollay, Bertha Rhoda 160
Poulston, Corporal William 117–23
Prentice, Thomas 22
Pretty, Harry 242
Price, Doris 251–4
Price, Kathleen Elizabeth 251–4
Prince, Samuel Henry 153–6

Quaine, James 72–4, 75, 84–5
Queen, John 52

Radonich, Albert 207
Raison, Charles 294–5
razor gangs 177–8, 180
Red Baron, *see* von Richthofen, Baron Manfred
Rich, Justice Sir George 25
Rogers, Justice Sir Percival Halse 269–70
Rollins, James 104–5
Rose, Albert Arthur Howard 108
Ross, Thomas D. 136–7
Ryan, Edward John Francis 57–8
Ryan, Francis Edward 118–19
Ryan, Henry 127
Ryan, Patrick 40

Sabine, Magistrate E.M. 160
Salvator, Lieutenant W.H. 235–6
Samson, Annie Elizabeth 241–4
Samson, Mary Jeanette 242
Samson, Stephen George 240, 244
Sands, Lord 105
Schmitzer, Constable 223
Schutt, Justice 166
Senior, Henry 105
Sexton, Private Gerald, *see* Buckley, Trooper Maurice
Seymour, Frederick Charles 127
Sharp, Ernest Edward 98–101
Shaw, Robert 70–1
Sheedy, Sydney Harold 118
shell shock 1, 277
Sheridan, Harold Alexander 83–4
Simpson, George Albert 246–7
Slater, Henry 195, 216
Small family 35
Sonenberg, Napthali Henry 165, 226
Speakman, Percy 199, 200
Stanley, Peter 3, 68–9
Steele, George 90
Stewart, Edward 127, 129
Stewart, G.R. 150
Stokes, Henry 'Harry' 194, 195, 196–8
Street, Arthur William 235

Taylor, Albert 203, 204–5
Taylor, Benjamin 204
Taylor, Claude Harold John 22–4, 203
Taylor, Leslie 'Squizzy' 9, 22, 44, 179, 180–1, 182, 189–91, 192, 198, 200, 201, 203, 206–8, 211, 216, 225
Taylor, Margaret 33–5, 36
Taylor, Rose 24, 204, 205
Taylor, Rosie 33–5
Taylor, Stanley 203, 204, 205, 206, 225
Tombe, Eric Gordon 228–32
Tombe, Reverend and Mrs 231–2
Towes, Christina 111
Tragheim, Florence Margaret 232–4
train of shame 109–25
training camps 25–7
    Blackboy Hill 25, 38, 41, 44, 129, 133, 181, 264
    Broadmeadows 25, 26
    Enoggera 26
    Liverpool 26
Twiss, Matilda, *see* Devine, Matilda 'Tilly'

Undesirables, the 185–6
Universal Service League 75
Ure, William Robert 41–2
Urquhart, Thomas George 132–6

Vardy, Alexander Leslie 133–6
Vaughan, Florence 66–7
Vaughan, George 66–7
venereal disease 15, 20, 43–5, 54–7, 59–60, 67, 68, 80, 93–5, 114–15, 117, 185, 192–3, 250, 276, 278, 290
    Bulford hospital 65, 192, 290
    in Egypt 45–6
    Langwarrin military camp 54–7, 58, 59–64, 179
von Richthofen, Baron Manfred, 140–2

Walker, Robert Jnr 28
Walker, Robert Snr 28
Wallace, George 9
Ward, Constable George Edward 70
Wark, Captain Blair Anderson 284–6, 297
Watson, George 249–52
Waulle, Madame Berthe 258
West, John Beaumont 110–14, 120, 124
White, Cyril Emanuel 287–92, 294–7
White, Georgina Jessie 291
White, Reverend William 151
Whiting, Edward 194–6
Whiting, Hilda 195–6
Wilkinson, Frank Barnaby 266–8
Williams, Christopher 22–3
Williams, Herbert 180
Williamson, Donald McCrae 249–50
Wilson, Charles 249–50
Wilson, Dolly 115
Wilson, Florence 129, 132
Wilson, Graham 48
Windsor, Albert John 217–18
Woinarski, Judge 172, 282
Woods, Edward 67–9
Worthington, Captain Sydney Herbert 50
Wren, John 59

Young, John George 110
Young, Robert 219